KU-506-291

WORKING FOR FULL EMPLOYMENT

Edited by John Philpott

London and New York

**HERTFORDSHIRE
LIBRARIES, ARTS
AND INFORMATION**

H31 670 0117	
HJ	2/97
339.5	14.99

First published 1997
by Routledge
11 New Fetter Lane, London EC4P 4EE

Simultaneously published in the USA and Canada
by Routledge
29 West 35th Street, New York, NY 10001

© 1997 Employment Policy Institute

Typeset in Garamond by Keystroke, Jacaranda Lodge, Wolverhampton
Printed and bound in Great Britain by
TJ Press (Padstow) Ltd, Padstow, Cornwall

All rights reserved. No part of this book may be reprinted or
reproduced or utilized in any form or by any electronic,
mechanical, or other means, now known or hereafter
invented, including photocopying and recording, or in any
information storage or retrieval system, without permission in
writing from the publishers.

British Library Cataloguing in Publication Data
A catalogue record for this book is available from the British Library

Library of Congress Cataloguing in Publication Data
A catalogue record for this book has been requested

ISBN 0–415–14347–0 (hbk)
ISBN 0–415–143489– (pbk)

A\12

W(

Full empl
marked b
employmc
jobs boom
is still atta

Working F
market ex
stimulatin
include:

- the
- the
- the
- wor
- how
- the
- refo

The book
and the '
themes in
economisi
changes.

John Phil

Please renew/return items by last date shown. Please call the number below:

Renewals and enquiries: 0300 123 4049

Textphone for hearing or
speech impaired users: 0300 123 4041

www.hertsdirect.org/librarycatalogue
L32

Hertfordshire

He has written widely on unemployment and labour market policy. His previous publications include *Stopping Unemployment* (with Richard Layard).

CONTENTS

CONTENTS

FIGURES AND TABLES

FIGURES

TABLES

CONTRIBUTORS

John Philpott is Director of the Employment Policy Institute (EPI), an independent think tank. An economist, he has worked as a consultant for various UK and international bodies including the United Nations and the International Labour Organization. Between 1993 and 1996 he was Specialist Adviser to the House of Commons Select Committee on Employment. Since joining the EPI in 1987 he has edited and contributed to the Institute's monthly publication, *Economic Report*.

Andrew Britton is Executive Secretary for the Churches' Enquiry into Unemployment and the Future of Work, which has the support of all the main Christian churches in Britain and Ireland and is due to report in early 1997. From 1982 to 1995 he was Director of the National Institute of Economic and Social Research and is also a former member of the Treasury panel of independent forecasters (the so-called 'wise men'). His main publications are *The Trade Cycle in Britain* and *Macroeconomic Policy in Britain*, (Cambridge University Press).

David Piachaud is Professor of Social Policy at the London School of Economics and Political Science. From 1968 to 1970 he worked at the Department of Health and Social Security and from 1974 to 1979 worked in the Prime Minister's Policy Unit. He has written widely on the causes of poverty, the costs of children, the redistribution of incomes, international comparisons of social security, work and welfare, and European social policy.

Jill Rubery is Professor of Comparative Employment Systems at the Manchester School of Management. She is also currently the co-ordinator of the European Commission's Network of Experts on the Situation of Women in the Labour Market which researches into women's employment for the Equal Opportunities Unit of the European Commission. She has published extensively on employer policies and the labour market.

Patricia Hewitt is Director of Research at Andersen Consulting. From 1992 to 1994 she was Deputy Chair of the Commission on Social Justice and is a former Deputy Director of the Institute for Public Policy Research (IPPR), of which she is now a Trustee. She is the author of numerous books and reports, including *About Time: The Revolution in Family Life*, and a regular broadcaster on TV and radio programmes.

Christine Greenhalgh is Fellow and Tutor at St Peter's College Oxford, and **Mary Gregory** is Fellow and Tutor in Economics at St Hilda's College Oxford. They are currently carrying out an analysis of the changing structure of UK output and employment based on input–output tables. Christine Greenhalgh has also examined the role of non-price factors in influencing UK trade perform-ance. Additionally she has published a variety of studies of microeconomic aspects of the UK labour market, most recently focusing on training. Mary Gregory's research interests centre on macroeconomic aspects of labour markets and she has published widely on pay and employment. She is currently working on an analysis of the impact of unemployment on the subsequent employment and earnings experience of British men.

Christopher Freeman is Professor at the Science Policy Research Unit (SPRU) at the University of Sussex. He started the SPRU in 1965 having moved from the National Institute of Economic and Social Research where he worked, among other things, on the economics of technical change. He retired in 1986 and since then has worked at the SPRU on a part-time basis and for the Maastricht Economic Research Institute on Innovation and Technology (MERIT) at the University of Lindburg in the Netherlands. He is author of various papers and books on technical change and economic policy. He is co-author, with Professor Luc Soate, of *Work for All or Mass Unemployment* (1994, Pinter).

Richard B. Freeman is Ascherman Professor of Economics at Harvard University and also Program Director of the National Bureau of Economic Research's Program in Labor Studies, Cambridge, Massachusetts. He is also Executive Programme Director of the Comparative Labour Market Institution's Programme at the Centre for Economic Performance, London School of Economics and Political Science. He has published over 200 articles and 16 books, including *Differences and Changes in Wage Structures* (1995), *Demand Side Policies for Low-Wage Labor Markets* (1996) and *Capitalism and Generosity: Non-Selfish Behaviour in a Selfish Economy* (1997).

Paul Ormerod is head of Post-Orthodox Economics, which he founded in 1992, and has been a visiting Professor of Economics at London and Manchester. In the 1970s he was Senior Forecaster at the National Institute of Economic and Social Research. He was head of the Economic Assessment Unit at the *Economist* and from 1982 to 1992 Director of Economics at the Henley Centre. His most recent book is the international best seller, *The Death of Economics.*

Chris Pond is Director of the Low Pay Unit and Honorary Visiting Professor at the University of Middlesex. He was previously Lecturer in Economics at the

Civil Service College, Visiting Lecturer in Economics at the University of Kent, Honorary Visiting Professor/Research Fellow at the University of Surrey and Consultant to the Open University. He has acted as adviser to the European Commission and European Parliament and has published widely on issues of poverty and inequality, employment, taxation and social policy. He is a regular TV and radio broadcaster.

David Marsden is Reader in Industrial Relations at the London School of Economics and Research Associate of the Centre for Economic Performance, LSE. The research on which his chapter in this book is based was a study of the possible effects of management practices on unemployment, carried out as one of the background studies for the OECD *Jobs Study* (1994). He is currently engaged in a study of public service pay reforms in Britain and Germany, funded by the Anglo-German Foundation.

Richard Layard is Professor of Economics at the London School of Economics and Political Science and Director of the Centre for Economic Performance. He has worked for many years on the problems of unemployment and inflation and is co-author (with Stephen Nickell and Richard Jackman) of *Unemployment: Macroeconomic Performance and the Labour Market* (1991, Oxford University Press). He is an Officer and Trustee of the Employment Policy Institute, which he founded. Since 1991 he has worked as a part-time adviser to the Russian government.

Chris Trinder is Chief Economist at the Chartered Institute of Public Finance and Accountancy (CIPFA) where he has worked since 1990. He is also a Visiting Fellow in Economics at the University of Leicester. In the 1980s he was in charge of labour market and public expenditure research at the National Institute of Economic and Social Research. From 1990 to 1993 he was Director of the Employment component of the Carnegie Inquiry into the Third Age and has been involved in the subsequent implementation phase. He has been a specialist adviser to the Social Security Advisory Committee and is a member of the Advisory Committee for the Centre for the Study of Regulated Industries (CRI).

William Brown is the Montague Burton Professor of Industrial Relations and Chair of the Faculty of Economics and Politics at the University of Cambridge. He was previously Director of the Economic and Social Research Council's Industrial Relations Research Unit at the University of Warwick. His research interests have been concerned with workplace bargaining, pay determination, incomes policy and the impact of legislation upon industrial relations. His publications include *Piecework Bargaining*, and *The Changing Contours of British Industrial Relations*.

FOREWORD

When the TUC and the Employment Policy Institute decided to hold a conference on full employment in 1994 we hoped to start a national debate on full employment and how it might be achieved.

In doing so we were challenging the conventional wisdom that had grown up over the past twenty years that mass unemployment was inevitable and that the answer to Britain's problems was reliance on the free market and deregulation.

Discussion on how to address the problems of unemployment and social exclusion has once again become part of the mainstream policy debate. That questioning is not confined to the issue of full employment. The issue of job insecurity and the deregulated labour market has come from the sidelines to become one of the central policy issues of the mid-1990s. The debate about the stakeholder economy and industrial competitiveness is just beginning.

The theme that unites these debates is that modern industrial economies and societies do not function well when unemployment and fear of unemployment come to dominate the workings of the labour market. Unemployment and insecurity make it harder to create competitive workforces based on flexible skills.

But challenging a well-established convention is never easy. Many still believe that the UK economic experiment in labour market deregulation is still the right policy direction – indeed some argue it should and could be taken much further. If the free market solutions applied to the British economy have been under question and challenge, so too has the social partnership model in the rest of the European Union.

It has been claimed that the more 'flexible' UK labour market has produced a better job performance and lower unemployment. Industry in the rest of Europe is said to be hampered by excessive regulation and employment protection and high wage and non-wage hiring costs, making firms less competitive and forcing up unemployment.

The truth is that the economies of Europe have created more jobs and had higher levels of investment than in Britain. British industry invests less, exports less and earns a lower rate on capital than German or French industry.

The compatibility between full employment and the drive towards economic and monetary union has been brought to the fore by recent events in France and Germany in particular. But while the present economic difficulties and high unemployment in Europe clearly pose a challenge, that challenge existed before the Maastricht Treaty and needed to be met. The new European model which is now being developed requires a strong policy priority towards growth, investment, job generation and a fully fledged social dimension.

Central to this approach is the creation of an economic and monetary union based on investment in people and new technologies, taking the high productivity route to job creation. At a time when growth is slow, there is naturally more interest in ideas which seek to create jobs by lowering productivity. As the main way to tackle unemployment, this would be a mistake. High productivity and high investment economies offer the best chance of creating more jobs and rising living standards in the long run. The creation of high productivity, high investment economies depends in turn on developing social partnership in the workplace and at national level.

Essential to this concept is that we should become a 'learning society'. There is a role for schemes at the margin to create high employment intensive activities, but this cannot be the way forward.

This was the central thrust behind the EU White Paper on *Growth, Competitiveness and Employment*, which had as its target the halving of European unemployment by the end of the century. The recent proposals by the European Commission to divert European budget resources towards investment in new infrastructure and new technologies is a welcome step in that direction. The blocking of this by the UK government among others is short-termism at its worst.

One area of the debate which has not yet taken off concerns the role of demand management. The orthodoxy has taken hold that demand management cannot be used to address the present unemployment problem, that unemployment is essentially structural in nature and must therefore be addressed by structural reforms of the labour market.

The 1980s' British alternative to social partnership is not an option. The British economic and monetary authorities may publicly subscribe to this view, but they remain unwilling to put the deregulation experiment to the final test. True believers in labour market deregulation would see no danger in expanding the economy to bring down unemployment to one million of the population or less. Wiser counsels are likely to guide policy for the foreseeable future.

Deregulation in Britain has instead helped to create a volatile labour market, strong on hire-and-fire attitudes and the short-term, weak in long-term investment in people and new capacity. There is no compelling evidence that deregulation has raised the long-run economic potential of the economy or has slain the inflationary dragon. The recent fall in UK unemployment could be easily reversed, as it was in 1990.

Higher levels of growth are of course essential to bring down unemployment. Without faster growth, supply side measures simply will not work. But if deregulation has not done the trick, there is also a limit to what can be done through growth alone.

Put simply, efforts to bring down unemployment through demand alone will eventually run into inflationary and balance of payments problems. This is hardly a new concept, but lay at the heart of the policy dilemmas for successive governments in the 1960s and 1970s. The same question arises today about what can be done to promote more growth and more jobs without inflation running out of control.

Part of the answer is to avoid across the board increases in demand that feed directly into consumption. The more increases in growth can be linked to higher investment and exports, the greater and longer the economic expansion that can be sustained.

Investment in the skills of the workforce through better training is central to raising industrial competitiveness and the efficiency of the economy. Had the same efforts gone into investment in people and addressing the problems created by short-term attitudes to investment by industry as were put into labour market deregulation then the British economy today would be in a much better position.

But these measures are long-term policies: they cannot be expected to have a major impact in the short-term. More promising as a short-term measure to complement an expansionary demand policy may be large-scale employment programmes targeted on groups such as the long-term unemployed. An important recent proposal by the Institute for Public Policy Research (IPPR) suggests it is quite feasible to put together a scheme at modest cost which could help reduce unemployment to 5 per cent without setting off inflationary pressures.

But getting unemployment below this figure requires more. Developing social partnership arrangements is central to making more progress. Experiences in Australia and Ireland show that it is possible to construct arrangements which give better economic outcomes. The Australian experience is especially instructive because of the contrast with the other great deregulator of the 1980s, New Zealand. On most conventional economic indicators, Australia clearly has done better. One area of particular success has been in agreeing and meeting national job creation targets over the period of the Hawke–Keating government.

Of course, these arrangements cannot simply be imported wholesale, even if there was general agreement that they are desirable. Economies with very different industrial, political and social institutions demand different solutions. But there may be important lessons to be learnt which could be applied in the British context. For example, the work done in Australia on improving industrial competitiveness, improving training and labour market measures would all repay more study.

Yet no matter how reasonable and sensible all these proposals may be, if they are to make a difference they involve some uncomfortable choices. Growth based on exports and investment is virtuous, but not as popular as growth based on consumption. Helping the unemployed by investing in the infrastructure, quality training and special labour market measures is good for social cohesion but cannot be afforded alongside tax cuts. Perhaps most difficult of all are some of the wider distributional choices that have to be made when it comes to incomes. The decline in the share of wages and salaries in national income is one distributional issue that needs to be faced, as even the CBI has accepted.

But equally importantly those in work – and especially but not exclusively those groups which have done best out of the massive growth in inequality over the past fifteen years – will have to accept that they will not get quite so big a share of the growth in national income if those without work and those who would like to work are to have jobs. The curbing of excessive salaries at the top – which drag up behind them many salaries below boardroom level – and the end of wage exploitation at the bottom through a national minimum wage will make an important contribution. So too would restrictions on excessive and increasingly unpaid overtime for many full-time workers.

These distributional questions are not simply important as social justice issues. They are central to developing successful economies in the future. The exclusion of a significant proportion of the population from the benefits of growth weakens the industrial base of the economy, most noticeably in the failure to invest in people. In contrast, policies aiming to reduce inequalities can also improve economic performance. There is no conflict between objectives aimed at fairness and economic success and competitiveness.

Distributional questions are also fundamental to reaching understandings on the allocation of resources. The words incomes policies have dropped from the debate and in the more decentralized labour markets of the 1990s a different form of understanding would have to be developed. The present policy debate in Britain falls short of developing a common understanding of how the economy works and what has to be done by all the social partners – government, employers and trade unions – to reach the long-term objectives of full and fair employment. The recent offer of the German trade unions to moderate wage increases in exchange for a commitment to job creation at a time of shared economic pressure is a good practical example of what social partnership is about.

How far that understanding can be developed over the next few years – both at national and European level – is critical to the realization of full employment as a practical policy objective. This book is an important contribution to that objective.

John Monks,
General Secretary,
Trades Union Congress

PREFACE AND
ACKNOWLEDGEMENTS

This book has its origins in a series of background papers prepared for a major conference held in London in July 1994 and attended by senior politicians of all parties as well as leading trade unionists and key figures from the business and finance communities. The conference, Looking Forward to Full Employment, organized jointly by the Trades Union Congress (TUC) and the Employment Policy Institute (EPI) at Congress House, marked the fiftieth anniversary of two landmark publications: the wartime coalition's 1944 White Paper *Employment Policy* (Cmnd 6527) and W. H. Beveridge's classic *Full Employment in a Free Society*.

Anniversaries are often little more than an excuse for nostalgia. But every now and then an anniversary provides a valuable reference point for contemporary debate. This was undoubtedly true in 1994, a year which saw the first clear signs of a renewed ground swell of interest in solutions to mass unemployment.

The European Commission circulated *Growth, Competitiveness and Employment* (first published at the end of 1993 and popularly known as the Delors White Paper). The G7 industrial nations held a wide-ranging Jobs Summit in Detroit, USA, and after two years of analysis the OECD published its detailed *Jobs Study*. In the southern hemisphere the Australian government released a White Paper on *Employment and Growth* and an accompanying policy report *Working Nation: Policies and Programmes*. The policy momentum at EU level was subsequently maintained at top level summits at Essen (1994) and Madrid (1995). Meanwhile, the International Labour Organization in its first *World Employment Report* (1995) called for a renewed international policy commitment to full employment, while the G7 announced that it would hold a second Jobs Summit in Lille, France, in 1996.

In Britain, these international developments were reflected in the return of employment policy to the forefront of political debate. The Labour Party, under the late John Smith, reaffirmed its commitment to the goal of full employment which had been gradually downplayed in the 1980s. Equally significant, however, was a change of mood in official policy circles as compared with the 1980s.

Mrs Thatcher's governments had abandoned the 1944 White Paper's historic commitment to 'maintain a high and stable level of employment'. The weapons of macroeconomic policy, which for a generation after 1944 were deployed to control unemployment, had only inflation in their sights. The Thatcher government's view, as stated by former Chancellor of the Exchequer Nigel Lawson in his 1984 Mais Lecture, was that unemployment was best tackled by microeconomic and supply side policy. But since this meant enabling markets to operate more freely, employment was left to find its own level. Unemployment, once the central concern of economic policy, was therefore effectively relegated to the status of a residual. ·

In the 1990s, however, under John Major's premiership, the emphasis began to change. Inflation remained the number one priority of macroeconomic policy but the Conservative government now seemed less prepared simply to tolerate mass unemployment. This was demonstrated most clearly by Chancellor of the Exchequer Kenneth Clarke in his Mais Lecture, delivered just days before the jubilee of the 1944 White Paper. Mr Clarke not only stated that unemployment must be the 'main preoccupation' of economic policy-makers in the 1990s but also that he shared in principle the commitment to maintain a high and stable level of employment.

Mr Clarke's view of how to meet this commitment is of course vastly different to that of the authors of the 1944 White Paper – not to mention Beveridge – and will no doubt fail to convince everybody today. It is nonetheless encouraging at least to see unemployment being given greater priority, a development reinforced by the emergence of vigorous debate on the centre-left of British politics – kick-started by the emergence of 'New Labour' under the leadership of Tony Blair – about the requirements of employment policy in the late 1990s and beyond. The debate has been fostered by a succession of major policy publications: The report of The (Borrie) Commission on Social Justice (October 1994); the Joseph Rowntree Foundation's *Inquiry into Income and Wealth* (March 1995); and the Report of the Dahrendorf Commission on *Wealth Creation and Social Cohesion* (July 1995).

The collection of papers brought together in this book makes an equally important contribution to the ongoing debate. The individual and self-contained chapters by leading experts in the fields of economics, employment and public policy span the entire range of policy issues that will need to be addressed if full employment is to be achieved. Most of the contributions are revised versions of the original conference papers. An exception is Chapter 2 by Andrew Britton which was delivered as a keynote address to the conference and is best read in that light.

Perhaps inevitably, the book focuses on British experience and offers a home-grown perspective on the conditions for regaining full employment. However, what might be called the centre-left political economy of full employment that permeates much of the book will find echoes in policy debates in the EU and most other Western industrialized countries. Moreover, while the starting-point for book was the policy debate of the 1940s and early post-war years the book's title indicates the importance of adapting policy to meet the needs of today and the generation to come. While it is useful for society to look back to Beveridge and the 1944 White Paper to re-enlist the intellectual rigour and moral zeal enshrined in the post-war commitment to full employment, we must be forward looking in our search for solutions.

As editor, I would like to thank all the contributors for their considerable efforts in preparing and subsequently revising their contributions. Thanks are also due to Alison Kirk, Economics Editor at Routledge, for her assistance. Special thanks are due to David Lea, Bill Callaghan, Ian Brinkley and Neil Stoessel at the TUC for their support, as well as to TUC General Secretary John Monks whose initial enthusiasm for the 1994 conference made this book possible. Last but not least I must thank my colleagues at the Employment Policy Institute – a small independent think tank – who have helped in this exercise: Peter Stokoe, Peter Harvey, Lucy Brooks and Nick Isles. Without their respective efforts the book would still be in preparation!

John Philpott
Employment Policy Institute
January 1996

1

LOOKING FORWARD TO FULL EMPLOYMENT

An overview

John Philpott

INTRODUCTION

Jobs are once again a serious item on the political agenda. In Britain as elsewhere, policy debate has been galvanized by the spread of unemployment – and feelings of job insecurity – beyond the traditionally affected blue-collar occupations to white-collar workers and those employed in managerial and professional grades. Conservative politicians who, like former Chancellor of the Exchequer Norman Lamont, might once have described unemployment as a 'price well worth paying' in the battle against inflation are now mindful of the fact that fear about jobs is evident throughout the Tory heartlands of 'middle Britain'. Rather than down-play the unemployment issue in the mid-1990s, the British right has instead sought to talk up Britain's jobs record within the EU. Deregulated free market Britain has been described as the 'enterprise centre of Europe', while interventionist economic and social policies (for example, minimum wage legislation or adherence to the general principles set out in the Social Chapter of the Maastricht Treaty on European Union) have been condemned as 'job destroyers'.

Politicians on the centre and left meanwhile have once again begun to talk of full employment as a policy goal, albeit often cautiously and with varying degrees of enthusiasm. While centre-left politicians agree that unemployment must be a policy priority, some are wary of promising too much while others – leastways in private – question whether the language of full employment is still appropriate in a modern technologically oriented free market economy. There are similar disagreements about the means of achieving full employment. Old style Keynesian solutions to unemployment – which emphasize the importance of expansionary macroeconomic policy – are still voiced but the views of so-called 'modernizers', who stress supply side reforms and the need to make individuals more employable, have recently been in the ascendant. Between these poles are those – sometimes referred to as 'New Keynesians' – who seek a sophisticated accommodation between demand management and supply side measures designed to create a socially inclusive and cohesive 'stakeholder

1

economy' able to sustain full employment without inflation whilst at the same time improving living standards for all citizens.

The subsequent chapters in this book will pick up different strands of the ongoing debate on unemployment and employment policy which provide the context for an understanding of the kinds of policies that will need to be introduced if Britain is once again to experience full employment. This introductory chapter provides a non-technical overview of the key underlying themes and policy issues.

Full employment and mass unemployment

According to Beveridge at the end of World War II, full employment would entail an unemployment rate of 3 per cent or less of the workforce in a 'sellers market' in which the number of job vacancies outstripped the number of jobless men (Beveridge 1944). Moreover, there should be no long-term unemployed. The margin of 3 per cent would 'consist of a shifting body of short-term unemployed who could be maintained without hardship by unemployment insurance'.

Beveridge, in line with the HM Government 1944 *Employment Policy* White Paper's less precise aim of maintaining a 'high and stable level of employment', considered the prime responsibility for achieving this to rest with the state. The principal instrument would be demand management; as Keynes had shown, it was essential that the state should use the tools of financial policy to maintain an adequate level of demand for goods and services. Yet it would be wrong to conclude that this was considered all that was needed to achieve full employment.

The White Paper, for example, warned about the inflationary pressures that might be associated with the maintenance of a high and stable level of employment and contains extensive reference to what we would nowadays call 'supply side' measures as a way of mitigating them. Indeed, according to the late Professor James Meade – Nobel Laureate and a key contributor to the White Paper – Keynes was concerned that inflationary pressures might build up in the post-war economy if the unemployment rate were to fall much below 8 per cent of the workforce (Meade 1994). Beveridge was also aware that the task of achieving full employment was far from straightforward and extended beyond demand management. He concluded his preface to *Full Employment in a Free Society* as follows:

> Unemployment cannot be conquered by a democracy until it is understood. Full productive employment in a free society is possible but it is not possible without taking pains. It cannot be won by waving a financial wand; it is a goal that can be reached only by conscious continuous organisation of all our productive resources under democratic control. To win full employment and keep it, we must will the end and must understand and will the means.
>
> (Beveridge 1944: 16)

2

As events turned out, Beveridge's optimism that the means and the will could be marshalled to fight unemployment was vindicated throughout much of the post-war era. Full employment without serious inflation was maintained in conditions of excess demand for a generation after the war, albeit as Andrew Britton points out (Chapter 2) this reflected a confluence of economic and social circumstances – not least a remarkable degree of restraint on the part of wage bargainers – as much as any skill on the part of policy-makers.

Unfortunately, matters have deteriorated during the past twenty years. The UK economy nowadays 'overheats' at well in excess of 3 per cent unemployment. Over the last business cycle the unemployment rate averaged 8 per cent – and long-term unemployment has re-emerged as a major social and economic problem (one in every three people currently unemployed have been without a job for at least a year). Although the lack of any upsurge in inflation as unemployment has fallen during the course of the 1990s economic recovery offers some hope that matters have improved more recently, few can be confident that the present recovery will on its own succeed where all those since the mid-1970s have failed and restore full employment as envisaged by Beveridge.

The cost of this failure is truly immense. Research shows that unemployment is a major source of unhappiness (Clark and Oswald 1994) and as David Piachaud outlines (Chapter 3) mass unemployment has bred poverty, damaged the health of individuals and whole communities and reduced social cohesion by fostering an emergent 'underclass'. It has also threatened to undermine the welfare state – the very existence of which was originally predicated by Beveridge on the assumption of full employment. According to Piachaud the burden on the taxpayer of maintaining between two and three million people on the dole in 1994–95 amounted to £26 billion or £9,000 per unemployed person. Piachaud calculates that if unemployment were reduced to its average level in the 1970s, the Exchequer cost would fall by the equivalent of 10 pence on the basic rate of income tax.

This is of course a big if. Yet Piachaud is surely right to conclude that mass unemployment should not be passively accepted as a *fait accompli*. As he concludes, 'Britain has a choice'. The initial task facing those who still aspire to full employment, however, is, as Andrew Britton also remarks in Chapter 2, to convince people in the 1990s that full employment is more than just a political slogan borrowed from the past – and to make clear the requirements and costs associated with a strategy to achieve it.

More than just a slogan?

If the opinion polls are to be believed most people in Britain today remain unconvinced that full employment can be achieved and many consider the objective a pipedream. This is unsurprising. One needs to be well over the age of majority to have any real memory of a time when finding a job was relatively easy. Nowadays few people feel fully secure in their employment and the common belief is that never again will there be sufficient jobs to go round, even during good times for the economy. In addition to pessimism, many are also confused by the language of full employment. It often conveys an impression of full-time male employees working flat out, which can seem outdated in the 1990s when women make up half the workforce and more people work part-time or are self-employed.

Jill Rubery (Chapter 4) is critical in particular of the 'gender blindness' evident in definitions of full employment and unemployment. Both Rubery and Patricia Hewitt (Chapter 5) agree that full employment must mean employment for both women and men. As Hewitt makes clear, however, while this will mean re-evaluating the assumptions surrounding Beveridge's historically specific definition of full employment, the definition in its broader numerical sense is still appropriate today. In other words, although the changed nature of the labour market in the 1990s has major implications for the policies society will have to adopt to achieve full employment – and means that a fully employed economy would look very different – the goal as set out by Beveridge remains valid.

If, for example, the demand for labour could once again be sustained at the level required to meet Beveridge's full employment target, modern day social preference – as mitigated by prevailing tax and benefit systems – would undoubtedly result in a very different pattern of employment (in terms of the mix of male and female and full-time and part-time workers, etc.) than that which prevailed under full employment in the post-war era. But we should not (as the growing number of 'future of work' gurus often do) confuse discussion of how society should respond to a changing pattern of employment with the issue of how to expand the volume of employment.

Common pessimism about the prospects for full employment would of course be justified if it were impossible to expand the volume of employment. If there were only a fixed amount of work to be done policy-makers would be virtually impotent in the face of, say, new technology or an increase in the number of people looking for jobs. At best all that could be hoped for would be to share the available work around. But in a world of mass desire, not to mention poverty and need, the belief that there can never again be jobs for all who seek them seems hard to sustain. The problem of mass unemployment instead lies in society's inability to maintain demand in the economy at a rate sufficient to absorb idle hands without stoking up inflation (and creating balance of payments problems). In order to translate full employment from a slogan into a set of practical propositions we must therefore – as Beveridge would certainly have appreciated – understand why so much unemployment is nowadays required to keep inflation in check.

'Core unemployment'

The crux of the post-war remedy for unemployment was to dampen fluctuations in the economic cycle in order to ensure that there was no prolonged deficiency in demand of the kind experienced during the inter-war years. Since the mid-1970s, however, although unemployment still rises and falls broadly in line with fluctuations in demand and output, increasing emphasis has tended to be placed upon the 'core' of unemployment around which fluctuations in the cycle occur. This has been especially true in Britain and most of the countries of the European Union. The EU countries as a whole have experienced a trend increase in the core rate of unemployment to around 10 per cent of the workforce. In the USA, by contrast, unemployment has fluctuated around a core rate of 7 per cent – now considerably lower than the EU average, having generally been higher in the 1950s and 1960s – while Japan has maintained both a low core unemployment rate of roughly 2 per cent and also prevented significant fluctuations of unemployment (Table 1.1).

'Core' unemployment is a less loaded term than the more commonly used term 'structural' unemployment. For some, structural unemployment means a mismatch between the skills or location of jobless people and the skill requirements and location of job vacancies. For others, it implies inflexibility in institutional arrangements that make the labour market more 'rigid' or more prone to inflation at any given level of demand. In particular, the term often implies that only supply side measures are appropriate for dealing with the problem. In general, this is probably a valid implication. But some economists would argue that macroeconomic measures operating on the demand as well as the supply side of the economy would have a role to play in any strategy for full employment. It is preferable to have an open mind on all of these issues so we shall stick with core unemployment (as Andrew Britton remarks in Chapter 2, unemployment is not a simple problem with one explanation and one cure).

The initial onset of the rise in the core unemployment problem in Britain as elsewhere is generally felt to be associated with the various economic 'shocks' of the 1970s and early 1980s – notably the sharp oil price hikes – and over the longer term 'strains' caused by structural change which have led to job losses in traditional industries and in particular caused a reduction in the demand for unskilled workers.

Table 1.1 Standardized unemployment rates in major OECD countries, 1974, 1983, 1994

	1974 %	*1983* %	*1994* %
USA	5.5	7.4	6.0
Japan	1.4	2.7	2.9
Germany (West)	1.6	7.1	6.9
France	2.8	9.7	12.5
Italy	5.3	9.4	12.0
UK	2.9	11.7	9.6

Source: OECD

Some explanations of the rising core point to interactions between periodic bouts of deficient demand and a deterioration in the strength of the supply side of the economy. The loss of industrial capacity and skills, combined with the creation of a large group of long-term unemployed who are not easily re-absorbed into jobs even during periods of economic recovery, weakens an economy's capacity to reduce unemployment substantially without a resurgence of inflation.

A related, albeit even more fundamental issue for Britain, is raised by Christine Greenhalgh and Mary Gregory (Chapter 6). They point to 'deindustrialization' leading to substantial job losses in manufacturing as a major cause not only of unemployment in Britain but also of the nation's general economic difficulties. Greenhalgh and Gregory show that over the period 1960–90 – and especially since 1979 – Britain shed manufacturing jobs at a far faster rate than any of the G5 major industrial nations.

This outcome could of course be viewed as a sign of success because manufacturing productivity has risen sharply. Improved productivity should serve as a boost to domestic output and, by increasing competitiveness in world markets, also assist export-led growth. This can generate sufficient prosperity to underpin job creation in the service sector if not manufacturing itself. However, as Greenhalgh and Gregory show, Britain's deindustrialization has corresponded with a loss of market share in both domestic and export markets for manufactured goods, while growth in manufacturing output has been weaker than that of any other G5 nation.

The central issue here as far as core unemployment is concerned is not that jobs are being lost from manufacturing – this will tend to occur come what may because new technology is continually providing scope for improvements in productivity. The issue is rather that of the consequences of the apparent lack of competitiveness of Britain's manufacturing sector.

Poor manufacturing performance makes it more difficult for Britain to maintain a healthy balance of trade and limits the scope for generating a sustained reduction in unemployment. For one thing, policy-makers will be reluctant to boost demand for goods and services for fear that balance of payments problems might lead to downward pressure on the pound and – because this would result in higher import prices in the shops – upward pressure on inflation. Moreover, Greenhalgh and Gregory point out that manufacturing sustains a far higher proportion of jobs throughout the economy than is measured by its share in total employment because it makes substantial purchases from the service sector. A weak manufacturing sector is therefore likely to result in a lower overall level of employment.

New technology and 'globalization'

A common explanation for the rise in core unemployment is an observed shift in the demand for labour favouring those with skills as against those without skills.

6

At present in Britain, for example, despite the fact that unemployment rates at all levels of skill are high as a hangover from the 1990s recession, rates for unskilled workers are five times as high as those for better skilled workers (Philpott 1994). Perhaps even more significant, the unskilled comprise roughly half of Britain's present (i.e. mid-1990s) pool of one million long-term unemployed, while many more unskilled people have left the workforce altogether. Roughly a third of unskilled men of working age are 'non-employed', either unemployed or existing outside the labour market (see Schmitt and Wadsworth 1994).

Christopher Freeman (Chapter 7) examines the role of technology in causing this shift. He focuses in particular on the dramatic impact of information and communications technology (ICT) which – like steam power or electrification in previous eras – represents a quantum leap in the prevailing mode of technology affecting not just a few products or services but every industry and every service. This change in the technological mode benefits most those workers skilled enough to perform higher level jobs, especially jobs requiring significant 'brain power' in order to fulfil so-called 'problem-solving' tasks. It causes difficulty, however, for those equipped only for traditional routine forms of work based on either simple 'muscle power' or the ability to operate within a fairly standard production line or service function setting. Opportunities for the unskilled and less skilled are thus diminishing, an outcome that is putting downward pressure on pay at the bottom end of the labour market and making it more likely that unskilled workers will lose their jobs and be unable to find new ones (see also Rifkin 1995).

Some economists, however, while not disputing the importance of technology, also argue that increased competition from low-cost developing countries – arising from the ever more 'globalized' pattern of investment, production and trade – has also been a major factor underlying the fall in demand for unskilled workers in developed economies (see, for example, Wood 1994; Minford 1994). Richard Freeman (Chapter 8) reviews the evidence for and against this trade effect on the labour market.

Economists' theories of international trade – which predict that in order to maximize the gains from trade a country will exploit its comparative advantage in available resources – suggest that the effect of globalized trade on the labour market prospects of low-skilled workers could be considerable. The developed economies are relatively more abundant in skilled workers so it makes sense for them to specialize in goods and services with a high skill content and rely on imports of less skill-intensive products from developing countries. As more cheap imports have become available, it is therefore argued, the general tendency of Western economies has thus been to shift even more in the direction of higher-skilled labour, reducing opportunities for the unskilled. Some economists suggest that just such a trade effect has led to a 20 per cent fall in demand for unskilled labour in the developed economies during the past thirty years (see Wood 1994).

Richard Freeman is agnostic on this issue. While concluding that globalization has, and probably will have, a much greater impact on unskilled labour in the

7

West than many economists have thus far estimated, he questions whether the effect has been as dramatic as some claim. One reason is simply that developed economies mostly trade among themselves, using broadly similar proportions of skilled and unskilled workers (according to the OECD *Jobs Study* 1994, exports from 'low wage countries' account for only 1.5 per cent of total expenditure on goods and services by the developed economies). Another reason is that the impact of globalization falls on the tradable sector (primarily manufacturing) which in most developed economies accounts for a relatively small share of total employment. Since unskilled workers are under pressure throughout the labour market the likelihood therefore is that their prospects are affected by technology and other factors as well as by trade (see also World Bank 1995).

The importance of being adaptable

The preceding discussion should not of course be taken to imply that trade and technology are things to be avoided. On the contrary, they are to be encouraged. By raising productivity, technological change helps lower costs and prices and enables people to buy more goods and services. Moreover, technology generates new investment, new forms of employment and new products – the demand for which, along with that for existing products, is boosted by the higher real pay and living standards afforded by improved productivity. Similarly, competition inspired by free trade benefits consumers in the form of lower prices while at the same time opening up new export markets. So trade agreements such as the General Agreement on Tariffs and Trade (GATT) should be supported.

However, while most of society stands to gain from these processes there will be losers if labour markets and related institutions fail to adapt to change. If the number of losers is simply allowed to rise, both they and other potential losers will become fearful of, and hostile to, change. Such hostility stands in the way of economic and social progress. Even more worryingly, it can give rise to political tensions that undermine the very foundations of democratic society. Some on the right (for example, Goldsmith 1994) and the left (Lang and Hines 1994) argue that in order to avoid this governments in Western industrialized countries should resort to some form of trade protectionism. A far better response, however, is to ensure that the labour market and economy more generally is adaptable in the face of increased competition. 'Adaptability' must therefore become the *sine qua non* of economic and employment policy.

Significantly, adaptability was the key theme of the wide ranging OECD *Jobs Study*. The study concluded that the way societies adapt to shocks and strains is what in the end matters for employment and unemployment, not the shocks and strains themselves. All the developed economies are affected by change in much the same way but some have fared better than others. Yet the OECD – while clearly having a preference for a policy approach to unemployment based upon deregulation – is careful not to single out any particular 'model' of adaptability since almost nowhere have labour markets adapted satisfactorily to change. The OECD prefers instead to set out policy options, based on multi-country experience, in the hope that countries will choose paths away from mass unemployment that both create jobs and maintain social cohesion.

The need for a 'middle way'

What sort of 'model' of adaptability would best suit Britain? It is often said that a choice has to be made between a deregulated/minimal welfare US-style model and a 'European Union' model comprising a more regulated labour market and generous welfare provision. In tabloid terms, the former model is said to be friendly to job creation, the latter a recipe for unemployment. This is something of a caricature. The EU after all is not a homogeneous entity and it is arguable that some 'social market' EU states, notably Germany, have performed better in terms of unemployment and adapting to change than the more 'free market' USA (see Goodhart 1994). The tabloid caricature nonetheless bears some resemblance to reality.

According to the OECD, the European Union has since the mid-1970s maintained strong productivity growth through shedding workers from traditional sectors but, with the exception of some increase in public sector employment, generated few new jobs. The result has been high unemployment and particularly long-term unemployment – half of those unemployed in the EU have been without employment for more than a year.

The US economy by contrast, although growing at a comparable rate, has been better at creating jobs – both high- and low-skilled – mostly in the private services sector. There is, however, some dispute over how to interpret the relative job creation perfomance of the US economy (see Glyn 1995). But productivity has grown only slowly and there have been profound implications for pay. Wage differentials have widened dramatically. Richard Freeman (Chapter 8 and Freeman 1994) notes that a man in the bottom tenth of the hourly earnings distribution in the USA earns just over a third as much as the average (i.e. median) man. In Europe, by contrast, a similarly placed man earns two-thirds of the average. However, the problem in the USA is not merely one of more unequal earnings – absolute poverty among the working poor has also grown to staggering proportions. Freeman calculates that an unemployed man in an advanced European country now has a higher living standard than a working man situated toward the bottom of the US pay league.

This outcome partly reflects developments in trade and technology of the kind discussed earlier. But as Paul Ormerod points out (Chapter 9) the US job creation record and the associated depression of wages is also to a large extent explained by a large influx of migrant labour from Mexico prepared to work for poverty pay. An indirect consequence of this has been increased 'non-employment' and rising crime; to avoid low-paid jobs many unskilled Americans have opted out of the legitimate labour market altogether (see also Balls and Gregg 1993).

The UK has spent the last seventeen years moving in the direction of the US model while attempting to maintain a semblance of the welfare state. Kenneth Clarke's 1994 Mais Lecture indicates that as a One Nation Conservative he believes such a 'hybrid' model offers a means of securing full employment without creating a class of working poor. However, Britain's record on jobs and inequality since 1979 offers little support for this view.

As Chris Pond notes (Chapter 10) earnings have become more unequal in Britain and the numbers in poverty have also risen (albeit to nothing like the same extent as in the USA). According to the Joseph Rowntree Foundation's (JRF) *Inquiry into Income and Wealth* (1995), hourly wages for the lowest paid men in the UK hardly changed in real terms between 1978 and 1992 (and by the latter year were lower than in 1975). Men on average pay, by contrast, saw their hourly earnings rise by a third while the highest paid men enjoyed a 50 per cent increase. The JRF Inquiry found that throughout the industrial world in the 1980s only New Zealand – which pursued a similar mix of free market policies – experienced a greater increase in income inequality than the UK. By 1990, British income inequality – reflecting much higher joblessness as well as more unequal earnings – was wider than at any time since World War II.

The rationale for this policy – which has involved cuts in the value of welfare benefits, severe curbs on the power of organized labour and the abolition of minimum wage protection – is that it improves work incentives. It is argued that by placing more emphasis on profits than pay, the economy's potential for investment, higher productivity and job creation is raised (the share of wages in national income in Britain has fallen to well below two-thirds, its lowest level for forty years). Despite this, however, rates of investment have been generally subdued and the pay-off in terms of extra jobs in Britain in the 1980s and 1990s has not been spectacular in European terms, let alone in comparison with the USA (Table 1.2).

It can of course be argued that an underlying improvement in the supply side potential for job creation in Britain has been masked by macroeconomic instability which has resulted in substantial job losses in the recessions of the early 1980s and 1990s. Indeed some economists – ironically mostly right-wing monetarists – argue that all that now stands between a return to a high investment, fully

Table 1.2 Employment growth, 1961–94 (percentage change on previous year)

	1961–73 %	1974–86 %	1987 %	1988 %	1989 %	1990 %	1991 %	1992 %	1993 %	1994 %
UK	0.3	−0.2	1.9	3.3	2.6	1.1	−3.1	−2.1	−1.6	0.3
France	0.7	0.1	0.3	0.9	1.3	1.0	0.1	−0.8	−1.1	0.1
EU	0.3	0.1	1.1	1.5	1.5	1.7	0.0	−1.3	−2.0	−0.5
USA	1.9	1.8	3.4	2.8	1.9	1.2	−1.0	−0.2	1.8	3.1
Japan	1.3	0.7	0.9	1.7	2.0	2.1	2.1	1.1	0.2	0.1

Source: European Commission

employed, low inflation economy is the failure of ultra-cautious policy-makers to recognize this underlying improvement and thus to relax macroeconomic policy accordingly (Minford and Riley 1994). But even accepting the proposition that the New Right policies pursued since 1979, and the attendant 'new inequality', have reduced core unemployment in Britain below the 8 per cent rate identified by the majority of economists in the 1980s, there are still few signs that Britain's new model labour market is functioning in a way that will provide opportunities for the chronic jobless in the 1990s in the absence of new forms of policy intervention.

Many of the new jobs created in Britain in the 1980s, for example, were part-time – and taken by women entering the labour market – or took the form of more people, men and women, in self-employment. Full-time employment, by contrast, contracted. Similarly, while the recovery of the 1990s has seen more 'good' jobs – i.e. in managerial, professional or technical occupations – created than low grade 'McJobs' (hamburger flipping and the like) a high proportion have offered only short-term contracts with the result that temporary work has grown by a quarter (EPI 1995). While there is nothing inherently inferior about part-time or temporary jobs and self-employment – indeed most people who work in this way want to do so – they fail to engage a substantial section of the labour force.

Unskilled men in particular have tended to be squeezed out of the jobs equation – lacking the ability to become self-employed or skilled 'portfolio workers' on several different temporary contracts, and unable or unwilling to work in low hours, unskilled jobs. Such men (and also to some extent more skilled former manual workers whose skills have been made redundant in the course of structural change) have tended to remain unemployed, existing on one form of meagre welfare benefit or another. Some are visible and 'officially' long-term jobless on unemployment related benefits, others 'non-employed' and – leastways prior to the introduction of Incapacity Benefit in 1995 – in receipt of sickness related benefits. The perversity of the benefits system (for reasons to be discussed in more detail later) has also meant that many of these jobless men have been joined on welfare by their female partners.

The tendency for the modern British labour market to leave a rump of non-employed people alongside a group of increasingly insecure people in work and a higher echelon of privileged workers has been highlighted by Hutton (1995) who concludes that the result has been the emergence of a fractured 'thirty– thirty–forty society'. The accuracy with which Hutton draws the contours and features of 'divided Britain' are a matter of debate (see, for example, Robinson 1995). But there is no doubting that Hutton's depiction conveys a deeper reality and is in tune with the more general observation that Britain's 'work and welfare' model seems to have created the worst of both worlds – more relatively poor people in work but also a high level of unemployment and a growing 'underclass' of welfare dependants.

In this context some on the New Right argue that the best route to more jobs would be to abandon the hybrid model that Kenneth Clarke defends in favour of further deregulation and draconian cuts in publicly provided welfare support. However, the social problems associated with a 'hire and fire' style flexible labour market are already apparent and a 'more of the same' approach could impose intolerable social costs. Moreover, those tempted to take this course ought to listen to what many Americans are saying about the fully deregulated approach: 'been there, don't like it, want something better' (for a detailed account of the economic and social consequences of the US approach see Freeman 1995).

New Democrats in the USA have sought to establish a new model – one that aims to create not just more jobs but also 'good' (i.e. skilled, well paid, 'problem-solving') jobs while at the same time supporting the incomes in work of those with low skills who can command only a low market wage. This 'middle way' approach is the brainchild of Robert Reich, Labor Secretary in the Clinton administration and was highlighted at the first G7 Jobs Summit (Reich 1991). The EU is also looking for a middle way that will create jobs and preserve social solidarity (European Commission 1993) as is Australia with its ambitious *Working Nation* programme. Britain should be flowing with this tide by developing its own progressive 'middle way' within the context of a strategy for full employment.

Key policy issues

From the contributions to this book and other available material it is possible to distil some policy ideas which, if knitted together, could form individual elements of a 'middle way' strategy for full employment. Here, rather than outline a specific strategy, we shall simply consider some of the key underlying policy issues as drawn from the papers. These are: labour market regulation; skills and competitiveness; employment taxes and benefit reform; active labour market policies; the role of the public sector and 'social employment'; macroeconomic issues; and pay and productivity.

Labour market regulation

The case for a deregulated labour market rests on the belief that regulation – in very broad terms employment protection and minimum wage legislation, plus adequate legal backing for trade unions – renders markets less flexible and less adaptable, thus driving up unemployment. This belief permeates the OECD's *Jobs Study* (the free market bias of which is more evident in its analysis of the causes of unemployment than its rather more catholic policy recommendations). However, the case for labour market deregulation can be questioned on a number of grounds.

The McKinsey Global Institute (MKI 1994), for example, suggests that the roots of high core unemployment in much of Europe lie not in labour market regulation but instead over-regulated product markets. The MKI thus concludes that product market deregulation represents the best way to promote across-the-board job creation; labour market deregulation simply leads to the creation of more low-grade, low wage jobs.

From a labour market perspective, radical (and highly controversial) new analysis by Blanchflower and Oswald (1995) appears to undermine the free market textbook economics upon which the case for labour market deregulation rests. Whereas conventional labour market theory predicts that high wages are associated with high unemployment, Blanchflower and Oswald find the opposite to be true in all manner of different countries (all other factors having been accounted for) although they accept that more work is needed in order to determine the precise relevance of this surprising finding for policy-makers. In a different vein, David Marsden (Chapter 11) also questions the assumptions underlying the case for deregulating the labour market (see also Mayhew 1994). The problem for policy-makers as Marsden sees matters is that the labour market is far from homogeneous. While regulation might harm employment prospects in some corners of the market – principally the low productivity end – it can enhance matters in those segments where what Marsden calls 'co-operative exchange' is important for creating productivity-enhancing relations between employers and workers.

This helps explain the equivocation of the OECD's *Jobs Study* itself on the subject of employment protection legislation. The OECD finds that while such legislation preserves jobs it also deters employers from hiring because of the costs of shedding labour (see also Layard *et al.* 1991). But it finds that by encouraging long-term relationships between employers and workers employment protection can increase the volume of on-the-job training in the economy. In terms of Marsden's analysis, crude deregulation right across the labour market may indeed boost low wage, low productivity jobs. But such a move can be counter-productive if what one wants is a high skill economy.

Marsden goes on to point out more generally that measures such as formal consultation procedures of the kind common in Germany enhance 'co-operative exchange' between workers and employers and thus make labour markets much more flexible and adaptable than is the case in the low trust, insecure environment of what might best be described as a 'hire and fire' culture. Others observing this situation – which bears some relation to the concept of the 'stake-holder company' – have concluded that the statutory imposition of consultation procedures on large European companies – as proposed under the Social Chapter of the Maastricht Treaty but opposed by the government and many employers in Britain – should thus be seen as a development to be embraced (see Balls 1994). More generally, however, Marsden implies that constructive dialogue between the social partners is ultimately more important than EU legislation.

The conclusion to be drawn from this discussion is not that all regulation is good and all deregulation bad, but rather that policy-makers should search for the right balance of intervention within a progressive policy of re-regulation. This balance should seek to ensure that low productivity jobs are not needlessly destroyed (or their creation wantonly prevented). But at the same time re-regulation should be used to gear the economy to compete at the high productivity end of world markets where Britain's comparative advantage surely lies.

As Jill Rubery and Patricia Hewitt also discuss (Chapters 4 and 5), appropriate re-regulation – backed up by other measures such as better child care to assist all mothers but especially jobless lone parents – would help to foster equal opportunities. Hewitt calls in particular for re-regulation to establish what she calls a new system of 'fair flexibility' in working time. This, Hewitt argues, could form part of a strategy for reducing unemployment and at the same time improve the quality of work and family life for both women and men. Hewitt believes that reform of working time would also enhance efficiency, a point backed up by Christopher Freeman in Chapter 7, who points out that the new mode of technology centred on information and communications is geared toward flexible forms of working. Regulations and benefit systems based upon traditional forms of working will thus hamper the ability of economies to adapt to change.

Skills and competitiveness

As Christopher Freeman's chapter also makes clear, the adjustment needed to create a high skill economy will involve improvements in education and training and related measures to assist the diffusion of information and computer technology. He advocates in particular substantial investment in 'information highways and byways' based upon digital technology. Such investment played an important part in the Clinton administration's plan for economic prosperity in the USA and – along with trans-European transport and energy networks – is a dominant theme in the European Union's competitiveness programme.

A highly skilled workforce will be crucial to exploiting the opportunities such technology offers for creating new markets and jobs. Everybody, of course, is in favour of education and training. Most people, for example, welcomed the principle behind the Modern Apprenticeship programme launched in Britain in 1994; it is vital that we stop producing wave after wave of young people too unskilled to hold down a properly paid job in a modern economy. Similarly, 'lifelong learning' and training for the unemployed are also seen as ways of preventing skills 'mismatches' of the kind that cause inflation to emerge even when unemployment is high. Some commentators, however, have described as vacuous the assertion that more skilled workers are needed. It is also necessary to ensure that the provision of skills is matched by the capacity and willingness of companies to use them. If not, costly investment could be wasted.

Keep and Mayhew (1995), for example, argue that while a proportion of British employers are already taking the high quality route to international competitiveness, too many remain wedded to low quality products because high quality strategies require substantial investment and radical changes in corporate organization. The underlying problem is the short-termism that bedevils so much of British industry with the quest for quick profits and dividends taking precedence over long-term planning and investment – a fundamental weakness powerfully exposed by Hutton (1995) in his influential critique *The State We're In.*

Ironically, it might be argued that this failure to make use of skills is good news for unskilled workers since it stems the shift in demand away from unskilled and toward skilled labour. The flaw in this argument, however, as Greenhalgh and Gregory's findings show, is that Britain's manufacturers have over time been losing out in world and domestic markets and manufacturing output has grown relatively sluggishly. So unskilled jobs are being lost notwithstanding the reluctance of many companies to move upmarket. Simply accepting the low quality scenario will only make matters worse. While it is tempting to argue that things can be improved if companies are able to become more price competitive (through currency devaluation or by reducing the cost of employing unskilled labour) this can be no more than a palliative. If British companies are to survive in the long-term they will have to upgrade the quality of their products.

Unfortunately, this leaves policy-makers with a problem. It is far from easy in a free market economy to persuade companies to behave differently. Exhortation through the Training and Enterprise Councils (TECs) may persuade more employers to become 'Investors in People' or participate in similar initiatives – but many employers still present a deaf ear. The Commission on Social Justice (CSJ) and the Labour Party have considered alternative routes – such as individual learning accounts, a 'learning bank' and a University of Industry – by which to promote the concept of skills through lifelong learning (CSJ 1994; Labour Party, June 1995). But it may be the case anyway that the emphasis on training or skills *per se* is misguided.

Keep and Mayhew (1995), for example, believe that more should be done in the first instance to encourage companies to think strategically – if they do this they are more likely to operate in ways designed to make use of skills. Whether this is a job for TECs is a moot point – perhaps the joint TEC/Chamber of Commerce model which some prefer offers a better institutional mechanism for promoting such change. Keep and Mayhew, also indicate that full-time education, rather than training, will assume increasing prominence as a way of altering the behaviour of companies. Similarly, Shackleton (1995) argues that the emphasis of policy should shift from specialist to general skills which are best inculcated through formal education rather than post-school training.

There has already been a rapid expansion in the numbers of young people staying on at school or moving into further and higher education before entering the labour market (which may represent a supply side response to the shift in demand away from unskilled labour). This supply side trend, it is sometimes argued, may so alter the incentives facing employers that many more will choose to adopt a high quality product strategy. Keep and Mayhew remain sceptical.

The conclusion to be drawn from this discussion is that one should be wary of arguments for full employment that blithely refer to the importance of education and training. A policy for skills must be wedded to a full-blown competitiveness package and industrial strategy. The latter, if directed at sustained investment would, over time, foster 'endogenous growth', thereby raising productivity and leading to more jobs and improved living standards (for a discussion of the links between investment and employment see Rowthorn 1995).

Greenhalgh and Gregory indicate that measures to enhance innovation and encourage ever greater use of technology as well as skills would have to be key components of a policy to rebuild Britain's manufacturing base. This view is reinforced by a recent analysis of British economic performance by a group of economists formerly employed at the now defunct National Economic Development Office (NEDO). This analysis highlights the need for wholesale institutional change in order to promote more effective financing and organization of British industry (see Buxton *et al.* 1994). Hutton (1995) argues that this will require rejection of the short-termist unstable liberal capitalism which has prevailed in Britain under successive Conservative governments since the late 1970s in favour of what he calls co-operative 'Stakeholder Capitalism' (see also Dahrendorf Commission 1995).

The series of 'Competitiveness' White Papers published by the Major government in the 1990s at the behest of Michael Heseltine MP, has displayed some recognition of the need for change. But the ascendancy of the Tory right and its opposition to anything that smacks of control over the affairs of the private sector has made it difficult for even forward looking Conservative politicians to admit to past policy failures. Irrespective of this, however, it is important to bear in mind that even if a competitiveness package were to succeed in creating more and better jobs the improvement would take some time, perhaps a generation, to emerge fully. Clearly, therefore, any strategy for full employment will also have to incorporate measures with a shorter pay-off time – and offer hope and opportunity to those whose natural capacity to learn may prevent them from ever obtaining highly skilled 'problem-solving' jobs.

Employment taxes and benefits reform

The choices which employers and individuals make in the labour market are influenced by the tax and benefit system. Some taxes, for example, employers' National Insurance contributions (NICs), directly raise the cost of labour over and above the amount employers have to pay out in wages to employees. This may affect the willingness of employers to hire labour, especially low-value, low-productivity workers. Such taxes also influence the pattern and structure of employment and unemployment as well as the overall demand for labour. For example, British employers at present (1996–7) pay no contributions on earnings of less than £61 per week – which acts as an implicit 'subsidy' to hire part-time workers. Such jobs may be acceptable to women who wish to combine employment with child care responsibilities but may not attract unskilled male 'breadwinners' who seek full-time jobs. The rules governing employers' NICs therefore play a part in tilting the structure of employment in favour of part-time women workers.

It is sometimes suggested that such taxes on labour should be substantially reduced to boost employment opportunities. Andrew Britton (Chapter 2), for example, considers whether large-scale adjustment of taxes of this kind might play a role in a full employment strategy. An obvious difficulty is loss of tax revenue to the Exchequer. This would be offset partly by savings in benefit as a consequence of lower unemployment, but Britton nonetheless expects the net cost having accounted for this to be considerable. Assuming these revenue losses have to be made up (to avoid cuts in public spending or higher borrowing) additional income tax or VAT would have to be raised.

This, of course, would be unpalatable for taxpayers – so some people argue instead that any compensatory revenue should be raised by taxing so-called 'anti-social activities', for example, the pollution which many companies cause as a byproduct of their production processes. This suggestion seems attractive. It would meet 'green' objectives in the process of helping the jobless – the so-called 'double dividend' (see Barker 1994; Jacobs 1995). But desirable though such a tax shift might be, it does not guarantee a 'free lunch'. The likelihood is that pollution taxes would, in full or in part, be passed on to consumers in the form of higher prices. Therefore, whether imposed on the consumer or the taxpayer, ultimately there would be some price to pay if policy-makers sought to create more jobs by slashing employers' NICs. Much then depends upon whether taxpayers (or consumers) consider the price worth paying. This is of course a matter of social choice as much as of economics. It is worth noting, however, that cutting tax contributions paid by employers on people they already employ would represent a deadweight loss to the Exchequer. When this loss is accounted for the net cost of each extra job created by such a tax cut often turns out to be much higher than that associated with an alternative job-creating use of the same amount of revenue.

The provision of benefits also affects the labour market. If the benefits system did not exist it is likely that there would be more low-paid employment. But the consequence would be mass poverty (and, in all likelihood, a still higher rate of crime as more people sought higher earnings from illegal activities). Nobody wants this in Britain, but neither do we want people to remain unemployed. The key issue therefore is to make the tax and benefit system more 'job friendly' without punishing those who comprise the poorest and most disadvantaged sections of the population. As the now hackneyed phrase – first used by John F. Kennedy in the 1960s and by British politicians of every political hue in the 1990s – puts it, there is a need to offer people 'a hand-up, rather than a hand-out'.

The Major government has implemented or experimented with different ways of improving work incentives. A lower rate tax band of 20 pence in the pound was introduced in 1992, while the less skilled, lower paid and long-term unemployed have been the focus of several changes to employee or employer National Insurance contributions (EPI 1995). In terms of benefit reform, aside from making welfare support less generous and more closely linked to job search, the switch from Unemployment Benefit to the Job Seeker's Allowance in 1996 being a prime example, ever greater stress has been placed on the use of in-work earnings supplements to encourage unemployed people into low-paid jobs (Duncan and Giles 1996; Whitehouse 1996). Around half a million people now receive Family Credit – at an annual cost of almost £1.5 billion – and experiments are ongoing on a new pilot in-work benefit, Earnings Top-Up, aimed at unemployed people without dependant children.

A fundamental problem with this approach is that the supplements are income related and give rise to the so-called 'poverty trap' – recipients of in-work supplements find that they are little better off if they try to raise their earnings because of the withdrawal of the supplement. Indeed, if one also adds the effect of tax rises as earnings rise it is possible for some people on benefits to experience marginal 'tax' rates in excess of 90 per cent.

Practical problems can also arise as a result of the bureaucracy involved in the administration of the benefits system. Family Credit, for example, is not payable until a person has been employed for a period often lasting several weeks (so that the details of the job can be processed) whereas Job Seeker's Allowance ceases to be paid as soon as an unemployed person enters work. The prospect of hardship during the interim period before moving on to Family Credit – not to mention the uncertainty surrounding the fact that the claim for the Credit might be turned down – may deter an unemployed person from giving up the meagre 'security' offered by out-of-work benefit (although recent reforms have attempted to overcome this problem). Further disincentives can also arise if, as is often the case nowadays, the low-paid jobs on offer are themselves relatively insecure. It takes time to process new claims for Income Support – unemployed people may therefore be reluctant to take a low-paid job, irrespective of the availability of Family Credit, because they fear that if the job were quickly to disappear it would be difficult to 'sign back on' for unemployment-related benefit (see McLaughlin 1992, 1994).

Hewitt in Chapter 5 emphasizes the importance of the changing pattern of employment in this respect. She argues that many families find themselves trapped between a so-called 'flexible' labour market creating more part-time and temporary jobs and a benefit system still geared to the post-war ('Beveridge style') labour market where most jobs were full-time and largely taken by men.

Both Hewitt and Rubery highlight the particular problems this causes for women. Means tested benefits (whether Income Support or Family Credit) are assessed on the basis of family incomes – the partners of unemployed men may therefore find that they will reduce the overall family income if they take a job offering less than sufficient to 'float' the family off benefit completely. Since most jobs being taken by women at present are part-time and/or relatively poorly paid this effectively shuts the women partners of unemployed men (or those receiving 'in-work' benefits) out of the labour market altogether.

A worrying side effect of this is a polarization in society between 'job rich' families where both partners work and 'job poor' families where neither partner

18

works – the wife of an unemployed man is two to three times less likely to be in employment than the wife of a man in work. This polarization has been demonstrated most by research undertaken by Gregg and Wadsworth (1995). They stress that jobless families on welfare are not feckless – indeed members of such families search harder for jobs than other people. The central problem is simply that 'entry level' jobs (i.e. of the kind open to people when they attempt to move from welfare to work) are increasingly very low paid in Britain. Half of all such entry jobs in the mid-1990s paid less than half average (median) earnings and a third below a quarter of the average, reinforcing the welfare trap.

The Labour Party has proposed measures that attempt to overcome some of these traps. A key proposal is to make the Inland Revenue responsible for automatic identification of those eligible for Family Credit. This could be a precursor to advocacy of a tax- rather than benefit-based system of income support, perhaps akin to the Earned Income Tax Credit that operates to a limited degree in the USA (Scholz 1996). Moreover, on the tax side there has been some talk of Labour proposing a lower rate tax band of just 10 pence in the pound to improve work incentives – a controversial suggestion that some argue would anyway have less impact than further benefit reform and, in tax terms, be less cost effective than a cut in personal tax allowances (Dilnot 1995). It may be that there will be renewed talk in the future of integration of the tax and benefit systems in order to operate a Negative Income Tax or perhaps a guaranteed Citizens' Income (the latter an idea supported in the past by Britain's Liberal Democrats).

Citizens' Income (CI) could in theory help overcome many of the problems associated with means tested benefits. CI would in effect act like a universal 'benefit' that every person in society would be entitled to as of right irrespective of what they earn (see Meade 1994, 1995). People could use this to supplement earnings but it would not vary with earnings or depend upon whether a person was employed or unemployed. Unfortunately, if provided at a reasonable level this would almost certainly prove to be very expensive – company profits or individual incomes would have to be taxed quite heavily to pay for it. A prerequisite of a CI would thus seem to be some acceptance on the part of the 'haves' that the 'have nots' should be provided with an equal stake in society. This is a laudable aspiration but cannot simply be taken for granted. Moreover, in economic terms any improvement in work incentives for the lowest paid could simply be displaced by reduced work incentives further up the earnings scale resulting from the imposition of higher marginal tax rates on better paid workers. However, it should be noted that the evidence of the effects of taxes on work effort is far from clear cut (see OECD 1995).

A less radical alternative to CI would be to provide more 'flexibility' within the Income Support system enabling unemployed people to work in temporary jobs for a small amount of money without losing benefit (in effect, extending the current British system of earnings disregards). This idea is in some ways attractive, although it would run the risk of creating a class of 'odd-jobbers' constantly part-dependent on the state for income. In particular, it could open up considerable scope for benefit fraud. Such a reform can nonetheless be recommended although it should really be seen as a palliative designed to cope with a labour market characterized by job scarcity and insecure forms of work, rather than something that would play a major role in any fully fledged strategy for full employment.

Finally, it is worth mentioning that any form of benefit top-up to wages (whether universal or means tested) will exert its effect upon employment by reinforcing downward pressure on wages levels at the lower end of the earnings scale (i.e. the purpose of the benefit is to 'price workers into jobs'). On economic grounds this may be of little concern so long as labour markets are competitive and the reduction in wage levels allows markets to clear at a higher level of employment. Some, however, like Britton in Chapter 2, may be concerned about the principle of having large numbers of people in work who are continually part-dependent on the state, while others fear that a side effect of in-work benefits is to support inefficient exploitative employers at the taxpayers' expense. The latter effect could be mitigated by a national minimum wage (NMW). The fear of course is that a NMW would itself destroy jobs, but the bulk of available evidence suggests that such fears are groundless so long as a NMW is implemented sensibly and not introduced at too high a level (Card and Kreuger 1995; IPPR 1995).

Active labour market policies

The above discussion might be taken to imply that the only problem with the benefit system is that many people on benefit are caught in the trap of being worse off if they take a job. Another problem with the benefit system, however, as Richard Layard argues (Chapter 12) is simply that people are allowed to stay on benefit for too long without being given adequate help back to work.

Once people have become long-term unemployed, employers are reluctant to hire them and they are rendered virtually unemployable. Therefore when demand for labour expands the labour market acts as though long-term un-employment did not exist and 'tightens' – thereby generating inflationary pressure – even when unemployment is very high. The build-up in long-term unemployment since the 1970s – when one in five jobless people had been without work for over a year compared with one in three at present – is therefore one reason why inflationary pressures emerge nowadays at much higher rates of unemployment.

Layard thus makes the case for more extensive use of active labour market policies to eliminate long-term unemployment which he considers to be a total waste of human resources. In a phrase that echoes Beveridge, Layard argues that the state should 'stop subsidising idleness and subsidise work instead'. Active labour market measures include improved employment services (to improve the amount and quality of job search undertaken by unemployed people) and training for the jobless. But in his chapter Layard stresses in particular the use of temporary employment as a means of preventing people becoming long-term unemployed. After a person has been unemployed for a year, Layard argues, the state should immediately take responsibility for providing that person with a temporary job as an alternative to providing benefit.

Layard counters the common objection that providing jobs for unemployed people in this way will merely take jobs away from other people. He posits that a period of work experience will mean that a long-term unemployed person becomes more employable than would be the case if he or she remained un-employed. Making the long-term unemployed more employable in this way means that employers have a larger pool of workers to choose from when seeking to fill vacancies. This reduces pressure on wages and prices and enables demand to expand farther than it otherwise would without stoking up inflation. The result is a higher level of employment overall.

The essential thing to ensure is that the temporary jobs offered to long-term unemployed people really make them more employable, which is why Layard is adamant that the jobs should be with regular employers. If the jobs are of a 'make work' kind, people employed in them will be little better off than had they simply remained on the dole. Unfortunately, this has too often been the case with the succession of temporary jobs programmes operated in Britain over the years. It is perhaps not surprising therefore that such programmes have often been viewed as little more than a means of 'disguising' the unemployment figures.

The same basic argument underlies the proposal by Snower (1994) for a 'Benefit Transfer Programme'. Snower advocates converting the value of benefits paid to unemployed people into a subsidy paid to employers. The unemployed person receives the normal rate for the job but the cost to the employer is reduced, thereby encouraging more recruitment. Snower's proposal has been implemented in a watered down fashion as the government's pilot 'Workstart' programme (see EPI 1993). The latter, however, is targeted at the very long-term unemployed whereas Snower, like Layard, argues that policy must aim to prevent people becoming long-term unemployed in the first place, otherwise it will prove more difficult – and more costly – to help them back to work.

The public sector and 'social employment'

Layard's proposals are compelling and seem to convey the considerable advantage of curing a major social and economic problem at little or no cost to the taxpayer – certainly in the medium term – once savings in benefit payments and tax revenue 'flowbacks' from lower unemployment are accounted for (for a more sceptical critique see Calmfors and Skedinger 1995). Some, however, would argue the social case for providing more jobs for the unemployed even if this did involve some additional sacrifice on the part of taxpayers or wage earners (Glyn 1995).

Paul Ormerod in Chapter 9, for example, argues that an economy's average rate of unemployment over the long-term is ultimately determined by prevailing social values and institutions. Hence the vastly different unemployment records of countries which have experienced comparable rates of economic growth. For Ormerod, therefore, technical economics tell us little of value about how to secure full employment. Neither counter-cyclical macroeconomic policies nor supply side policies designed to raise the growth potential of an economy – worthwhile though these may be – are likely to eat into core unemployment. What matters instead is the degree to which a society is prepared to ensure that the fruits of growth are fairly distributed.

Ormerod cites Japan as an example of a society which has been willing to bear the cost of a relatively inefficient private service sector providing jobs for low-productivity people who in Britain and many other European Union countries would remain unemployed. Elsewhere, the same outcome has been achieved by way of the state acting as 'employer of last resort'. As an alternative, Ormerod suggests that voluntary 'work sharing' linked to income sharing could perform a similar redistributive function and help Britain back to full employment. But – as with a Citizens' Income – the task of achieving the necessary shift in social values would be considerable and extend well beyond the realm of economics.

Chris Trinder (Chapter 13) illustrates that for much of the post-war period the public sector in Britain performed a similar sort of 'social safety valve' function in the labour market by preserving jobs at times when private sector employers were shedding them. However, successive privatizations and the drive for public sector managers to emulate those in the private sector has in recent years undermined this role. Trinder considers it short-sighted for the public sector to 'downsize' during recessions because any savings the Exchequer makes on labour costs are offset by the cost of keeping people unemployed. The perversity of this is that the burden of unemployment – made worse by private sector job losses – drives up public borrowing with the result that the government has to look for further cost savings. One consequence has been the prolonged freeze on public sector pay bills in the 1990s which means that already low-paid public employees are forced to choose between higher pay or the possibility of further job losses.

Trinder suggests that this approach ought to be re-evaluated, especially when one considers that while making public sector workers redundant from regular jobs, the government is having to finance temporary (and generally inferior) jobs for the long-term unemployed under programmes such as 'Community Action'. Trinder instead argues that there is considerable scope for increasing normal public sector employment to meet pressing social and economic need, providing this can be financed. Once again, this raises serious issues. If net public spending is required to finance more public sector jobs this will have to be financed by cuts in other forms of public expenditure or by higher taxation or borrowing. Each of these financing options will have different implications for jobs elsewhere in the economy and possibly also long-run consequences for the overall performance of the economy. Moreover, the higher tax option – again like Citizens' Income or work sharing – raises distributional issues.

The success of any such job creation policy would depend crucially upon the willingness of employed 'insiders' to fund the provision of jobs for unemployed 'outsiders' – in effect the policy would involve a transfer of income from the employed to the jobless. And since many of the insiders are themselves low paid and just managing to survive within work, the prime target for the redistribution would have to be the more affluent and secure insiders who have seen their real incomes rise as inequality has widened during the past two decades. However, while one can argue that those insiders who have reaped the benefits of economic growth ought to bear a higher burden of taxation, the political task of persuading them to do so would be far from easy. While it may be comforting to think that all that is needed is to 'tax the rich' or close tax loopholes, the reality is that a large part of the burden of extra taxation would have to fall upon people on around average incomes and above, many of whom, although 'comfortable', do not think of themselves as affluent (and are themselves increasingly concerned about their own job and income security).

One 'sales pitch' for policy-makers would be to emphasize the advantages of lower unemployment – for example, higher output of public services and reduced social problems, like crime. Alternatively, policy-makers could place most stress on the moral or social case for cutting unemployment. The latter argument becomes stronger if it is assumed that the value of potential output of the majority of unemployed people – and especially the long-term unemployed – is low and that the main benefit to flow from lower unemployment is greater social cohesion (Dilnot and Blastland 1995).

In addition, however, it would be important to ensure that any such approach operates in tandem with a broader full employment strategy designed to create jobs in the private as well as the public sector. Notwithstanding the basic merit in the argument for what might be called 'social solidarity', if public sector employment is seen as no more than an instrument for mopping up unemployment caused by broader economic failure then taxpayers may prove reluctant to finance it. If insiders believe the price of low unemployment is not worth paying, or are unwilling to pay it, they will either resist tax rises through the ballot box or press for compensatory wage rises which could sabotage any move toward full employment.

Macroeconomic issues

It is common nowadays for macroeconomics to lurk in the background of debate on employment policy, while discussion of macro-issues often ignores employment. But one should not be swept away by current fashion which suggests that 'full employability' – admirable though the aim might be – is a substitute for 'full employment'. For example, for all our earlier discussion of supply side problems and the causes of the rise in core unemployment, it is worth noting that some economists argue that the fall in the relative demand for unskilled labour contributed only 20 per cent of the long-run increase in unemployment in Britain up to the 1980s (Nickell and Bell 1995).

The levers of demand must be made sensitive to supply side improvements. To cut through unemployment it is necessary to use the twin scissors of demand and supply side policies (both of which will interact). As the OECD *Jobs Study* (1995) remarks, employment policy will be better adjusted if there is a 'synergy' between macroeconomic and supply side policy.

Most people are in general agreement that a stable macroeconomic background is essential for steady, sustained growth, enabling investment in capacity and skills. However, the nature of macroeconomic policy is also important. Meade (1995), for example, argues that macroeconomic policy is at present too wedded to simple monetary-based inflation targets when what one really wants is a policy that controls inflation without incurring a major sacrifice of output and employment. He therefore suggests that government should attempt to control aggregate expenditure in the economy using both monetary and fiscal instruments in order to instil a greater sense of the importance of the real economy into macroeconomic policy (see also Corry and Holtham 1995). Meade, of course, is also concerned with policies to reduce what we have earlier called core unemployment. But in the absence of effective demand management, supply side measures, however important, cannot prove fully effective (see also CEPR 1995).

The role of macroeconomic policy in causing mass unemployment has been highlighted by the International Labour Organization (ILO) in its major *World Employment Report* (1995). The ILO points above all else to developments at the level of international macroeconomics. According to the ILO, the deregulation of world financial and capital markets that has been ongoing since the 1970s has driven up real interest rates, deterred investment and forced countries to pursue deflationary domestic monetary and fiscal policies. The result has been economic growth at rates far below those needed to maintain full employment. In this context, says the ILO, observed international differences in unemployment and job creation performance (which provide the focus of the OECD *Jobs Study*) merely reflect differential responses to the more fundamental problem of slow growth.

The conclusion to be drawn from the ILO study is that economies seeking to achieve full employment should be adaptable in their approach to the conduct of domestic and international macroeconomic policy, as well as in their efforts to overcome structural or supply side rigidities. With regard to the European Union, the ILO calls for a co-ordinated expansion of demand, arguing that there is sufficient spare capacity in most EU economies to allow unemployment to fall well below the rates prevailing in the mid-1990s without causing an upsurge in inflation (see also Michie and Grieve-Smith 1994). Yet while such an approach finds clear echoes within some EU policy statements, the model of European Economic and Monetary Union (EMU) enshrined in the Maastricht Treaty of

1991 is underpinned by a fairly crude form of deflationary Euro-monetarism. Unless the current conditions for the operation of the proposed European single currency are recast it will thus be difficult to reconcile EMU with the twin goals of full employment and the preservation of social cohesion.

Pay and productivity

Whatever the chosen mix of supply and demand side policies within a full employment strategy one issue remains outstanding – how to handle the possibility of a pay–price 'spiral' as demand expands. Beveridge and the authors of the 1944 White Paper were well aware of the potential difficulties that could be caused by what is sometimes referred to as the British 'pay problem' (see Bayliss 1993). For much of the post-war period a succession of prices and incomes policies sought to overcome this problem. Unfortunately, formal incomes policies proved difficult to sustain and have fallen out of fashion since the 1970s.

Workers and trade unions are rightly perplexed when they hear it suggested that Britain has a 'pay problem', since on average real pay in Britain is low by international standards. Indeed, during the course of the 1990s recovery many workers have experienced little or no real increase in the size of their pay packets. It is important, however, to distinguish the issue of real pay from that of pay inflation. Real pay is relatively low in Britain because on average productivity is low. Over time, productivity rises enabling growth in real pay. The 'pay problem' arises simply because of a tendency for pay increases to grow at a faster rate than productivity. This is especially true when demand for labour is buoyant (and even more so when skill shortages are significant and the long-term un-employed are very numerous). When this occurs, the result is (unit) wage cost inflation and (usually) price inflation. Although the higher price inflation will tend to diminish the real value of a pay rise, those who are employed may nonetheless find themselves to be better off. But there will also be losers if the government responds to the inflation by depressing demand and allowing unemployment to rise.

A major reason why 'core' unemployment has risen in Britain since the 1970s is precisely because the government has resorted to unemployment as a means of keeping inflation in check. This is the worst kind of 'incomes policy'. A strategy for full employment would need to develop an alternative. Economy wide insti-tutions are required that can help ensure that pay (i.e. 'earnings', not just wage settlements) rises on average no faster than the economy can afford. Sadly, as William Brown shows (Chapter 14) economic and industrial relations institutions have become less conducive to keeping pay in step with productivity since the late 1970s. Pay bargaining has become more fragmented in both the private and public sectors, while government has been generally hostile to national forums – such as the National Economic Development Office (NEDO) – where the issues surrounding pay and productivity could be discussed by the 'social partners'.

Some commentators would challenge Brown's conclusion in the light of the failure of pay pressures to materialize during the course of the economic recovery of the 1990s. The annual rate of growth of average earnings remained remarkably stable throughout 1993, 1994 and 1995, at a very subdued 3–4 per cent. It is far too soon, however, to conclude that Britain's pay problem is a thing of the past. A more deregulated labour market with weaker trade unions may mean that less unemployment is now needed to keep pay pressures in check. But at the time of writing the jury is still out on this issue. Although having fallen during the recovery, the unemployment rate was still above 8 per cent at the end of 1995. And it requires considerable optimism indeed to conclude that pay pressures would not re-emerge if unemployment were to fall to a much lower rate.

Brown argues that building a full employment policy will require a renaissance of collective institutions – albeit not a simple resurrection of old ones – for employers, for employees and for bargaining between them. Social partnership will be an essential requirement. One might add that it will also be necessary to ensure that any new institutions are seen as a means of fostering prospects for long-run improvements in real pay as well as bringing about an accommodation between short-run movements in pay and productivity. Otherwise there is a danger that attention will focus too narrowly on pay and ignore the broader problem of poor economic performance.

Setting targets?

Having considered some of the issues that would surround the development of a strategy for full employment it is worth concluding by giving some thought to the sort of time scale involved for attaining the goal. The 3 per cent unemployment rate envisaged by Beveridge is achievable but will, in a free market economy, require painstaking effort over many years to achieve. It is twenty years since full employment was last attained; few can be confident that full employment could be re-attained in less than ten to fifteen years. Moreover, the future is uncertain – even the best of policies must accept the possibility of as yet unforeseen shocks or strains on the system. What is vitally important, however, is that the necessary measures are set in train immediately.

The uncertainty surrounding the future makes it difficult to guarantee that any precise target set for full employment could be met. Targets – such as the aim set out in the European Commission's 1993 White Paper on jobs to cut EU unemployment in half by the year 2000, which already looks highly ambitious – are nonetheless useful because they offer a benchmark against which progress can be measured.

Detailed work needs to be done to calculate a precise job creation target for full employment. A rough calculation of the numbers currently in the labour market and those who would enter in more buoyant times suggests a target figure of 3–4 million net new jobs (other things being equal). This is a tall order, although one must not forget that when demand expanded rapidly during the 'Lawson boom' of the late 1980s, and again in 1994, jobs were created at a remarkable rate. The difficult problem is not so much creating jobs as sustaining them.

Looking forward to full employment

Reducing unemployment by the required amount will certainly involve some sacrifices. In particular, society will have to face up to the fact that investment – private and public, in industrial capacity and in people – must take priority over consumption for a period of years. Economic renewal and the need to offer every citizen a full stake in society demands this. Social justice also demands that the burden of the adjustment from a largely acquisitive society to one that seeks to further the common good must fall primarily upon those most able to bear it.

These truths may be difficult for politicians to convey to the electorate in a modern free society even though success would ultimately pay a handsome economic and social dividend. It will therefore be necessary to spell out that the dividend would accrue to all, not just those currently at risk of social exclusion. Whether our political leaders are prepared to spell out the hard choices remains to be seen although fortunately, for the first time in years, the relatively more prosperous may be more receptive to the message of full employment now that the 'culture of contentment' has given way to a 'culture of anxiety'.

Many in the prosperous 'middle third' of society, who in the 1980s thought themselves immune from unemployment and job insecurity, have faced a rude awakening in the 1990s. Having taken for granted the ability to cover long-term mortgage commitments and forge a reasonable lifestyle, many are uncertain about the future. A practical strategy for tackling unemployment and adapting to change in the labour market would thus garner support from all sections of society. It is time to develop such a strategy. It is time to look forward to full employment.

REFERENCES

Balls, E. (1994) 'Looking beyond the flexibility rhetoric', the *Guardian*, 6 June.

Balls, E. and Gregg, P. (1993) *Work and Welfare*, London: Institute for Public Policy Research.

Barker, T (1994) 'Taxing pollution instead of jobs', *Employment Policy Institute Economic Report* 8 (11), November.

Bayliss, F. J. (1993) *Does Britain Still Have A Pay Problem?*, London: Employment Policy Institute.

Beveridge, W. H. (1944) *Full Employment in a Free Society*, London: Unwin.

Blanchflower, D. and Oswald, A. (1995) *The Wage Curve*, London: MIT Press.

Buxton, T., Chapman, P. and Temple, P. (1994) *Britain's Economic Performance*, London: Routledge.

Calmfors, L. and Skedinger, P. (1995) 'Does active labour market policy increase employment? Theoretical considerations and some empirical evidence from Sweden', *Oxford Review of Economic Policy* 11 (1), Spring.

Card, D. and Kreuger, A. (1995) *The New Economics of the Minimum Wage*, Princeton, NJ: Princeton University Press.

Centre for Economic Policy Research (CEPR) (1995) *Unemployment: Choices for Europe*, London: CEPR.

Clark, A. and Oswald, A. (1994) 'Unhappiness and Unemployment', *Economic Journal* 104, May.

Clarke, K. (1994) 'The changing world of work in the 1990s', Fifteenth Annual Mais Lecture, London: City University Business School.

Commission on Social Justice (CSJ) (1994) *Social Justice: Strategies for National Renewal*, London: IPPR/Vintage.

Corry, D. and Holtham, G. (1995) *Growth with Stability: Progressive Macroeconomic Policy*, London: IPPR.

Dahrendorf Commission (1995) *Report on Wealth Creation and Social Cohesion in a Free Society*, London: Dahrendorf Commission.

Dilnot, A. (1995) 'Brown's tax plan fails to aid those in poverty trap', the *Daily Telegraph*, 20 November.

Dilnot, A. and Blastland, M. (1995) 'The moral case for cutting joblessness', *The Financial Times*, 22 June.

Duncan, A. and Giles, C. (1996) 'Labour supply incentives and recent family credit reforms', *Economic Journal* 106 (434).

Employment Policy Institute (EPI) (1993) 'Making workstart work', *EPI Economic Report* 7 (8), April.

—— (1995) 'Conundrum upon conundrum', *EPI Economic Report*, 9 (2), February.

European Commission (1993) *Growth, Competitiveness and Employment* (Delors White Paper), Brussels: European Commission.

Freeman, R. (1994) 'Jobs in the USA', *New Economy* 1 (1).

—— (1995) 'The limits of wage flexibility to curing unemployment', *Oxford Review of Economic Policy* 11 (1), Spring.

Glyn, A. (1995) 'The assessment: unemployment and inequality', *Oxford Review of Economic Policy* 11 (1), Spring.

Goldsmith, J. (1994) *The Trap*, London and Basingstoke: Macmillan.

Goodhart, D. (1994) *The Reshaping of the German Social Market*, London: Institute for Public Policy Research.

Gregg, P. and Wadsworth, J. (1995) 'The Importance of Making Work Pay', London: Employment Policy Institute Budget Briefing, November.

—— (1995) 'Making Work Pay', *New Economy* 2 (4).

HM Government (1944) *Employment Policy*, Cmnd 6527, London: HMSO.

Hutton, W. (1995) *The State We're In*, London: Jonathan Cape (revised edition 1996, Vintage).

Institute for Public Policy Research (IPPR) (1995) *New Economy* 2 (4).

International Labour Organisation (ILO) (1995) *World Employment Report*, ILO: Geneva.

Jacobs, M. (1995) 'Do environmental policies cost jobs?', *Employment Policy Institute Economic Report* 9 (8), October.

Keep, E. and Mayhew, K. (1995) 'UK training policy – assumptions and reality', in A. Booth and D. Snower (eds) *The Skills Gap and Economic Activity*, Cambridge: Cambridge University Press.

Labour Party (1995) *A New Economic Future for Britain*, London: Labour Party.

Lang, T. and Hines, T. (1994) *The New Protectionism*, London: Earthscan.

Layard, P. R. G., Nickell, S. J. and Jackman, R. (1991) *Unemployment*, Oxford: Oxford University Press.

McKinsey Global Institute (MKI) (1994) *Employment Performance*, Washington DC: MKI.

McLaughlin, E. (1992) 'Towards active labour market policies', in E. McLaughlin (ed.) *Understanding Unemployment*, London: Routledge.

—— (1994) *Flexibility in Work and Benefits*, London: Institute for Public Policy Research.

Mayhew, K. (1994) 'Labour market woes', *New Economy* 1 (2)

Meade, J. E. (1994) *Full Employment Without Inflation*, London: Employment Policy Institute and Social Market Foundation.

—— (1995) *Full Employment Regained? An Agathotopian Dream*, University of Cambridge, Department of Applied Economics Occasional Paper 61.

Michie, J. and Grieve-Smith, J. (1994) *Unemployment in Europe*, London: Academic Press.

Minford, P. (1994) 'Unemployment in the OECD and its remedies', University of Liverpool (mimeo).

Minford, P. and Riley, J. (1994) 'The UK labour market: micro rigidities and macro obstructions', in R. Barrell (ed.) *The UK Labour Market*, Cambridge: Cambridge University Press.

Nickell, S. and Bell, B. (1995) 'The collapse in demand for the unskilled and unemployment across the OECD', *Oxford Review of Economic Policy* 11 (1), Spring.

Organization For Economic Co-operation and Development (1994) *OECD Jobs Study: Facts, Analysis, Strategies*, Paris: OECD.

—— (1994) *Evidence and Explanations*, Paris: OECD.

—— (1995) *OECD Jobs Study: Taxation, Employment and Unemployment*, Paris: OECD.

Philpott, J. (1994) 'The incidence and cost of unemployment', in A. Glyn and D. Miliband (eds) *Paying for Inequality: the Economic Cost of Social Injustice*, London: Rivers Oram Press/Institute for Public Policy Research.

Reich, R. (1991) *The Work of Nations*, New York: Simon and Schuster.

Rifkin, J. (1995) *The End of Work*, New York: Jeremy P. Tarcher/Putnam.

Robinson, P. (1995) 'Evolution not revolution', *New Economy* 3 (3).

Rowntree Foundation (1995) *Inquiry into Income and Wealth*, vols 1 and 2, York: Joseph Rowntree Foundation.

Rowthorn, R. (1995) 'Capital formation and unemployment', *Oxford Review of Economic Policy* 11 (1), Spring.

Schmitt, J. and Wadsworth, J. (1994) 'The rise in economic inactivity', in A. Glyn and D. Miliband (eds) *Paying for Inequality: the Economic Cost of Social Injustice*, London: Rivers Oram Press/IPPR.

Scholz, J. K. (1996) 'In work benefits in the US: the earned income tax credit', *Economic Journal* 106 (434).

Shackleton, J. R. (1995) 'The skills mirage', *Employment Policy Institute Economic Report* 9 (9), November.

Snower, D. (1994) 'Converting unemployment benefits into employment subsidies', *American Economic Review* 84 (2).

Whitehouse, E. (1996) 'Designing and implementing in-work benefits', *Economic Journal* 106 (434).

Wood, A. (1994) *North–South Trade, Employment and Inequality*,' Oxford: Clarendon Press.

World Bank (1995) *The Employment Crisis: Is International Integration to Blame?*, Background Paper accompanying *World Development Report* (1995), Washington DC: World Bank.

2

FULL EMPLOYMENT IN A MARKET ECONOMY[1]

Andrew Britton

INTRODUCTION

One of the key historical reference points for this discussion of full employment is the White Paper *Employment Policy*, Cmnd 6527, presented by the Minister of Reconstruction to Parliament in May 1944. It is a short paper, just thirty-one pages long, and much of that length is devoted to the special difficulties in the labour market that were expected during the transition from war to peace. The detailed policy proposals set out in the White Paper were not implemented in quite the way that was foreseen. Nevertheless, this slim document did signal a new approach to economic policy quite different to the approach of governments pre-war. The most important sentence is the first: 'The Government accept as one of their primary aims and responsibilities the maintenance of a high and stable level of employment after the war.' The Paper would have been a landmark in the history of economic policy if it had said no more than that.

To understand the significance of the commitment contained in the White Paper, we should turn to a very influential book, also published in 1944, *Full Employment in a Free Society* by William Beveridge. There we can find the reason for the commitment being made and also a fuller account of the methods by which it was hoped that full employment would be maintained. That will be my starting-point for an overview of the successes and failures of economic policy, then and now. Why was full employment adopted as an objective of policy? Why was it achieved and maintained so successfully for more than twenty years after the White Paper was published? Why has it not been maintained since the 1970s? Should the commitment to full employment be reiterated today? What does it mean in today's circumstances? And, since there is no point in making commitments which cannot be fulfilled, what policy actions should follow?

This chapter is entitled 'Full Employment in a Market Economy' to emphasize the difference between the circumstances of today and those in which Beveridge wrote fifty years ago. Whether we welcome the fact or not, the organization of economic life is very different now from that of the post-war years. There is no question of turning back the clock. If there is something in the commitment to full employment which still seems right, even compelling, today, then we need to face some hard and difficult choices if we are to convince a contemporary audience that this is more than a political slogan.

POST-WAR CONSENSUS

The long periods of high unemployment between the wars had been the cause of poverty of a kind we no longer know in this country. The unemployed and their families had experienced severe hardship, even hunger. One of the main concerns of Beveridge and of the wartime coalition government was that a social security system should be established which would prevent this happening again. Such provision, it was recognized, would be difficult to finance unless the level of unemployment was kept low. But that was not the main reason for making the commitment to full employment.

To quote Beveridge (1944: 20): 'Idleness is not the same as want, but a separate evil, which men do not escape by having an income. They must also have the chance of rendering useful service and of feeling that they are doing so.' He also wrote: 'A person who has difficulty in buying the labour that he wants suffers inconvenience or reduction of profits. A person who cannot sell his labour is in effect told that he is of no use. The first difficulty causes annoyance or loss. The other is a personal catastrophe.'

He gave three further reasons why full employment should be maintained: to prevent the growth of restrictive practices; to make structural change in the economy more acceptable; and to provide a stimulus to technical progress and the more productive use of labour. No doubt behind this lay also a profound unease as to the political implications of high unemployment. On the title page of his book Beveridge put the quotation 'misery generates hate'. That had indeed been the experience of the inter-war years. The rise of the dictatorships owed much to the perceived failure of liberal democracies to provide prosperity and jobs. It had to be demonstrated that a free society was capable of delivering full employment. The alternative to a free society was to imitate either Nazi Germany or Soviet Russia. The political consensus over economic policy after the war rested on the belief that full employment was essential to the survival of the freedoms that were believed to be fundamental by all the major political parties, and which the war had been fought to preserve.

The importance of wartime experience should never be underestimated as an explanation of post-war economic policies. In war, of course, full employment had been achieved. Useful work was found for everyone as part of a national effort, even those who had been thought unemployable turned out to be good soldiers or munitions workers after all. It could all be put down to good planning and a general willingness to co-operate. Workers and management found themselves, most of the time at least, on the same side. Much of economic life was regulated in the interests of the war effort, and despite some absurdities, regulation seemed to work well. The stimulus for efficiency or initiative came mainly from the need to serve a common purpose. Those who made profits for themselves were regarded as selfish and anti-social. The sense of a common purpose remained after the war was won and helped to support the continued existence of regulations and restrictions on economic life which might otherwise have been found to be intolerable.

Beveridge was well aware of the need for voluntary co-operation if full employment was to be made compatible with economic freedom. He wrote:

> The degree of liberty . . . which can be left to agencies independent of the State, without imperilling the policy of full employment, depends on the responsibility and public spirit with which those liberties are exercised. There is no reason to doubt that that responsibility and public spirit will be forthcoming.
>
> (Beveridge 1944: 19)

But the main requirement for full employment, according to the White Paper or to Beveridge, was neither regulation nor public spirit; these on their own would not be sufficient. What was essential, according to the post-war intellectual consensus, was an adequate level of aggregate demand. The diagnosis put forward by Maynard Keynes of the cause of unemployment between the wars led to an obvious prescription. The second paragraph of the White Paper begins thus: 'A country will not suffer from mass unemployment so long as the total demand for its goods and services is maintained at a high level.' The implications of this are set out later in the Paper: 'The Government are prepared to accept in future the responsibility for taking action at the earliest possible stage to avert a threatened slump. This involves a new approach and a new responsibility for the State.'

The new approach is well described by Beveridge as the creation of a 'seller's market' for labour. He defined full employment as being a state in which there were 'more vacant jobs than unemployed men'. Moreover these should be 'jobs at fair wages of such a kind, and so located that the unemployed men can reasonably be expected to take them'. It is important to recognize that this is what full employment meant for Beveridge: not a state of balance or equilibrium in the labour market, but rather a state of labour scarcity, so that anyone who wanted work would not have to look for long to find it. Of course he realized the danger of inflation in such a situation, but he relied on the public spirit and responsibility of employers and especially of trade unions to keep this tendency in check.

The main instruments for securing an adequate level of demand were according to Beveridge to be extra public spending, both current and capital, and the regulation of private investment by a National Investment Board. He criticized the White Paper as too timid, in its reluctance to intervene in the private sector and for its continuing concern with the scale of public sector debt. Very little was said either by Beveridge or in the White Paper about monetary policy. It was widely believed at the time that the rate of interest had little effect on saving or investment. Hence it was on fiscal policy that the architects of full employment relied for the management of aggregate demand.

Demand management was the main post-war policy innovation that supported the commitment to full employment, but it was not the only one. The White Paper also discussed regional or local unemployment and proposed to tackle it in three ways: by encouraging firms to locate in 'development areas'; by removing obstacles to labour mobility; and by providing facilities for training.

Looking back fifty years later we cannot but admire the courage with which the commitment to full employment was made. It was by no means clear at the time that the objective could be achieved. Indeed, all recent history suggested that it could not. In fact the White Paper was quite cautious in its wording, speaking of 'a high and stable level of employment' rather than the more emotive words used by Beveridge. And Beveridge himself thought that a reasonable target to aim at would be 3 per cent unemployment, or at that time 550,000: 'This margin would consist of a shifting body of short-term unemployed who could be maintained without hardship by unemployment insurance.' In fact unemployment was below that level throughout the 1950s and for most of the 1960s as well.

THE YEARS OF FULL EMPLOYMENT

In 1964, twenty years after the White Paper was issued, the National Institute of Economic and Social Research published a historical study, *The Management of the British Economy, 1945–60* by Christopher Dow. In his conclusions he wrote:

> In terms of its fundamental aim – the desire so to manage the economy as to prevent the heavy unemployment that accompanied the pre-war trade cycle – modern economic policy has clearly been a success. For some years after the war, high employment required no specific intervention: wartime arrears of demand were more than enough to ensure full employment. In the decade of the fifties, however, there probably would have been more unemployment if the Government had not intervened to increase demand when unemployment showed signs of increasing: and, perhaps equally important, if the world of business had not acquired some confidence that governments could and would so intervene when necessary.
>
> (Dow 1964: 233)

He then goes on to point out other economic problems, such as slow but persistent inflation, frequent balance-of-payments weakness, and growth rather slower than in many other countries. But he adds: 'Failure in these respects has been relative failure only.' At that stage the main emphasis was, quite rightly, on what went right, and not on the early signs of what would later go sadly wrong.

We cannot be certain even now why it was that demand remained so strong for so many years after the war. It was not because the government, following the teachings of Keynes and Beveridge, borrowed heavily to finance extra spending. They did not need to, because private expenditure was buoyant most

33

of the time. Initially private sector demand may have been strengthened by the low level of interest rates and by the devaluation of sterling in 1949. But this is not enough to explain the continuing buoyancy of expenditure well into the 1960s, by which time the authorities were more inclined to rein it back than to urge it forward.

We are concerned here with a phenomenon which affected most advanced industrial countries, not just the UK. Initially it may be attributed to making good the damage done by the war to building and equipment both in the public and private sectors. The Cold War and the Korean War stimulated military spending. Consumers for many years were running down the savings accumulated during the years of rationing, then borrowing to acquire new durable goods as they became available. The expansion of international trade was catching up with opportunities lost, not only in wartime but also as a result of trade restrictions in the 1930s.

The point I would wish to stress however is that demand and supply were not matched exactly together by some extraordinary skill on the part of policy-makers, nor indeed by any flexibility in the workings of the market mechanism. What seems to have characterized the period rather was a condition of persistently high, and at times excess, demand. We did have, as Beveridge intended, a 'seller's market' for labour.

It becomes important therefore to ask what were the restraints which prevented wages and prices rising to remove the excess demand, as would be expected in a market economy. Part of the answer may be with the size of the public sector, as well as the continued regulation of credit, foreign exchange and investment. But I am also prepared to recognize the importance of what Beveridge called 'responsibility and public spirit' as a restraint on inflationary pressure. There was a very general agreement on the priority to be given to full employment, and memories of the inter-war years were still fresh. In national wage bargaining there was some recognition of the potential conflict between the national aims of full employment and price stability. Perhaps the trade unions did not at first realize the strength of their bargaining position in a 'seller's market' for labour, or they chose not to use that strength. Either way, they were contributing to the persistence of what now appears to us as a golden age. By the mid-1960s it was already becoming clear that the problems with inflation, the balance of payments and international competitiveness were getting progressively more serious. Since the early 1970s the commitment to 'a high and stable level of employment', although never formally abandoned, has never actually been fulfilled.

WHAT WENT WRONG?

I hardly need to rehearse again the history of unemployment in the UK since 1970. The trend has been strongly upward, at least until the mid-1980s. The fluctuations from year to year have also become much more severe. For much of the time inflation has been very high and very variable, although it is low and stable now. The experience of other countries has been varied, but also generally unhappy. In most European countries the trend of unemployment has been strongly upward; in the USA the level has generally been high although the increase is not so marked. There is no consensus among economists about the explanation of these developments; on the contrary the period has been one of confusion, controversy and disarray.

It is helpful to distinguish between cyclical and structural unemployment. There is plenty of evidence that the pressure of demand rises and falls from year to year and that unemployment moves in sympathy with that cycle. For example, unemployment fell sharply following the boom in the late 1980s, rose again during the recession of the early 1990s, and is now falling again. This cyclical movement does seem to be related to the adequacy of demand in the economy as a whole, in much the way that Keynes described. However, this cyclical movement, troublesome though it may be, is not the main issue. The main issue is the high level around which this fluctuation occurs, and the dramatic increase in the average level of unemployment in the 1970s and 1980s.

It is difficult to argue that this increase was attributable in any simple way to a deficiency of aggregate demand, since it was not matched by other indications of increasing spare capacity and since it was accompanied by bursts of rapid inflation. We must therefore address the problem of 'structural unemployment', or an increase in the NAIRU (the level of unemployment at which inflation is held constant) or an increase in the equilibrium or 'natural' rate of unemployment. But attaching labels to unemployment tells us little or nothing about its origin, or its remedy. I shall summarize the possible explanations of structural unemployment under three headings: hysteresis, sclerosis and skedasticity. If these sound like the names of serious diseases, that is appropriate enough, because they all represent something going seriously wrong with the workings of the economy.

Hysteresis

Hysteresis in this context means the long-lasting, perhaps even the permanent, effect of an accident or stress to the system. Thus the shocks caused by the two increases in world oil prices during the 1970s each produced a sharp contraction of activity in most countries, including the UK, with cyclical downturns much larger than those of the 1950s and 1960s. The hysteresis theories turn on the idea that the associated sharp rises in unemployment were difficult even impossible to reverse. For example, the investment, training and even the technical improvements which should have taken place during the years of recession may not have been made good, even when growth was resumed. Another theory of the same kind suggests that the workers made redundant in a recession lose contact with the labour market, are no longer protected by their union, are regarded with suspicion by employers and become demoralized or demotivated. If this kind of theory is correct we do not need a different theory for the trend from the cycle.

A succession of severe cycles would be enough to explain the whole story. My own view is that this explanation, although it is important, is not enough to account for all of the upward trend.

Sclerosis

Sclerosis blames the rise in unemployment on a lack of flexibility. It is the main explanation given by the OECD in its 1994 *Jobs Study*. According to this view the difficulty is one of matching demand and supply for labour. Relative wages do not change quickly enough to clear the market, if indeed they move at all. Workers are reluctant to change their location or occupation, or to learn new skills. According to this view there does exist a labour market equilibrium at which full employment would be restored, but the market takes a very long time indeed to reach it, especially in Europe.

Those who favour sclerosis theories would claim that the problem has got much worse since the 1960s. The need for adjustment has become greater, but the ability to adjust has become less. They point to rigidities introduced into labour markets, especially in Europe, in the 1960s and 1970s. These include increased union power, increased regulation of terms and conditions of employment, greater job security (which ironically could increase unemployment by making firms reluctant to take on new staff) and the statutory enforcement of minimum wages. The weakness of the theory is that the economy was highly regulated, and in a sense inflexible, during the war and for some time afterwards; yet then we had full employment. I am in favour of flexibility, of course, but I am not convinced that an increase in inflexibility can explain the rise in unemployment since the 1960s, at least so far as the UK is concerned.

Skedasticity

Skedasticity is a term I have invented to describe those theories which emphasize the variation or inequality of earning power in the labour force. Suppose that this inequality has increased for some reason, but that the inequality of actual wages cannot increase, because of minimum wage provisions or the level of unemployment benefits. The result will be higher unemployment. The possible reasons for a widening in the dispersion of earning power are many and various. Some blame international trade, especially imports from low-wage countries; some blame new technology, which benefits the average worker but not the least skilled; some blame the increased participation of women, especially in relatively low-paid jobs, others blame an actual deterioration in training and education. The situation could be made worse by increased competition between firms obliging them to eliminate any job which is not essential, and to make quite sure that none of their employees are paid any more than a strict assessment of their contribution to the business would justify.

I should emphasize that these theories do not suggest that trade, technology, competition and so on are bad for the economy as a whole. On the contrary, the point is that they do raise average living standards and average pay, but this means that the minimum level of pay which employers will offer or workers accept also goes up – and that leaves a significant minority with no work at all. I suspect that theories which emphasize the problems of inequality and low skills do explain a good deal of the increase in unemployment particularly in the UK.

So we do not lack explanations of the rise in unemployment, nor suggestions for policies to reverse it. As inflation and unemployment rose from the mid-1960s to the late 1970s the initial response of policy was to try to repair the post-war consensus. By this stage it was evident that the problems of rising prices and balance-of-payments deficits were so serious that the government could not restore full employment simply by adding to demand. For the twenty years or so after the war it was possible to maintain a 'seller's market' for labour, as Beveridge had wished. But this could continue only so long as a combination of regulation and co-operation kept the lid on price and wage inflation. The lid was blown off in the 1970s and no attempt to put it back on again has succeeded for long. We have had to reduce the temperature, that is to say the pressure of demand in the economy. A market economy cannot operate with a persistent excess of demand.

A great deal has changed in the labour market since we last experienced full employment. New developments of technology, especially information technology, have transformed working conditions requiring new skills and making old skills obsolete. The participation of women has increased and with that has grown the practice of part-time working. Self-employment has become much more widespread. Job changes have become more frequent, and employment has become less secure. The influence of trade unions in wage bargaining has declined, although they still have an important role to play and still have popular support. Management has become more scientific (at least the jargon it uses sounds more scientific) and its approach to employment has become more businesslike – perhaps because competition between firms has become more intense. To sum up, we have seen the evolution of a market economy in this country, much more like the market described in economic textbooks, and it is in that context that the issue of full employment must now be addressed.

WHAT DOES FULL EMPLOYMENT MEAN NOW?

Since Beveridge wrote about full employment much has changed, but much also remains the same. It is still true that enforced idleness destroys self-respect and that 'misery generates hate'. There is still the same need to belong to society, to serve and to be valued. For most people, indeed for more of the population than in earlier generations, this need to belong can be satisfied only by participation in the economy, in paid work, part-time or full-time, permanent or temporary, for an employer or for your own business. High levels of unemployment have not destroyed liberal democracy as seemed possible in the 1940s, but they have divided society and alienated a substantial minority. We have to ask what kind of society we want to live in. I think that most people would say that they want a society in which everyone is able to participate, in which there is effective access for all to work in exchange for an income. The work is important as well as the income, because it is still true, as Beveridge said, that idleness is a separate evil from want and that no one should be told by society that they have nothing useful to contribute.

Looking into the far distant future we can perhaps imagine a world in which the need for work has been almost eliminated, a world in which machines have taken over most of the jobs now done by human hands or brains. In such a world, if it ever exists, and I am not sure it will, most of the population would in a sense be idle most of the time. But it would be idleness of a very different kind from that now experienced by the unemployed. It would be voluntary idleness, a life of leisure chosen in preference to work, or indeed a life of voluntary work undertaken for its own sake and with no financial reward. Because it would affect the workforce as a whole it would not be socially divisive. It may be useful to speculate about such possibilities and to consider their implications for society, sometime in the twenty-first century. But this does not help us to solve the urgent problem of involuntary unemployment today and the need for all who wish to participate in economic life to be given an opportunity to do so.

We cannot be certain that this need to participate will necessarily be satisfied in a market economy. In the property market buildings can stand empty for years; in the market for consumer goods some of the stock has to be written off. If we treat labour as simply another commodity to be bought and sold, then it is human lives that will sometimes be written off and declared to be redundant. It is appropriate to use emotive language, because the issue here is one of feelings rather than calculation. We want the labour market to be humane in its treatment of individuals, as well as efficient, and we may fear that it is becoming less so. This is in part a matter of the way in which employers and employees choose to behave towards one another, but it is a matter of public policy as well.

For many professional economists unemployment is the most important policy issue of all. We see our role as contributing to the solution of a social problem, not just making the economy more productive. We would be most reluctant to abandon the objective of full employment, because it points beyond economics to a goal which is not just increasing individual utility but also the cohesion of society as a whole.

Setting full employment as a policy objective, even in the context of a market economy, makes it clear that society as a whole has an interest in the way that individuals are treated. It does involve the concept of a community and something which Beveridge called 'public spirit'. We need, in the very different circumstances of today, to find the institutional setting within which that common purpose can be achieved.

Clearly there is no way in which society can underwrite the continued existence of particular jobs or even occupations. Neither can there be a right to a job of one's own choosing at a wage one considers fair. A commitment to full employment will leave many individual ambitions unsatisfied and hopes disappointed. There will still be closures and redundancies, but perhaps we can find a better way of dealing with the consequences. Perhaps we can prevent people being too dependent on the continuation of a particular job and widen the opportunities they have to recover from misfortune when it hits them.

If this is to be achieved then in practice something may well have to be given up in return. The recipe for full employment proposed by Keynes was in effect a 'free lunch'. By making good the deficiency in demand everyone could be better off. If, however, unemployment is now a structural problem then it is unlikely that a painless cure can be found for it. One interpretation of the rise in unemployment is that society has given up the aim of full employment because it found the cost in terms of other objectives was too great. Perhaps no such conscious choice was ever actually made. If, however, we are now to make the deliberate choice that full employment is to be given priority then we need to know what else is being given up. To make a choice between aims we need to know the means that will be adopted. I turn therefore to the question of how a commitment to full employment in a market economy might actually be fulfilled.

There is no shortage of recent studies of unemployment, certainly no shortage of policy recommendations. In the last two years extensive work has been done on the subject both by the European Commission and by the OECD. The latter organization has produced not one solution to the problem but sixty. It may be inevitable that international organizations, which have to take account of the very different situations in all their member states, will produce recommendations with no clear single focus. Moreover, there is a natural tendency, not confined to international organizations, to include within the policy menu a large number of reforms, which could be thought worthwhile in their own right, but which are at best of marginal value in relation to unemployment. Those who favour causes as diverse as privatization, European integration, or nursery education will want to argue that they have something to offer as part of the package. Those who are looking around for attractive ingredients to put in the package will find these offers difficult to resist. But if we are serious about achieving full employment then we must concentrate on the search for policies which will really make a big difference.

MACROECONOMIC POLICY

It follows from what I have already written that the problem of unemployment cannot be solved by macroeconomic policy on its own, simply by more public spending, by tax cuts or lower interest rates. We have quite recent evidence of the effects of stimulating aggregate demand. In the late 1980s, partly as a result of credit liberalization, partly as a result of tax cuts, both consumer spending and fixed investment accelerated. The result for a few years was a rapid growth of output. In some parts of the UK at least there was briefly a 'seller's market' for many kinds of labour, as national unemployment fell sharply and skill shortages developed. But the consequences were rapid growth of imports, renewed inflation and an increase in interest rates. The expansion had to be stopped and there followed one of the most severe recessions since the war.

We are now in the recovery phase of the cycle, with unemployment falling again and capacity utilization rising. Macroeconomic policy became expansionary after sterling was forced out of the Exchange Rate Mechanism, and the impetus given by the depreciation and reduction in interest rates is still carrying the economy forward despite the tax increases coming into effect this year. There is some purely cyclical fall in unemployment still to come, but on the basis of past experience I do not think that the level can be held much below two to two-and-a-half millions. Several years of really rapid growth of output, unless accompanied by improved competitiveness and growth of capacity, would lead only to fresh problems of inflation and for the balance of payments. There are some optimists who believe that the level of structural unemployment, the NAIRU or the equilibrium rate (whatever term one uses) is already much lower than that, perhaps no more than one million, thanks to the free market policies introduced since 1979. There is not much evidence from the behaviour of the aggregate economy to support that view. I would like to believe it is true, but I shall proceed on the assumption that it is not.

If structural unemployment is indeed of the order of two to two-and-a-half millions then there is not much more that can be achieved by demand expansion. The management of demand does, nevertheless, still have an important part to play in a strategy to achieve full employment. As has already been indicated, one theory of structural unemployment sees it as a legacy of past recessions. If it were possible to keep the economy growing steadily, with no recessions, and no unsustainable booms either, then it is more likely that the damage done by the instability of the last twenty years can gradually be put right.

A great deal has been learnt about the management of demand since the White Paper was issued fifty years ago. Far more statistical information is available and econometric models have been developed to improve forecasting methods. Nevertheless, the record of demand management has been disappointing. We know, from many years of experience, the inevitable limitations of economic forecasting, and hence the difficulty of taking timely action to offset the economic cycle. The White Paper said in 1944 that 'the Government are prepared to accept in the future the responsibility for taking action at the earliest possible stage to avert a threatened slump'. I think the government is still prepared to play that role if it can, and that a long drawn out slump could probably be corrected, but clearly it is not always possible to avert a sharp recession

Given the limits of demand management it would be beneficial if more stability could be built into the economic system itself. A relatively free market economy may be more prone to cyclical variation than the more regulated economy of the post-war period. The British economy seems to have had a more bumpy ride than most other economies in Europe. Possible reasons for this include the structure of financial markets and the importance of home owner-ship. These considerations are relevant to the problem of unemployment, and need to be considered in that context, but obviously more direct action is needed as well, if a commitment to full employment is to be fulfilled.

INDUSTRIAL POLICY AND INTERNATIONAL COMPETITIVENESS

The foreword to the 1944 White Paper ends with the following sentence:

> But the success of the policy outlined in this Paper will ultimately depend on the understanding and support of the community as a whole – and especially on the efforts of employers and workers in industry; for without a rising standard of industrial efficiency we cannot achieve a high level of employment combined with a rising standard of living.

The point is an important one and still valid today. There are those who believe that the whole economy needs to be strengthened and reformed before full employment can be achieved. They stress the need for greater industrial efficiency and competitiveness if Britain is to participate in the open markets of Europe and the world as a whole. This broad approach is particularly attractive if it could make possible an increase in industrial employment at the same time as real wages were rising. Moreover the potential constraint on growth arising from the deficit on the balance of payments would be lifted if Britain's trade performance were improved.

The White Paper published by the European Commission in 1993 put great emphasis on improved industrial competitiveness as the best approach to job creation. Implicitly it assumes that Europe can gain employment at the expense of other industrial countries, for example, the USA and Japan. (The OECD *Jobs Study* prepared for the governments of all industrial countries jointly on the other hand could not make recommendations which would help some member states at the expense of others.) In considering policy options for the UK we must remember that considerable scope remains for raising our standards of perform-ance and productivity to match those of our continental neighbours. Indeed a considerable effort may be needed to ensure that we do not fall further behind.

Having accepted all this, it would nevertheless be wrong to concentrate too much attention in this chapter on industrial policy. In the first place there is no agreement as to the actual policy measures which are most likely to achieve the desired result of improving Britain's competitiveness and efficiency. While some economists argue for a 'developmental' approach, which would involve some kind of national planning, others regard that with disdain and see the proper role of the state as confined to regulation – and no more of that than is unavoidable. I do not need to take sides in that debate here.

The second reason for placing the main emphasis elsewhere is real doubt as to the scale of effects on unemployment which could be achieved by industrial policy of any kind. One could imagine a successful industrial policy which achieved its main goal of improving international competitiveness, while leaving the problem of structural unemployment largely unsolved. The theories of what I have called 'skedasticity' attribute unemployment to the distribution within the workforce of skills and other characteristics relevant to employment. If this approach is right we need to concentrate on the lower end of that distribution, not on the midpoint. It is to policies with that focus that I turn next.

LABOUR MARKET POLICIES

We now have a great deal of experience of special employment measures in the UK and plenty of examples to draw on from the experience of other countries as well if we wish. The list of schemes gets longer and longer, although many of the new ones turn out to be variations on themes which have been tried out before. There have been selective employment subsidies and schemes to promote employment in the public sector. More recently the emphasis has been more on help with searching for work and tightening up the conditions for the receipt of benefit. At the most, these schemes may have reduced unemployment by a few hundred thousand each year since the mid-1970s.

Proposals to introduce similar schemes on a much larger scale run into problems of administrative feasibility. If unemployment was low, say half a million or a million in total, then it would be possible to consider each case individually and to show a genuine care on behalf of society. Training and counselling could be provided on a generous scale. Every effort could be made to find or to create jobs within the capability of each unemployed person. It might even be right, in that context, to insist that job offers are not refused. One could readily imagine an employment 'fallback' provision, even an employment guarantee of some kind to cope with a relatively small number of people who for one reason or another have difficulty in finding or keeping employment. But I do not think that mass unemployment, running to two millions or more, can be tackled in this way. The task becomes unmanageable and the expense becomes prohibitive.

It might be possible by something akin to conscription to create work of a kind for even two million unemployed, but there would be no question of giving individual attention to the needs or the potential abilities of such vast numbers. It would mean creating a large regimented sector clearly differentiated from the rest of the economy. This is not at all what Beveridge had in mind when he wrote about full employment. The underlying purpose of renewing that commitment today could not be fulfilled by special employment measures on a gigantic scale. The social marginalization and alienation caused by unemployment would remain and the need to feel that everyone belongs to the community would not be satisfied. On a small scale, special employment measures undoubtedly have an important part to play and it matters a great deal how that role is performed. But they cannot be the main means by which a promise to restore full employment would be kept.

TAXES AND SUBSIDIES

In a market economy economic policy works best by influencing relative costs and prices, by creating incentives for individuals or firms to behave in a socially desired way. Thus the burning of fuel which may threaten the environment is not prohibited or rationed, but it is taxed. Energy saving is not made compulsory, but it is encouraged by subsidies. A similar approach could work in the labour market.

The aim is not to encourage employment as such, but to increase the employment opportunities for those who, for any reason, are likely to earn wages well below the average. This relates to the dispersion or skedasticity theory of unemployment. We want to offset the widening in the range of earning power which seems to be one reason for the upward trend in unemployment. Chancellor of the Exchequer Kenneth Clarke took a first small step in that direction in the November 1993 Budget when he reduced by one per cent the national insurance contributions of lower paid employees and widened the 20p income tax band. Could the same approach, on a very much larger scale, be the centrepiece of a strategy to restore full employment?

Taxes and subsidies apply to the population as a whole, not just to particular individuals identified as requiring individual attention. The state operates at arms length. No one has to be identified as requiring special help; there is no need to interfere in their lives or question their motivation. Unlike special employment measures, taxes and benefits can operate on a very large scale without the danger of stigma or marginalization.

If the intention is to encourage employment creation then the natural place to start reform is with national insurance contributions. I shall not attempt to go into any detail, but two general points can be made. The first is that employees' contributions must in the long run influence employment prospects just as much as do employers' contributions. The need is to improve incentives to seek employment as well as incentives to provide it. If the employers' contribution is cut then there will be a tendency for wages to rise because the demand for labour will increase, and if the employees' contribution is cut there will be a tendency for wages to fall because the supply of labour will increase. The net effect on labour costs and take-home pay should be much the same in the end – and both employers and employees would benefit. The second point to make is that the graduation of contributions should relate to pay per hour. The intention is to improve the employment prospects for those most at risk of unemployment, that is those whose earning power is relatively low, whether they work full-time or part-time.

While national insurance contributions are the natural place to start, the reforms could affect other forms of taxation as well. Income tax thresholds could be raised. But if the wish is to focus specifically on earned income then there would need to be a new form of tax allowance designed with that in mind. This too would need to be related to pay per hour – an innovation so far as the tax system is concerned.

Instead of cutting national insurance contributions, a very similar result could be achieved by subsidies to employers, also related to pay per hour. For the lowest paid it might be necessary for the subsidy to represent a large proportion of the wage before sufficient growth of employment could be induced.

One of the merits of a general tax cut or employment subsidy for the low paid is that we do not have to know in advance where the new jobs will be created. That can be left to the market to decide, so long as the state does not stand in the way. My own guess is that many of them would be in services, and more generally in sectors which do not compete with imports. This inevitably points to activities, for example, health and education, which are largely in the public sector. If this approach is to be effective, then employment by central and local government must be allowed to increase even if total public spending is left unchanged. It would be absurd to adopt a target of full employment and then to say that the public sector is not allowed to contribute to its achievement.

If the problem of employment is addressed in this way it is bound to be expensive in terms of revenue; there can be no disguising that. Large sums of money must be involved if a large effect is to be achieved. If the reform succeeded in its aim of reducing unemployment permanently to a tolerable level then there would be substantial savings on benefits now paid to those out of work. That would be an important offset to the gross cost of the reform to the Exchequer. Nevertheless I suspect that the net cost would still be large. The political process must indicate whether society is prepared to pay that cost, and if so in what form the revenue should be raised. Options worth considering would include higher NI contributions from the better paid, higher rates of VAT or taxes on energy. None of these would be popular, but many people would say it was a price worth paying for full employment. Over a number of years significant changes in the impact of taxes and spending do take place, so we should not dismiss this type of policy option simply because the numbers involved are big.

THE BENEFIT SYSTEM AND MINIMUM WAGES

In the UK, unlike many other industrial countries, the ratio of unemployment benefits to wages has been falling since the 1960s. If the rates of benefit were to be cut this might well reduce the numbers of claimants but at the expense of increased poverty for those who remain out of work. Most people would consider this a price not worth paying.

The replacement ratio could also be reduced however by paying benefits to workers on low pay, which would of course tend to reduce poverty rather than to increase it. Family Credit already does this and the scheme has many admirers.

Some would like to develop this approach much further and make it a major element in a strategy to achieve full employment. Certainly it merits careful examination and it is possible that it is the best option available.

As compared however with the alternative of reforming NI contributions and employment subsidies it has two disadvantages. The first is simply that it approaches the main problem we are concerned with indirectly rather than directly, by focusing on individual or household income when it should focus on job creation. The second disadvantage is that most of the schemes considered require some form of means test for the individual or the household so as to keep down their cost. A relationship of dependency is unavoidable between the recipients and the state as the donor. This may be right and proper as a temporary relationship for individuals or households in times of particular adversity, but it is not so appropriate as a permanent relationship between the state and perhaps millions of less skilled workers. I do not think that Beveridge would have approved at all.

The attraction of paying benefits to those in work reflects the increase in the dispersion of wages over the past decade, adding to the prevalence of low pay, often of pay so low that workers gain little compared to their benefit entitlements. The same increase in dispersion has not been observed in much of continental Europe, partly because of minimum wage regulations.

Where minimum wages are high relative to rates of benefit they must reduce the possibility of creating relatively low-paid jobs for relatively low-skilled workers. The countries concerned therefore face a difficult choice between better pay and more jobs, with a conflict of interest between the employed and the unemployed to be resolved. The issue has, of course, been much discussed in the UK in recent times. The main issue so far as unemployment is concerned is not whether there should be a minimum wage or not, but the level at which the minimum is set if we do have one. If it was set high enough to require the wages now paid to a large number of workers to be raised, then some, though not all, of the jobs concerned would be lost.

The situation could be helped by the reforms to national insurance contributions or the introduction of employment subsidies. By cutting total unit wage costs for those offering relatively low-skilled jobs the incidence of very low pay should be reduced. The need for minimum wage regulation would then be less, and so also would be the loss of jobs if a minimum wage was in fact introduced.

EDUCATION AND TRAINING

I have left until last what is perhaps the ideal solution to the problem of unemployment. If only we could make the labour force more productive, then of course the economy would be more competitive, real wages and living standards would rise, and the prospects for employment would improve as well. Everyone is in favour of better education and training, for these reasons and many more.

45

In the context of structural unemployment however we should look not just at the average level of education and training but at its variation across the workforce. It is striking that in the UK the variation of educational achievement is greater than in most other European countries. In the context of the distribution of 'earning power' and its relation to unemployment this is an important and disturbing fact. The widening seems to begin at an early age, with very different rates of progress of children at primary school. It may then be self-reinforcing as the children who have not benefited fully from one stage in their education get left further and further behind. It is also true that in the UK we have been relatively good at providing higher education opportunities for the academic elite and relatively bad at organizing craft training or vocational qualifications for the population at large. Public awareness of these issues has increased over the past ten years and new policies have been introduced. This is not the occasion for a critique, but the intention behind these reforms is clearly to address long-standing problems that have contributed to the high level of unemployment in Britain.

In reviewing the various forms of policy action which might help reduce unemployment we must keep in mind the very different time horizons over which they might be effective. The reform of education and training for the population as a whole will mainly affect the employment opportunities of the next generation. That does not make them any the less important or urgent, but it means that on their own they are not a sufficient response to unemployment today. If the government made a commitment to full employment it would be reasonable to ask to what time period the commitment referred. If the answer was well into the twenty-first century, then the popular endorsement would not be so enthusiastic.

CONCLUSIONS

It is remarkable how support of the objective of full employment has survived despite the failure for over twenty years to achieve it. Clearly it accords with a popular perception of the responsibility of the state and the well-being of society. Self-interest may also be involved now that so few people can feel really secure in their possession of jobs. The concerns which led to the commitment made in the 1944 White Paper are no less relevant today. A job is still, for most people, the basis for participation in the community and to be deprived of a job is to be rejected or pushed to the margins.

The full employment of the post-war period reflected a condition of persistent excess demand in the labour market in which inflation was suppressed by regulation and by restraint in the use of market power. It also depended on a consensus, not just between political parties about the conduct of policy, but also between employers and employees about the priority of jobs as against pay.

Those tacit agreements broke down in the 1960s and attempts to replace them with the formal structure of prices and incomes policies have all been unsuccessful. Structural unemployment has developed for a combination of reasons, which may include the lasting effects of three severe recessions, a lack of flexibility in relative rates of pay and a widening in the dispersion of potential earnings within the labour force. Since 1979 (but not only because of the change in government) the British economy has been transformed from a largely corporatist to a free market system. This is the context within which a new commitment to full employment would now be made.

It would be a cruel deception to speak of full employment as an objective if there were no way of achieving it. My own view is that full employment is possible, although only at a considerable cost. Some form of taxation would have to be increased or some form of public expenditure cut. The sums involved could be large. The question remains therefore whether political support can be found in the country for the measures which would be needed. There is no lack of support for the objective, but the real challenge is to build support for a sustained effort over many years and for some sacrifice in the interests of social solidarity.

Steady, non-cyclical, growth, if it can be achieved, would be a great help, but on its own it will not result in full employment. A successful industrial policy, if that can be achieved, would also be of value both in supporting real wages and escaping from a balance of payments constraint. The employment problem could be greatly eased by improvements in education and training, and for the long term this is the most attractive solution. But the group most likely to be helped by such reforms would consist of new entrants to the labour force, so as a means of achieving full employment, this may take us well into the next century.

Special employment measures, targeted on the unemployed, to improve their job prospects on an individual basis, will always be of value if they are well designed. But they cannot be expected to cope with mass unemployment as we have known it since the 1970s. Extending them to a much larger scale would run the risk of creating another form of marginalization, not very different in its social implications from unemployment itself.

In a market economy the main instrument for increasing job opportunities for those at risk of unemployment should be incentives and relative costs. These can be influenced by changes in the system of national insurance contributions, changes in income taxation or public spending on transfers and subsidies. The reforms needed to bring about full employment by this method would be on a large scale and involve substantial costs to the general taxpayer. It is best to aim as directly as possible at the objective of creating more jobs, and for that reason reform of national insurance contributions and subsidies for low-skill employment seem more appropriate than benefits paid to low income individuals or households. They also avoid the intrusiveness and sense of dependency, which are always associated with a means test. They would have to be introduced gradually and the scale of change needed could not be calculated accurately in advance. Suppose however that the reform was continued to the point where the cost of employing the lowest paid workers fell mainly on the community as a whole rather than on the employer. If one went to that extreme then I have little doubt that full employment would be the result.

There may be other means of reaching the same objective, not covered in this chapter. I hope I will have provoked some of my professional colleagues to continue the debate by responding to the points I have made. I hope that most of them would agree that full employment is a very worthwhile aim and that, given a high enough priority, it is an aim that we can achieve.

NOTE

1 This Chapter was originally delivered as a keynote address to the TUC/EPI Conference, Looking Forward to Full Employment, Congress House, 5 July 1994.

REFERENCES

Beveridge, W. H. (1944) *Full Employment in a Free Society*, London: Unwin.
Dow, C. (1964) *The Management of the British Economy 1945–60*, Cambridge: Cambridge University Press.
European Commission (1993) *Growth, Competitiveness and Employment*, Brussels.
H M Government (1944) *Employment Policy*, Cmnd 6527, London: HMSO.
Organization for Economic Co-operation and Development (OECD) (1994) *Jobs Study: Facts, Analysis, Strategies*, Paris: OECD.

3

A PRICE WORTH PAYING?
THE COSTS OF
UNEMPLOYMENT

David Piachaud

INTRODUCTION

The average numbers unemployed in the last four decades were:

- 1950s – 338,000
- 1960s – 459,000
- 1970s – 976,000
- 1980s – 2,714,000

Even if unemployment is now falling slightly, it remains at a level massively greater than that experienced during most of the post-war period. This chapter seeks to explore and where possible quantify the costs of unemployment so that those who tolerate and perpetuate current levels and think it a price worth paying may at least understand what that price is. To many the human costs of unemployment seem self-evident; it is, perhaps, a sad reflection on our times that these costs need to be spelled out. Unemployment has consequences for individuals, their families, the wider society and the economy. It affects poverty and health, children and family break-up, crime and racism. This chapter reviews the evidence on each of these in turn. It draws on and updates a number of excellent reviews of the effects of unemployment by Sinfield (1981), Hakim (1982), the House of Lords (1982), Taylor (1987) and McLaughlin (1992). In particular it attempts to extend previous reviews with respect to the consequences of unemployment for poverty, the question of whether unemployment is creating an underclass, and the economic burden imposed by mass unemployment.

There is abundant evidence that unemployment is not uniformly distributed in society. As unemployment generally has risen, it has increased disproportionately among those lacking skills, those with disabilities, and among ethnic minorities. The costs are most unequally borne, which is, perhaps, why mass unemployment has lasted so long.

POVERTY

Poverty is defined here as those living below half the average income level. The government's own statistics are used, based on the latest available statistics which refer to 1990–91. More precisely, the poor are defined as those living in households where the income, adjusted for household size and after taking account of housing costs, was below 50 per cent of average income. For 1991 this level (expressed in 1993 prices) represented £61.33 per week for a single person and £160.56 for a couple with two children (aged 6 and 8 years). While the British government does not officially recognize this as a poverty line, it is a definition frequently used in the European Union and it serves as an appropriate benchmark.

The number and proportion of individuals in poverty in Britain is shown in Table 3.1(a). It can be seen that between 1979 and 1991 the number in poverty rose from 5 million to 13.5 million and constituted nearly one-quarter of all individuals in Britain in 1991. In Table 3.1(b) only those individuals where the family head was unemployed are shown. In total the number of poor individuals due to unemployment nearly tripled between 1979 and 1991 to over two million.

Table 3.1 Unemployment and poverty

		1979	1991
(a)	Individuals below half average income		
	Number	5.0m	13.5m
	Proportion	9%	24%
(b)	Individuals below half average income where family head is unemployed (relative terms)		
	Number	0.8m	2.2m
(c)	Individuals below half average income where family head is unemployed (absolute terms)		
	Number	0.8m	1.6m
(d)	Proportion of bottom tenth whose family head is unemployed	16%	28%
	Proportion of bottom fifth whose family head is unemployed	10%	18%
(e)	Proportion of individuals below half average income Status of family head:		
	Unemployed	58%	72%
	Lone parent	19%	60%
	Pensioner	17%	37%
	Full-time worker	2%	7%

Source: Department of Social Security 1993a

So far the poverty standard used has been a 'relative' standard, namely half of average income in each year. As average incomes rise, such a relative poverty standard increases in real terms. An alternative is to use a fixed, 'absolute' poverty line. The changes in poverty using half of 1979 average income as a fixed poverty line are shown in Table 3.l(c). Overall the number in absolute poverty rose slightly between 1979 and 1991. By contrast, the number below a fixed poverty line in unemployed families doubled. Thus using either a relative poverty level – as is most appropriate and is shown in Table 3.l(b) – or using an absolute standard – as shown in Table 3.1 (c) – poverty in unemployed families has very greatly increased.

The extent to which unemployment contributed to the lowest income groups is shown in Table 3.l(d). In 1979,16 per cent of the bottom tenth of the income distribution was in unemployed families; in 1991 it was 28 per cent. Of the bottom fifth, the unemployed made up a smaller proportion which again grew substantially between 1979 and 1991.

The incidence of poverty is directly related to the economic status of the family head. Where the family head is a full-time worker only a very small proportion are in poverty – although that proportion has substantially increased. In Table 3.1(e) it can be seen that 7 per cent of those in families of full-time workers were poor in 1991, compared with only 2 per cent in 1979. By contrast, the very highest risk of poverty occurred in families with an unemployed head – where 72 per cent were poor – a higher proportion than for any other status and a substantially higher proportion than in 1979.

For the unemployed, the 1980s have been a period of growing selectivity in social security. The earnings-related supplement was abolished and a growing proportion of unemployed people became dependent on means tested income support (or its predecessor, supplementary benefit). In 1992, 70 per cent of unemployed men and over half of unemployed women were dependent on income support. The value of both contributory and means tested benefits has changed little in real terms, as is shown in Table 3.2. The decline in value relative to the incomes of those in work has been very marked. The other, and most drastic, change has been the decline in income support for those aged under 25 for whom the real level of benefits has been cut by one-fifth or more. Overall then the real level of support provided by the social security system for the unemployed has declined during the 1980s. It is no wonder that unemployment has made such a massive contribution to the growth in poverty.

The most detailed recent investigation of the effects of unemployment on living standards was a series of case studies that complemented a large-scale survey of the unemployed; a sample was interviewed in 1983–4 and again in 1988 (Ritchie 1990). It was found that the benefit system was rarely seen as an adequate safety net for providing financial security, or relieving insecurity, in the longer term. Even expenditure which was a priority, like food, heating, clothes or other things for the children, or tobacco, had to be curtailed in unemployment and gave rise to concerns about health, the deprivation of the educational

51

Table 3.2 Value of social security benefits

	1979	1993
Unemployment benefit		
At April 1993 prices		
Single person	£43.17	£44.65
Married couple	£69.89	£72.20
Benefit as proportion of average earnings		
Single person	18.4%	14.1%
Married couple	29.8%	22.8%
Benefit as proportion of net income of average earner		
Single person	23.2%	17.4%
Married couple	35.8%	27.3%
Supplementary benefit/Income support		
At April 1993 prices		
Single person aged 18–24	£42.70	£34.80
Single person aged 25+	£42.70	£44.00
Married couple	£69.31	£69.00

Source: Department of Social Security 1993b

or social needs of children and the general impact on family life. Spending on low priorities was minimal or non-existent. In general, self-esteem appeared to be more affected by the lack of employed status and occupation than by the financial consequences of unemployment. Nevertheless, for some families the consequences of unemployment – a depleted domestic stock of personal possessions, the absence of choice in expenditure, the inability to mix socially, the onset of debt or arrears – affected people's feelings of pride and respect in themselves.

HEALTH

Without work all life goes rotten.

(Albert Camus)

Unemployed people are less healthy, both physically and mentally than people in work. The relationship of unemployment and health has been examined in many studies; these have been reviewed by Smith (1987), Taylor (1991) and Fryer (1992).

The links between unemployment and health are not, however, as obvious as might appear. Unemployment, as has been seen, causes poverty. Poverty in turn may lead to poor nutrition, inadequate heating and bad housing, all of which can affect health. Poverty also contributes to financial stress and anxiety which are damaging psychologically. Thus many of the health consequences of unemployment may be linked to poverty rather than to unemployment on its own.

While there are numerous studies showing that physical and mental health are worse among the unemployed and in areas of high unemployment, the statistical association is no proof that unemployment is the cause of the health problems. People in poor health may be more prone to become unemployed and have more difficulty in finding work than those in better health. Poor health may, thus, be the cause of unemployment, rather than the other way round. It is also important to bear in mind that work, as well as the lack of it, may damage health through stress or unhealthy working conditions. Nevertheless there is strong evidence that on balance unemployment does damage health. Studying men unemployed in the week before the 1971 Census, Moser *et al.* (1984) found that unemployment raised the chance that a man would die in the next decade by about a third; for those in middle age the chance doubled. Beales and Nethercott (1985) found that when redundancy threatened, GP consultations and referrals rose significantly.

It is on mental health that unemployment has the most striking effects. Gallie, Marsh and Vogler (1994) found that: 'The unemployed were in relatively segregated networks in which their friends also tended to be unemployed. They therefore had weaker social support systems to help with both psychological and material problems.' Explanations for the psychological effects of unemployment differ. Some (e.g. Jahoda 1979) argue that work is psychologically supportive, imposing a structure on the day, providing contacts, experience and goals outside the individual and his or her family, and giving status and identity to the individual; the absence of these latent functions of work makes unemployment destructive. Others (e.g. Warr 1987) argue that there are other aspects as well – such as financial anxiety, insecurity, rejection and loss of control over one's life – which may lead to psychological deterioration. Whatever the explanation, the damage that unemployment does to mental health cannot be doubted.

FAMILY

If a single person is unemployed only one person is directly affected. If a sole earner with a spouse and three children is unemployed then five people are directly affected. Thus the incidence of unemployment in families of different sizes is important. Unfortunately, from this perspective, it is in the largest families that unemployment is highest and where it has risen fastest: between 1979 and 1990 the proportion of married men who were unemployed rose from 2 per cent to 3 per cent where there was no child, but from 6 per cent to 10 per cent where there were three or more children (General Household Surveys, 1979 and 1990).

The result has been that the proportion of children in married couples with an unemployed husband doubled during the 1980s from 3 to 6 per cent. This is the proportion at a given time; the number in families experiencing unemployment at some time is much larger. Thus, more and more children have been brought up with unemployment as a central influence on their lives. Much evidence exists showing a relationship between unemployment and marital dissolution. Thornes and Collard (1979) found that the average total duration of all spells of unemployment among divorcing couples was double that for stable marriages. Payne (1989) noted that in 1985 the proportion of widowed, divorced and separated men aged 16–64 who were unemployed was approximately twice that for married men in the same age group. Lampard (1994) found that:

> A bout of unemployment during one calendar year raised the chances of dissolution during the following calendar year by approximately 70 per cent. . . . In short, it appears that postmarital unemployment caused a significant number of marital dissolutions which would otherwise either not have occurred at all, or would have occurred at a later date.
>
> (Lampard 1994: 89)

CRIME

Many see the relationship between unemployment and crime as self-evident: there can be no law and order in a society where many are excluded. Yet many social scientists have cast grave doubt on this relationship. For example, Fox (1978) wrote: 'The absence of an impact of the unemployment rate on the rate of crime appears at this time to be unequivocal.' More recent evidence points to a different conclusion. There are several reasons for caution in analysing and interpreting any relationship between unemployment and crime.

First, as Radzinowicz pointed out long ago (1939), any relationship between employment conditions and crime is likely to differ across types of crime and social groups. Second, the relationship is by no means straightforward. The years of high unemployment during the 1930s were a period of rising crime rates, but so too were the 1960s when unemployment was low. While unemployment may affect overall levels of certain crimes, the effect is not direct: many who are not unemployed commit crimes and most who are unemployed do not commit crimes. Indeed Farrington *et al.* (1986) found that unemployment did not seem to cause 'basically law-abiding youths to commit crimes'. Third, as Cantor and Land (1985) have argued, unemployment may simultaneously increase the motivation for crime but decrease the opportunity. Fourth, the direction of causality may not be only from unemployment to crime; involvement in crime or a criminal record may cause unemployment. Fifth, the measurement of both crime and unemployment is difficult and controversial. Finally, associations may be established but they do not necessarily indicate causation. Thus, for a number of reasons, the relationship between unemployment and crime is likely to be complex and hard to elucidate.

The most extensive recent review of research evidence, nearly all based on the USA, by Chiricos (1987), questions the prevailing 'consensus of doubt' about the relationship of unemployment and crime. He concludes that:

For the present, it is appropriate to argue that evidence favors the existence
of a positive, frequently significant unemployment crime relationship. . . .
And, while the relationship between unemployment and crime rates is far
from perfect, it is sufficient to put jobs back on the agenda for dealing
with crime.

(Chiricos 1987: 57)

Important recent work by Dickinson (1994) analysed male burglary offenders
by age in relation to age-specific unemployment rates for Britain: when
unemployment rose, the number of burglary offenders rose but, more strikingly,
when unemployment fell from 1983 to 1989, these offenders also fell. Dickinson
concluded that:

The association between unemployment and criminal activity amongst
young men, shown for domestic burglary, is clear. . . . No claim is made
that there is a simple relationship between unemployment and crime, but
unemployment must be regarded as a major factor motivating crime.
While unemployment alone may not be sufficient to result in criminal
behaviour it may well be the catalyst for those having least educational
and economic opportunities and who are, as a result, least affected by
social restraints. Worryingly, unemployment may well erode those social
restraints where they do exist.

(Dickinson 1994: 24)

An increasingly important aspect of the link between unemployment and
crime is drug use. Parker et al. (1988) examining heroin use found that 'high
unemployment serves to foster drug use'. The areas of the Wirral with the
highest rates of known opioid use averaged 20 per cent unemployment, whereas
the areas with no opioid problem averaged 6 per cent unemployment. Most
known users relied on illegal means to finance the habit. Thus the causal links
between unemployment, heroin use and crime seem clearly established.

RACISM

There can be no doubt that one of the most far-reaching and evil consequences
of mass unemployment in the 1920s and 1930s was the growth of racism. There
is no reason to think that the same threat does not exist today in Britain, as in
Germany and France. Unfortunately, however, there is little up-to-date evidence
on the relationship of unemployment and racism in Britain. A notable exception
was the study by Husbands (1983) of racial exclusionism and the growth of the
National Front. He found that:

There is a strong suggestion in the data of the greater susceptibility to
the NF of the unemployed, certainly of the female unemployed. The
proportion of respondents mentioning unemployment among whites as
among the main changes that black people have brought to the way of life

in Britain was, not surprisingly, substantially higher among National Front sympathisers than among the rest of the population. . . . Most of these data were collected at a time when the national number of unemployed was 1.6 million; it is not necessary to labour the possible implications of this finding at a time when unemployment is officially at 3.3 million, especially if some movement similarly oriented to the NF were successfully to replace it.

(Husbands 1983: 137)

UNEMPLOYMENT AND AN UNDERCLASS

In recent years the idea that there is an underclass in Britain which has caused or been caused by unemployment has been gaining ground. This makes it all the more important to examine the evidence. Since the concept of underclass has often been used loosely and emotively it is important to be clear about terms and circumspect about what the evidence does and does not show.

The term 'underclass' like so much in modern Britain is an import from the USA. There writing on an underclass is extensive (for example, Wilson 1987; Jencks and Peterson 1991). Macnicol (1987) has shown that the idea of an underclass has been around in Britain for over a century; even if the term is new, the concept is not. For example, Marx's lumpenproletariat had much in common with some notions of an underclass. Dahrendorf (1987) argued that, as a result of unemployment and underemployment, an underclass was developing with a lifestyle 'which has little in common with the values of the work society around'. Field (1989) in a more extensive discussion saw the underclass as being recruited from three groups:

First, the recruiting sergeant has been active in the ranks of the long-term unemployed. . . . A second distinct group of claimants with little hope of freeing themselves from dependence on welfare are single parent families . . . . The third group of very poor claimants . . . are elderly pensioners. It is this hard core of unemployment – that is, those who have been out of work longest – that makes up a large part of the new underclass.

(Field 1989: 68)

The writer who has achieved most prominence – a colour supplement devoted to his work by *The Sunday Times* who financed his tour of Britain – is an American, Charles Murray. Murray (1990) saw the underclass as having three dimensions: illegitimacy, crime and unemployment, particularly of young men. On unemployment Murray wrote:

The theme that I heard from a variety of people in Birkenhead and Easterhouse was that the youths who came of age in the late 1970s are in danger of being a lost generation. All of them did indeed ascribe the problem to the surge in unemployment at the end of the 1970s. 'They came out of school at the wrong time', as one older resident of Easterhouse put it, and have never in their lives held a real job. They are now in their late twenties. As economic times improve, they are competing for the same entry level jobs as people 10 years younger, and employers prefer to hire the youngsters. But it's more complicated than that, he added. 'They've lost the picture of what they're going to be doing.' When he was growing up, he could see himself in his father's job. Not these young men.

(Murray 1990: 10)

The question facing Britain is the same, haunting question facing the USA: how contagious is this disease? Is it going to spread indefinitely, or will it be self-containing? One source of some of the heat about an underclass is that much discussion is on causation and even blame – Murray's judgements are as liberal in quantity as they are illiberal in quality. Whether an underclass, if it exists, is due to an inadequate welfare state, the culture of poverty, perverse government incentives or changes in the inner city economy (as Peterson 1991 discusses) raises many interesting and important questions. But seeking causes presupposes that the phenomenon exists, which is certainly not well established in Britain. Another source of heat is that the underclass is such a slippery concept – 'hopelessly polluted in meaning', as Wilson (1990) put it – which is perhaps why it has spread so fast. As far as this chapter is concerned, the only relevant question is whether there is solid evidence that an underclass has caused or been caused by mass unemployment. Walker (1990) argues that Murray 'fails to provide any scientific proof that an underclass exists. Substituting for such evidence are innuendos, assertions and anecdotes'. Similarly, Marmor and Plowden's (1991) verdict on Murray's argument that social benefits 'encouraged young men to withdraw from the labour market, young women to become pregnant outside marriage, and young fathers to decline to marry the mothers of their babies' was that: 'This is rubbish, as literally scores of serious reviews made clear.'

One of the important assumptions about an underclass in the writing of Dahrendorf and Murray is that it is spatially concentrated in run down, inner city council estates. It seems evident to many that there are particular estates or districts in which the underclass is concentrated and that such areas should be the focus for an investigation of an underclass. Yet what may appear to be evident may also be misleading.

Unemployment is associated with poverty, rent arrears and debt. Poverty generally results in lack of choice over where to live. Council policies on the allocation of housing and on rehousing of those in rent arrears determine the composition of particular estates in terms of age, employment history and other characteristics. Thus, unemployed people may be spatially concentrated as a result of their unemployment and its consequences. This is the opposite causation to that suggested by Murray who saw the attitude of people in particular areas as being the cause of their unemployment. Focusing on small areas may, therefore, tell us more about the results of poverty and of council housing policies than about the existence of an underclass.

To shed some empirical light on the underclass controversy, Piachaud (1992) examined two questions based on Britain's unemployment experience in the 1980s. First, when unemployment generally fell was there a group which failed to benefit? What the evidence suggested was that lower unemployment generally appeared to benefit all groups. Second, was there a group for which earlier experience of unemployment affected the extent of unemployment at a later date? The evidence on this suggested that prior levels of unemployment did appear to affect later levels of unemployment of age cohorts. The latter evidence does suggest that an unemployed underclass may now exist, although it hardly amounts to clear-cut and indisputable evidence (see also Smith 1992).

The most valuable recent findings are those of Gallie, Marsh and Vogler (1994) which are based on research arising from the ESRC's Social Change and Economic Life Initiative. On an underclass, Gallie and Marsh wrote:

> In general, the evidence marshalled in this volume suggests that the unemployed form a distinctive group at the bottom of the social heap, who experience recurrent difficulties. However, it would be a cruel step to move from this descriptive statement to the conclusion that they were in this condition through some fault of their own or as a result of the operation of the system of welfare. Rather the results of this volume suggest that people may be caught in a spiral of disadvantage in which small events may have large repercussions. Through an initial accident of job loss, a person may get trapped in a cycle of further unemployment. Unemployment frequently leads to depression, family break-up, and social isolation, which in turn makes the next job more difficult to find. After the event we may identify a group with a distinct life-style at the bottom of the heap, but they were not destined to be there, and under different labour market conditions, as the work history analysis shows us, they would not have been there.
>
> (Gallie and Marsh 1994: 79)

It seems clear that the idea of an underclass must be treated with great caution, particularly if the idea extends beyond description to causation.

ECONOMIC COSTS

The most obvious cost of unemployment is the expenditure on social security benefits to unemployed people. This expenditure grew from £3,371 million in 1979–80 to £9,290 million in 1992–3 measured in constant 1992–3 prices (DSS 1993b). Thus, real expenditure directly on the unemployed nearly tripled over this period. In 1994–5 social security benefits for the unemployed were expected to amount to nearly £11 billion in current prices. The direct expenditure on benefits for the unemployed is, however, far from the full measure of the costs to the Exchequer.

First, there are extra benefits to the long-term sick and disabled that result from increases in unemployment generally. It seems probable that at least one-third of the growth in expenditure on the long-term sick and disabled is due to the growth in unemployment. Second, there is the cost of administering benefits to the unemployed, amounting to about 6 per cent of benefit expenditure. Third, there are revenues foregone. There is the loss of direct taxes – income tax and national insurance (NI) contributions that would have been received if the unemployed had been earning. There is the loss of employers' NI contributions that would have been paid. There is the loss of indirect taxes that would have been paid since consumer expenditure would have been higher if the unemployed had been in work. Estimates were made of all these Exchequer costs for 1994–5; they are shown in Table 3.3.

Table 3.3 Estimated Exchequer costs of unemployment, 1994

Social security	
Benefits to unemployed[1]	£10,816m
Extra benefits to long-term sick and disabled[2]	£4,004m
Administration[3]	£640m
Taxes foregone	
Direct taxes[4]	£4,581m
Employers' NI contributions [5]	£3,371m
Indirect taxes[6]	£3,164m
Total Exchequer cost	£26,576m

Notes:
Method of calculation
1 Figures derived from Cm 2213, *The government's expenditure plans 1993–94 to 1995–96, Social Security*, London: HMSO,1993, uprated by 4 per cent to convert from 1992–3 to 1994 prices.
2 During the period 1979–80 to 1992–93, expenditure on this group rose on average by 9.8 per cent per annum when unemployment was rising and by 5.5 per cent per annum when unemployment was falling. One-third of the growth in expenditure on this group between 1979–80 and 1992–3 is attributable to the rise in unemployment.
3 As 1 above.
1–5 and 6 These figures were derived as follows: first the loss of earnings due to unemployment was estimated. The earnings lost by the unemployed (previous earnings less earnings while unemployed) were taken from the most recent survey of incomes in and out of work by SCPR (Erens and Hedges 1990). These data related to those becoming unemployed rather than the stock of the unemployed but it is probably the best indication of lost earnings. The unemployed, who were for this exercise divided by sex and manual/non-manual, had approximately three-quarters average earnings. These figures relating to 1987 were updated using the change in average earnings 1987–94.
  Second, lost direct taxes were estimated applying the average tax rate for the bottom quintile of non-retired households in the latest available year – namely 14.6 per cent – to the lost earnings (*Economic Trends*, May 1993); tax foregone on unemployment benefits (assuming all unemployment benefit is taxed at the basic rate) was deducted.
  Third, lost employers' national insurance contributions are estimated based on the current rate – 10 per cent – applied to lost earnings.
  Fourth, the loss of disposable income was estimated from the SCPR 1987 survey, uprated to 1994. The average rate of indirect tax for all non-retired households – namely 19.5 per cent – was applied to this (*Economic Trends*, May 1993). This certainly understates the loss of indirect taxes since the rates of indirect taxes on the lower quintiles are considerably higher than the average and indirect taxes have increased in the last year.

Not all Exchequer costs have been included. Unemployment has consequences for health, personal social services and for policing and the criminal justice system. No estimates have been made of the costs unemployment imposes for each of these.

While some of the methods and estimating assumptions differ from earlier estimates, the results are consistent with the earlier estimates of the Exchequer costs made for the House of Lords Select Committee on Employment (1982) and they are close to the estimates made by Taylor (1993). The total Exchequer cost of unemployment now amounts to over £26 billion, or over £9,000 per unemployed person. If unemployment were reduced to one million, the Exchequer cost would fall by some £16 billion which would allow the basic rate of income tax to fall by about 10 pence in the pound. Thus, it is realistic to think of unemployment as imposing a tax equivalent to 10 pence on basic rate tax.

The overall loss to the economy is however greater than this. The result of unemployment is that people who could be producing goods and services are not doing so. An indication of the lost output may be obtained by estimating the loss of earnings resulting from unemployment. Philpott (1994) estimated that the output lost in 1992–3, when unemployment was slightly higher than in 1994, amounted to at least 8 per cent of gross domestic product. On the basis of the calculations used here, the loss of earnings – and of output – would have amounted to some £34 billion in 1994, which is just over 5 per cent of gross domestic product. While the precise loss is inevitably somewhat uncertain, what is indisputable is the massive scale of the output lost – literally the waste of unemployment.

A choice has to be made as to whether the costs of mass unemployment outlined here – and the future costs about which one can only speculate – are a price worth paying. Are the costs of bringing down unemployment so high that the benefits to individuals, families, society and the economy of doing so are unattainable? The ultimate weakness is to suggest we have no control over the future. Britain has a choice.

REFERENCES

Beales, N. R. and Nethercott, S. (1985) 'Job loss and family morbidity – a factory closure study in general practice', *Journal of the Royal College of General Practitioners* 35: 332–51.

Cantor, D. and Land, K. C. (1985) 'Unemployment and crime rates', *American Sociological Review* 50.

Chiricos, T. G. (1987) 'Rates of crime and unemployment', *Social Problems* 34 (2): 92–115

Dahrendorf, R. (1987) 'The erosion of citizenship and its consequences for us all', *New Statesman*, 12 June.

Department of Social Security (1993a) *Households Below Average Income*, London: HMSO.

—— (1993b) *Abstract of Statistics for Social Security Benefits and Contributions and the Indices of Retail Prices and Average Earnings*, London: HMSO.

Dickinson, D. (1994) *Crime and Unemployment*, Cambridge: Department of Applied Economics, University of Cambridge.

Erens, B. and Hedges, B. (1990) *Survey of Incomes In and Out of Work*, London: Social and Community Planning Research.

Farrington, D. P., Gallagher, B., Morley, L., St Ledger, R. J. and West, D. (1986) 'Unemployment, school-leaving and crime', *British Journal of Criminology* 26 (4):30–42.

Field, F. (1989) *Losing Out: The Emergence of Britain's Underclass*, Oxford: Basil Blackwell.

Fox, J. A. (1978) *Forecasting Crime Data*, Lexington: Lexington Books.

Fryer, D. (1992) *The Psychological Effects of Unemployment*, Leicester: British Psychological Society.

Gallie, D. and Marsh C. (1994) 'The experience of unemployment', in D. Gallie, C. Marsh and C. Vogler, *Social Change and the Experience of Unemployment*, Oxford: Oxford University Press.

Gallie, D., Gershuny, J. and Vogler, C. (1994) 'Unemployment, the household and social networks', in D. Gallie, C. Marsh and C. Vogler, *Social Change and the Experience of Unemployment*, Oxford: Oxford University Press.

Gallie, D., Marsh, C. and Vogler, C. (1994) *Social Change and the Experience of Unemployment*, Oxford: Oxford University Press.

General Household Survey (1979), London: HMSO.

General Household Survey (1990), London: HMSO.

Hakim, C. (1982) 'The social consequences of high unemployment', *Journal of Social Policy* 11 (4): 5–62.

House of Lords (1982) *Report from the Select Committee on Unemployment*, Paper 142, London: HMSO.

Husbands, C. (1983) *Racial Exclusionism and the City*, London: George Allen and Unwin.

Jahoda, M. (1979) 'The impact of unemployment in the 1930s and the 1970s', *Bulletin of the British Psychological Society* 32: 40–52.

Jencks, C. (1991) 'Is the American underclass growing?' in C. Jencks and P. E. Peterson (eds) *The Urban Underclass*, Washington DC: Brookings Institute.

Jencks, C. and Peterson, P. E. (eds) (1991) *The Urban Underclass*, Washington, DC: Brookings Institution.

Lampard, R. (1994) 'An examination of the relationship between marital dissolution and unemployment', in D. Gallie, C. Marsh and C. Vogler, *Social Change and the Experience of Unemployment*, Oxford: Oxford University Press.

McLaughlin, E. (ed.) (1992) *Understanding Unemployment*, London: Routledge.

Macnicol, J. (1987) 'In pursuit of the underclass', *Journal of Social Policy* 16 (3): 562–90.

Marmor, T. R. and Plowden, W. (1991) 'Spreading the sickness', *Times Higher Education Supplement*, 25 October.

Moser, K., Fox, A. and Jones, D. (1984) 'Unemployment and mortality in the OPCS longitudinal study', *The Lancet* ii: 1324–9.

Murray, C. (1990) *The Emerging British Underclass*, London: IEA Health and Welfare Unit.

Parker, H., Bakx, K. and Newcombe, R. (1988) *Living with Heroin*, Milton Keynes: Open University Press.

Payne, R. L. (1989) 'A longitudinal study of the psychological well being of unemployed men', *Human Relations* 41 (2): 119–38.

Peterson, P. E. (1991) 'The urban underclass and the poverty paradox', in C. Jencks and P. E. Peterson (eds) *The Urban Underclass*, Washington DC: Brookings Institution.

Piachaud, D. (1992) 'Mass unemployment and the underclass debate', *Campaign for Work Research Report* 4 (3).

Philpott, J. (1994) 'Unemployment, inequality and inefficiency', in A. Glyn and D. Miliband *Paying for Inequality*, London: IPPR/Rivers Orams Press.

61

Radzinowicz, L. (1939) 'The influence of economic conditions on crime', *Sociological Review* 33: 20–32.

Ritchie, J. (1990) *Thirty Families: Their Living Standards in Unemployment*, Department of Social Security Research Report No. 1, London: HMSO.

Sinfield, A. (1981) *What Unemployment Means*, Oxford: Martin Robertson.

Smith, D. J. (1992) *Understanding the Underclass*, London: Policy Studies Institute.

Smith, R. (1987) 'Without work all life goes rotten', *British Medical Journal* 305: 972.

Taylor, D. (1987) 'Living with unemployment', in A. Walker and C. Walker (eds) *The Growing Divide*, London: Child Poverty Action Group.

—— (1993) 'The cost of unemployment', Unemployment Unit Monthly Briefing, October.

Taylor, P. (1991) 'Unemployment and health', *Campaign for Work Research Report* 3 (6).

Thornes, B. and Collard, B. (1979) *Who Divorces?*, London: Routledge and Kegan Paul.

Walker, A. (1990) 'Blaming the victims', in C. Murray *The Emerging British Underclass*, London: IEA Health and Welfare Unit.

Warr, P. B. (1987) *Work, Unemployment and Mental Health*, Oxford: Clarendon Press.

Wilson, W. J. (1987) *The Truly Disadvantaged: The Inner City, the Underclass, and Public Policy*, Chicago: University of Chicago Press.

—— (1990) Quoted in Jason DeParle 'What to call the poorest poor', *New York Times*, 26 August.

4

WHAT DO WOMEN WANT
FROM FULL EMPLOYMENT?[1]

Jill Rubery

INTRODUCTION

Full employment . . . means having always more vacant jobs than unemployed men, not slightly fewer jobs. It means that the jobs are at fair
wages, of such a kind, and so located that the unemployed men can
reasonably be expected to take them.

(Beveridge 1944: 18)

What do women want from full employment? First and foremost, and most
obviously, they want to be included in the definition. This inclusion involves
more than simply replacing 'men' by 'persons' or 'people'; it involves rethinking
the definition of unemployment, and the associated definitions of 'fair wages'
and what constitutes 'reasonable expectations' with respect to the behaviour of
the unemployed. The inclusion of women into the definition of and analysis
of unemployment has so far largely been restricted to the first cosmetic-type
approach; unemployment statistics include women. But the fundamental
rethink of definitions has not yet occurred. When problems of unemployment
are discussed it is the unemployed male with a dependent family, or the young
unemployed male without access to proper training that policy-makers and
analysts focus upon.

For example, the proposal to abolish unemployment benefit and replace it
with a six months only Job Seekers' Allowance was heralded in the media
as a policy designed to remove benefits from those, mainly men, with large
redundancy pay-offs. The likelihood that primarily it would be women who
would suffer from the changes passed most analysts by. Redundant men, at least
below a certain age, in fact tend to find new jobs relatively rapidly and do not
constitute a high share of the long-term unemployed (Daniel 1990). The long-
term unemployed to suffer most under the new policy regime would be women
because they are more likely to be living in households with another wage earner,
thereby making them ineligible for income support. In the case of the male long-
term unemployed it is often not worthwhile for their spouses to enter or remain
in part-time and/or low-paid employment because of the loss of benefits. But
the employed spouses of unemployed women are more likely to be earning a

high enough wage to make working worthwhile, despite the loss of benefits. Women thus suffer from two kinds of unemployment: from direct unemployment, that is the loss of their own jobs; and enforced retirement as a result of their partners' unemployment.

Gender blindness with respect to the definition and analysis of unemployment is not a condition or problem that has been overcome in the past fifty years. Current policies still fail to provide for equal rights for women to work, and present-day analysts fail to observe the most obvious gender dimensions to unemployment issues. Such omissions may be regarded as more 'understandable' fifty years ago, until one remembers the key role that women were playing in the wartime economy. Beveridge failed to reflect upon the possibility that this mobilization of the female 'reserve army' might lead to long-term changes in women's relationship to the labour market. Instead, he assumed that women would continue to provide an essential but entirely flexible reserve to deal with any further national emergencies.

> Finally, as the war has shown, there are many people not dependent on employment and not normally in the labour market, such as pensioners and married women, who can be drawn into employment at need. . . . Full employment at normal hours for all who are normally available for work is consistent with carrying an adequate reserve for variation in the total demand and for the emergencies of war.
>
> (Beveridge 1944: 130)

The experience of the war is drawn upon as demonstrating the possibility for men of genuine full employment: 'the experience of the two wars has shown that it is possible to have a human society in which every man's effort is wanted and none need stand idle and unpaid' (Beveridge 1944: 249). But for women this mobilization is not assumed to have any learning effect, nor to change their expectations of involvement in paid work.

Progress undoubtedly has been made since Beveridge in making women's work, both paid and unpaid, more visible. In 1944 there would not have been two chapters in a book such as this on women and full employment. However, the acid test of progress is to see how many contributions to the unemployment debate, not specifically directed at women's employment, address the issue in any depth, or whether, for example, a standard breakdown of statistics by gender is regarded as adequate treatment. This chapter now reviews some of the main issues that are raised by introducing a gender dimension to the analysis and definition of full employment.

While the first part of a women's agenda must be to become visible and integrated into the analysis, the second must be to move beyond analysis and to identify in what ways women would like to see changes in the operation of the labour market and in the concept of full employment. These changes, if fully implemented, might reduce the extent of differences between men and women in the labour market, thereby apparently diminishing the need to maintain and develop a gender perspective. Nevertheless, these two aspects of the agenda for women's equality must be kept analytically separate. Unless the labour market is analysed from a gender perspective it is impossible to understand how it currently operates and thereby to develop appropriate policies. Making women visible is an essential precondition for any move towards reducing or eliminating gender differences in the labour market. But the achievement of the elimination of discrimination, even as a long-term goal, may be regarded as in doubt. Even if there is a move towards greater equivalence in labour market outcomes between the sexes there will still be a need for gender-specific analysis to enhance understanding and to ensure that such equivalence is maintained.

RETHINKING THE EMPLOYMENT RATE

Full employment is usually defined with respect to the number of jobs relative to the number of unemployed persons. However, full employment could also be taken to imply a high rate of employment. These two perspectives are by no means the same. Countries can have a low rate of open unemployment and a low employment rate (measured as the share of the population in work). Focusing on the employment rate, instead of the unemployment rate, draws attention to a whole range of questions that need to be asked, but which can be ignored or sidestepped if only the unemployment rate is looked at.

What is the appropriate length of time that young people should spend in education and to what extent has the recent expansion of education served more to disguise the problems of achieving full employment than to increase the effective skills of the labour force? How should such periods of education be financed: through the state, the family or through casual employment; and should therefore the demand for casual work by students be included in the definition of full employment? What is the appropriate retirement age and should there be incentives to combine part-time work with retirement? Should pensioners' desire for paid work be included in the full employment equation?

Questions such as these are central to understanding the system of social and economic life underpinning the current levels of employment and unemployment and the current systems of income distribution between those in and outside the labour market. Above all, however, analysis of the employment rate raises the issue of female participation. Most differences in employment rates between advanced countries are probably attributable to differences in women's participation rates; and certainly differences in employment rates of the core working age populations, for example, between ages 20 to 60 years, are linked primarily to differences in female employment rates.

Figures 4.1 and 4.2 show that within Europe the female employment rates follows the same pattern as the total employment rate: the countries are ranked by total employment rate, but there is a notable downward trend to the right for the female employment rate graph as well as for the total employment rate. Moreover, there is more variation in female employment rates than in total

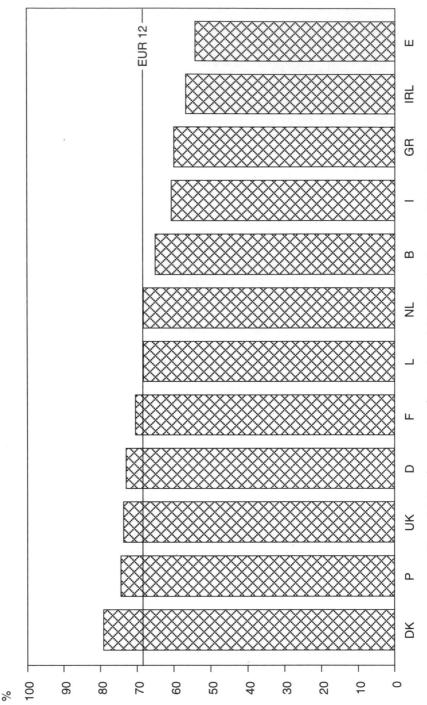

Figure 4.1 Employment rates for people aged 20–59 in the European Union, 1991
Source: European Labour Force Survey 1991, data provided by Eurostat

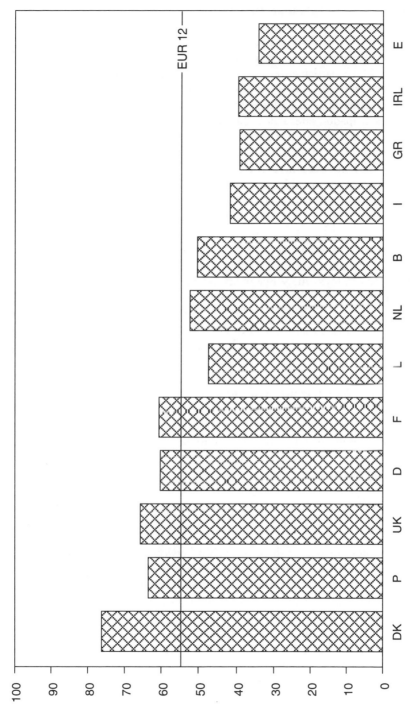

Figure 4.2 Employment rates for women aged 20–59 in the European Union, 1991
Source: European Labour Force Survey 1991, data provided by Eurostat

employment rates, indicating the potential wide range of possible patterns of participation.

This range of patterns is not adequately described by reference to average female participation rates. There are also wide differences, for example, in the extent to which participation is continuous or discontinous (that is involving breaks for childbirth), based on part-time or full-time work, or affected more by marriage, number of children or age of youngest child. Moreover, current average participation rates reflect differences between generations or cohorts. In some countries it seems as if older women are not interested in changing their current economic and social roles as housewives or participants in the informal economy and increases in participation rates for younger women have had little spill-over effect on older generations. In other countries, including the UK, the increase in female participation has been more pervasive, with major rises in participation, albeit on a mainly part-time basis, for older as well as younger cohorts.

This type of generational analysis is important in order to understand and predict the potential or 'hidden' labour supply of the future and thus the full demand for employment. While in several European countries the main impact of the changing generational composition on the labour supply will be to bring more women into the labour market, the main effect for Britain, for example, may be to change the share of women who work or seek work on a full-time basis, as more younger women seem to be adopting the continuous employment, full-time career path, whether or not they have children.

These changes in behaviour may clash with the evolution of the demand side of the labour market, which seems to be moving towards more part-time jobs. One possible outcome of this clash is an increase in the share of men in low-paid and part-time jobs. Such a scenario implies an homogenization of the labour market at the bottom end. Such a development may be misconstrued as a victory for equality, but this misconception arises again out of a gender-blind instead of a gender-neutral analysis of labour market structures.

RETHINKING THE RELATIONSHIP BETWEEN WAGE LEVELS, WORKING TIME AND UNEMPLOYMENT

Most economic analysis of the relationship betweem wages and unemployment focuses on the level of labour market wages in comparison to the level of unemployment benefit. Benefits are considered to be too high if they provide an incentive for the unemployed to continue their 'search' of the labour market for a better job, rather than accept the wages on offer in current vacancies. These analyses tend to assume an homogenization of benefit levels, wage levels and working time attached to jobs. The reality is a much more fragmented structure, in which gender plays an important role in both access to benefit levels and the characteristics of jobs, measured by hourly pay rates and by working time. The benefit levels that individuals are entitled to claim depend upon both a record of continouous employment (arguably a male model of employment) and on means tested income at the household level. For both reasons, women are less likely to be entitled to benefits than men and to be in receipt of lower benefits.

Thus women, under any economic theory, must be regarded as less likely to turn down a job because it offers too low a wage relative to benefits, for many receive no benefits and few receive more than the standard individual unemployment benefit(except for single mothers). The relevant comparison for women is between expected earnings in the job and the additional costs of wage work that women are likely to incur, including direct child care and the cost in terms of leisure of adding wage work to their non-wage work commitments. Time perhaps takes on a greater importance in women's assessments of available jobs than is the case with men.

It is the combination of these effects – the low access to benefits and the greater importance attached to time – that perhaps leads to the proliferation of low-paid and part-time jobs for women. The low income generated by these jobs may still be regarded as preferable to no income, but this is not because women do not value what they do with their time. It is the absence of alternative sources of income for those women constrained by domestic responsibilities which may force them to accept low hourly rates of pay.

This analysis suggests that the traditional view that those with low work commitment are willing to work for low wages (the notorious 'pin money' argument) is misplaced on two counts. First, it seems highly improbable that those not committed to work would be willing to trade their working time for a low wage. Second, it is the welfare system that assumes that women are dependent upon their partners (and that rights to insurance against unemployment should not be provided to those with discontinuous employment patterns because of domestic responsibilities) which therefore limits the opportunity for women to contribute to family wage income other than through the acceptance of low-wage jobs. The effects of the continuation of the 'male breadwinner' model as the basis for social welfare provision are to provide a supply of labour, particularly that of married women, for jobs generating low hourly and low weekly wages. Without comprehensive access to unemployment benefit and without minimum wage protection, the only protection against wages falling even further is provided by the extra costs that women incur from working, such as child care.

Into this 'gendered world' of wages and benefit systems, the Conservative government appears to have decided to introduce gender equality by requiring all the unemployed to consider jobs involving sixteen hours or more of wage work, but with no minimum hourly wage level attached. This push from unemployment benefit into low-paid, part-time work, has been matched by a pull from the Family Credit system, whereby those with dependants are subsidized by the state. The effect of this system is to break down the notion of a 'family wage' for unemployed men at the bottom of the labour market. No longer are they to be allowed to search for a job, beyond a specified period, that pays either a reasonable hourly wage, or even a reasonable total weekly income (generated perhaps through long hours even if at low hourly wages). Part-time work has come to be identified as a normal part of the labour market and not as a sector organized and designed around the employment of second income earners, including women, pensioners and students; except of course that the Family Credit system then seeks to re-establish the notion of the male breadwinner household providing subsidies to those with dependants, and thereby allowing employers to expand the range of jobs in which pay levels do not even have to match benefit entitlements.

The impact of these policies has so far been limited by the problems that the unemployed face in making the transition from benefit status to Family Credit claimants; few unemployed can survive the intervening weeks while the new claim is being processed (McLaughlin 1994). Nevertheless, Chancellor of the Exchequer Kenneth Clarke's 1994 Mais Lecture – in which he heralded part-time work as part of the new flexible working order to which the unemployed must adapt, albeit supported by a welfare state, suggests that this push to place unemployed men into atypical jobs will continue.

This 'homogenization' at the bottom of the labour market contradicts the principle that equality of opportunity should be achieved through a levelling up and not a levelling down of pay and benefit entitlements (Jones 1993). Moreover, the basis for the low wage levels is found not in the free operation of a labour market of individuals, but in the embedded system of household organization and assumptions of income sharing and economic dependency of women.

The abolition of the Wages Councils in 1993, coupled with high levels of unemployment, served to exacerbate these problems. When Beveridge wrote about full employment in 1994 it is clear that he did not envisage men being forced into part-time employment paid at 'women's wages'. Moreover, the publication of the 1944 White Paper *Employment Policy* coincided with an extension of minimum wage protection to trades in which, even then, were female dominated occupations, such as retail, catering, hairdressing and the like (Routh 1980). The minimum wage levels set in Wages Councils were increasingly tied to the female labour market, with relatively few men found employed at these wage rates. Nevertheless, they provided some kind of stability at the bottom of the labour market, a floor below which the minimum hourly wage that the unemployed might be required to accept could not fall (Rubery 1987). In the absence of any mininum wage in the mid-1990s this floor disappeared, affecting many women still in work, and a growing share of jobless men and women who came under pressure to accept whatever jobs were available to them.

RETHINKING THE NOTIONS OF CLOSED AND OPEN LABOUR MARKETS

In most considerations of the task of moving to full employment the emphasis is placed primarily on generating jobs and on getting the unemployed or inactive into a job; the quality of the job and the likelihood of moving back into unemployment or inactivity come second. If jobs are organized on a casual and short-term basis with high rates of job destruction as well as creation, then getting a job is only the beginning of the problem for the individual. In the unstable jobs market, they face a repeated struggle to find work and to escape the danger of falling between jobs and sliding eventually into long-term unemployment (Daniel 1990). Under these conditions it might be argued that it is better to have relatively few job openings, but to ensure that once someone has obtained a job and left unemployment or inactivity they could be reasonably certain of remaining in work. It might involve longer initial spells of unemployment as people queue for jobs, but fewer repeated spells and less long-term anxiety and insecurity.

However, the problem with this latter approach is that the labour market does not work like an orderly queue and waiting patiently on benefit for a secure job to materialize is not a viable option in many cases. The fact of being unemployed for a long time rules one out of consideration for most secure jobs and the unemployed are constantly bypassed in the queue. It is for that reason that so-called 'free' or 'open' labour markets are regarded by some as preferable for the jobless than the 'closed' labour markets which offer long-term employment security but only to the relatively advantaged.

A similar dilemma is faced when the opportunities for female employment are analysed. On the one hand an open and casual labour market opens up opportunities for women to leave to have children and to re-enter after childbirth. However, it also often results in the female labour market being organized on a casual and low-paid basis, with few opportunities for promotion out of the 'ghetto' through internal labour market systems or even through occupational or external labour markets offering career advancement. Yet the more closed labour markets offer a stark choice between continuous employment careers, with or without children, or exclusion from the labour market and perhaps confinement to informal activities or domestic work.

All those removed from the current access to employment face comparable problems. To improve access increases the chances of obtaining a job but at the expense of job quality and with much of the burden of greater job insecurity placed on those operating at the bottom of the labour market, where most new entrants and re-entrants are located. Moreover, the majority of those employed in low-paid jobs in the UK and many other countries are women; policies that are adopted to increase the flexibility of the labour market and opportunities for the jobless to move into work often have negative effects on those already in work in similar employment areas.

Thus flexibilization policies are by no means gender neutral. Even if the policies had a positive effect on creating opportunities for men and women to enter work – and even if these opportunities were to benefit women equally or perhaps even more than men – these apparent benefits have to be set against the negative impact of flexibilization policies on men and women in work. Here the balance is likely to be skewed against women...

society. For women, participation in the informal and domestic economy was regarded as the 'normal' and desirable model; but for men there was a need for formal and public recognition of their contribution to the family economy. These differences in social values persist today. It may be that in some senses there are more acceptable alternatives for women to formal wage work than there are for men, perhaps reducing the stark contrast between employed and non-employed women and certainly blurring the distinction between the unemployed and economically inactive. However, this greater acceptability of informal work and domestic work, of activity in the private sphere, reflects the poor rewards to women available still in the public sphere, and the continuing responsibility placed on them to provide much of the labour required within the private sphere to maintain standards of life for all family members.

In these respects there is considerable continuity between the 1940s and the 1990s; yet perhaps the major social change to have occurred over the past fifty years is the progressive rejection of the notion that women's appropriate role is in the private sphere and men's in the public. This trend is found in all advanced countries and has taken on its own dynamic, independent of particular economic circumstances or the level of employment demand (Humphries and Rubery 1984). To regard female labour thus as a reserve, to be turned on in times of economic necessity or as an opportunistic labour supply, entering the market when demand is high but settling for non-wage activities when demand is low, is neither appropriate nor tenable.

Those that hold to these views are constantly surprised by the tendencies for most new jobs to be taken by those not currently in the labour market, that is by the constant revelation that we have a large hidden supply of labour, whose demands for and aspirations within the world of wage work have yet to be satisfied. An implicit recognition of this phenomenon is perhaps found in the continued failure to develop nursery provision in Britain, despite the evidence of the educational and social benefits that this brings for children. Such provision would probably increase the open unemployment rate at a stroke. Yet even here women are confounding the policy-makers and providers; the largest increase in participation over recent years has occurred among mothers of young children, in spite of the lack of child care provision.

Nevertheless, even though women have been making their demands for access to the public sphere of wage work increasingly more evident, and at the same time reassessing their responsibilities for domestic work (even if not necessarily successfully reassigning them), these changes have undoubtedly been hampered and constrained by continuing inequalities between men and women in the wage labour market. Even neoclassical economists concede that individual families may be constrained in their choices over who is to 'specialize' in domestic and who in wage work, if the two partners face different opportunities in the wage labour market.

These differences in opportunities may not in any way reflect individual potential; instead women are constrained in their access to jobs and income by the sex-segregated labour market, which tends to undervalue women's work and limit access to men's work, often justified by attributing 'second income earner' characteristics even to those women who wish to become the main income earner for the family. However, these constraints on family 'choices' do not necessarily result in women accepting dependency on men; social change can in fact move ahead of economic change. Thus while the labour market still treats women as subordinate second income earners with access to income supplements from the family, in reality many women are seeking their own independence, through setting up independent households. The result of this clash between social change and out-of-date economic structures is, as the USA has already demonstrated, a major increase in the share of women living in poverty.

In thinking about what women want from full employment, it is therefore imperative to focus not only on access to wage work, but also on access to independent income. The ideal of what a fully employed society would entail can be extended to include a world in which women as well as men seek access to wage work to enhance their self-esteem and to feel valued by society. However, just to provide women with 'a little job', to 'get them out of the house', is not an appropriate or satisfactory definition of full employment. Women also want the option to be economically independent and to have the possibility of making a full contribution to household income. Only if that possibility exists can negotiations over how the domestic responsibilities may be shared start off from a level playing field, in contrast to the present situation in which men's superior options in the labour market give them the possibility of arguing that the division of labour in the household is not only economically rational but also fair. Full employment for women thus means not only access to some form of wage work, but also access to reasonable levels of wage income, sufficient to provide at least for themselves and to contribute towards dependants. Thus the agenda of what women want from full employment cannot be divorced from the agenda of improving women's pay in the labour market.

BENEFIT REFORM AND RE-REGULATION

Economic independence for women depends not only on full employment and improvements in pay but also on a reform of the benefits system. The system of very low individual entitlements for the unemployed but the opportunity for a reasonable level of total benefits based on means tested household income creates conditions under which women living with unemployed men are effectively denied the right to continue their economic activity or to restart their involvement in the labour market (McLaughlin 1994). Such disincentives also exist when an unemployed man finds low-wage or part-time work as access to top up Family Credit is affected by the existence of a second income earner in the household. These disincentives to women to work contribute to social exclusion of the unemployed and reinforce society's perception of women's economic activity as subordinate and contingent on household activities, instead of women enjoying an independent right to work regardless of their household circumstances. Of course in principle the benefit rules apply symmetrically to men and to women, but women's lower wage earning opportunities mean that rarely is it possible for a family to escape from the welfare benefit system on the basis of the women's paid labour market activity. Thus to the extent that the benefit system discriminates against the economic activity of partners it is women's activity that is likely to be suppressed.

These problems should not be solved through reductions in benefits but through a restructuring of the benefit system towards higher individual entitlements and greater scope for earned income of spouses to be discounted in determining access to any remaining means tested benefits. Eligibility for individual benefits should also be improved through extension of social security cover to those with part-time or discontinuous work records. Any reform of a benefit system has its costs and benefits, but included in the assessment of reform proposals must be the question of whether it gives women the right to independent economic activity.

The other side of a women's agenda for economic independence and escape from subordination is the right to enjoy their personal and family life. As Beveridge pointed out, the purpose of employment is to be able to enjoy a stable and satisfying life, and commitment to work should not be at the expense of commitment to families and personal relationships. In this agenda there is potentially much to be gained for men as well as for women. However, the trends in the labour market tend to be pushing in the opposite direction. The much vaunted choice within the UK labour market over hours of work, demonstrated apparently by the wide distribution of working hours in Britain, in fact often disguises increasing pressure on individuals to work whatever hours are necessary to complete increasing work loads. Individualization of contracts and moves towards performance-related pay for higher level workers may act to break down the notion of employment contracts related to time. Task-related pay seems likely to take over from time-related pay, with 'promotability' based on evidence of work commitment, that is willingness to work extra hours whenever necessary.

These types of contracts which are spreading down the occupational hierarchy blur the distinction between wage work and family and home life, thereby making it more difficult for individuals and couples to manage their work and domestic responsibilities. At the other end of the job spectrum the downward pressure on hourly wage levels, particularly for manual workers, leads to increasing need to work long hours to maintain living standards. Britain now has the longest working hours in Europe for full-time employees (Bercusson 1994; see Table 4.1), a factor considerably restricting women's choice to opt out of part-time and into full-time work – both because of the hours of work of their partners and because outside clerical work women can also be called upon to work these long hours (Rubery *et al.* 1994). Under these circumstances families are called upon to 'put children first' (Leach 1994) and to put their careers on

Table 4.1 Average usual hours of work for full-time employees in the EU member states, 1991

Ranked by average usual hours all full-time employees	Employees working full-time			Share of full-time employees usually working more than 45 hours per week (%)		
	All	Males	Females	All	Males	Females
UK	43.4	45.2	40.1	29.5	34.8	9.6
Portugal	41.5	42.7	39.8	4.5	5.8	1.8
Spain	40.5	40.9	39.6	3.6	3.9	2.0
Ireland	40.4	41.7	38.3	10.1	12.5	–
Greece	40.3	41.0	38.8	10.9	12.4	6.7
Germany	39.8	40.0	39.3	4.2	4.8	2.2
Luxembourg	39.8	40.4	38.3	(2.8)	(3.1)	–
France	39.7	40.4	38.7	5.2	6.2	2.3
Netherlands	38.9	39.1	38.3	1.1	1.2	–
Italy	38.7	39.8	36.6	7.4	8.6	3.4
Denmark	38.4	38.9	37.6	3.2	3.8	–
Belgium	38.0	38.5	36.9	2.2	2.5	–

Source: Labour Force Survey 1991, Eurostat
Note: – indicates too small a sample for reliable estimates

hold while the children are young, and for an appropriate framework for child care to be established. However, perhaps what needs to be done first is to reverse trends in the labour market which are increasing the problems of reconciling family and work commitments.

Re-regulation of the labour market is needed to limit the hours that can be asked of individuals and for these restrictions if possible to start with the higher level jobs. Much of the discussion about work sharing focuses on manual workers but it is the increasing hours of managers and professional workers where perhaps concern should be focused (Gregg 1994) as this represents a small elite capturing an ever increasing share of the available high-paid labour hours. These long working hours may or may not be voluntary under current work and family arrangements, but a change of climate or attitude is needed such that work re-distribution starts at the top and not at the bottom of the labour market where the income constraints are greatest. At the bottom of the labour market perhaps the best way to reduce pressure on low-paid men to work long hours is to raise the pay of their female partners, thus enabling families to achieve a reasonable standard of living without excessive overtime hours.

Another alternative often cited to a general reduction in working time commitment is to provide all workers with greater flexibility or choice in their working hours, including choice over daily and weekly hours and options for breaks in employment through their working lives (Hewitt 1993; see also Chapter 5). The problem here is that flexibility of working time in advance of greater equality between the sexes in domestic and work spheres is likely to maintain or even increase segmentation between the sexes at work. In the absence of any likelihood of policy to reduce general working time, it may well be argued, and understandably, that the opportunity to work part-time in one's current career is better than not to be able to work at all. But such a policy should not be confused with a strategy likely to result in equality. Flexible working time options are likely to be used to increase divisions within occupations, into those on career tracks and those who are job stayers with limited promotion opportunities. The freedom for women to make effective choices over working time is only likely to arise if they have first moved a great deal further towards equality of power, influence and income in the public sphere.

This agenda of what women want from full employment clearly involves major changes in all the key institutions and characteristics of the labour market, from benefit systems to pay structures and working time patterns. However, this is the 'long agenda' of equal opportunities policies (Cockburn 1989). The 'short agenda' recognizes the need for incremental change within existing structures and institutions. What is important within the short agenda is that the move towards incremental change should be in the right direction.

One of the problems that we have identified in recent trends is that these may be moving the system further away from equal opportunities, by increasing working hours, reducing pay for part-timers, and homogenizing the labour market more through a reduction in rights for men than through improvements for women. A necessary but not sufficient condition for the direction of change to be in the right direction is that the economy should move further towards instead of away from full employment. In a more buoyant economy it is easier for change that benefits labour to be accommodated and for employers to recognize a need to take into account workers' personal and family lives in their design of employment systems. Moreover, the ever increasing supplies of well-qualified women stand to gain most from temporary labour shortages in jobs previously dominated by men. Thus a process of dynamic expansion and change is probably the best scenario within which existing gender segmentation and inequalities can be challenged and restructured. Yet without the re-regulation of the labour market, including a reform of the benefit system and the establishment of a floor to wages in the labour market, these benefits may be captured by the more advantaged women in the labour market.

CONCLUSIONS

Beveridge in 1944 had the honesty to discuss the case for full employment from the explicit perspective of men. The social and economic changes since Beveridge have ruled out this option; instead the divisions between the sexes in the labour market are often glossed over for the sake of presenting a gender-neutral analysis in which the sexes of the victims or beneficiaries of various polices are not identified. This myth of gender neutrality is maintained in the analysis of the benefit system and the wage structure, even though the means tested benefit system and the low-wage part-time work both reflect the deeply embedded model of the male breadwinner household. The failure to make these relationships explicit has enabled the government to apply 'gender neutral' rules to the unemployed, forcing men to abandon the search for employment offering a family wage and to take up part-time or low-paid work, without the root and branch review of both benefit and pay structures that a move towards gender equality (or economic independence for women without poverty) would imply.

Making women visible and thereby highlighting the gendered nature of labour market and social protection institutions is an essential step on the long road towards the agenda of real equality of opportunity. The current deregulated labour market does not operate in a value-free way but reflects outdated and outmoded institutions, which in the absence of reform are likely to generate increasing poverty and income inequality for both men and women at the bottom of the labour market (Rubery 1992). Expansion of employment opportunities would provide a much more favourable context in which such reforms could be initiated and institutionalized, but even the prospect of a sustained cyclical upturn would be unlikely to be sufficient to bring about the restructuring of labour market institutions in line with current social structures and women's aspirations for economic independence and equality. The institutions which protected men's wages at the bottom of the labour market and safeguarded the unemployed from being forced into low-paid work and poverty have been dismantled and fragmented but have yet to be replaced by a new system of institutions appropriate to current social organization. Fragmentation and deregulation of the labour market leads to the application of wages appropriate for 'second income earners' to 'primary income earners', so that men who become displaced from their jobs face the prospect of sharing in the low wage levels previously reserved for dependants of prime age working men.

This pessimistic scenario can provide one glimmer of hope. The dismantling of the social protection system for prime age male workers means that there is now a greater communality of interests between the sexes. This communality of interests between the sexes and the importance of women's rights to the re-regulation of the labour market was recognized by the Transport and General Workers Union (TGWU) in its submission to the Commission on Social Justice. It called for improvements in child benefits, shorter working weeks, a woman's right to an independent income, a national framework for affordable child care and a statutory obligation for single parents to be given priority in housing (*Guardian* 4 April 1994). This list mirrors very closely the agenda set out above. This communality of interests between the sexes perhaps applies above all in the need to re-establish a floor to wages in the labour market. The escape out of poverty for working-class men and their families in the past may have been thought to have resided in the protection of a male breadwinner model in the labour market and in the social welfare system. Whatever the merits of this approach to wage and social protection, future security against poverty in working-class families is likely to lie more in the establishment of reasonable

78

wage levels for both male and female partners and for single-parent families of whatever sex.

Also important in the fight against increasing social exclusion of whole families would be the ending of discrimination in the welfare system against women participating in the labour market when living with unemployed men. In this segment of the market, women's opportunities for wage employment may be as great if not greater than those of their male partners, but the wage structure and benefit system currently creates strong disincentives to their participation in the labour market. Greater attention is paid in the media to the psychological damage to male egos if women are working when their partners are not, than to the psychological benefits to the adults and also to the children if at least one member of the family is integrated into the wage economy. Under this analysis greater equality between the sexes in the labour market and in the benefit system, brought about through an improvement in the individual floor of rights, could provide a source of greater social cohesion and stability, in contrast to the clichéd view that pressure for gender equality will lead to the destruction of 'family values' and the undermining of British institutions. Social and labour market institutions have already changed and what is needed is reform and reconstruction to provide the security and freedom from fear envisaged by Beveridge, albeit through an androcentric lens, some fifty years ago.

ACKNOWLEDGEMENTS

The author is grateful to Colette Fagan and Mark Smith from the Manchester School of Management for assistance in the analysis of the working-time data.

NOTE

1 The opinions expressed in this chapter are the personal views of the author.

REFERENCES

Bercusson, B. (1994) *Working Time in Britain: Towards a European Model*, part 1 and 2, London: The Institute of Employment Rights.

Beveridge, W. H. (1944) *Report on Full Employment in a Free Society*, White Paper, London: HMSO.

Cockburn, C. (1989) 'Equal opportunities: the short and the long agenda', *Industrial Relations Journal* 20 (3): 213–25

Daniel, W. W. (1990) *The Unemployed Flow* London: PSI.

Gregg, P. (1994) 'Share and share alike', *New Economy* 1 (1): 13–19.

Hewitt, P. (1993) *About Time: the Revolution in Work and Family Life*, London: IPPR/Rivers Oram Press.

HM Government (1944) *Employment Policy*, Cmnd 6527, London: HMSO.

Humphries, J. and Rubery, J. (1984) 'The reconstitution of the supply side of the labour market: the relative autonomy of social reproduction', *Cambridge Journal of Economics* 8 (4): 331–47.

Jones, B. (1993) *Working Document in Connection with the Memorandum on Equal Pay for Work of Equal Value*, Luxembourg: Equal Opportunities Unit DGV, European Commission V/6108/93-EN.

Leach, P. (1994) *Children First*, London: Michael Joseph.

McLaughlin, E. (1994) 'Employment, unemployment and social security', in A. Glyn and D. Miliband (eds) *Paying for Inequality*, London: IPPR/Rivers Oram Press.

Routh, G. (1980) *Occupation and Pay in Great Britain 1906–79*, London: Macmillan.

Rubery, J. (1987) 'Flexibility of labour costs in non union firms', in R. Tarling (ed.) *Flexibility and the Labour Market*, London: Academic Press.

—— (1992) *The Economics of Equal Value*, Manchester: Equal Opportunities Commission Discussion Series.

Rubery, J., Smith, M. and Fagan, C. (1994) 'The redistribution of work: taking into account gender and country-specific differences', Paper presented to the Second European Labour Market Congress, Berlin, March.

5

FULL EMPLOYMENT FOR MEN AND WOMEN

Patricia Hewitt

INTRODUCTION

A new vision of full employment must take into account the profound changes which have occurred in the working lives of men and women over the last fifty years. An effective strategy for full and fulfilling employment should not only tackle the severe problems of uncontrolled 'flexibility', but seek to make the most of the opportunities created by new working time patterns. The Beveridge model simply does not fit the modern world. Women now account for half of all British employees, and their numbers will continue to grow as those at home with children re-enter employment and those now in employment take shorter breaks when they have children. In future, full employment must mean employment for women as well as men. Furthermore, with a majority of women working part-time for part of their lives – and a growing minority of men doing the same – full employment must include part-time as well as full-time employment. Routinely used phrases such as 'back to full employment' can betray old, inappropriate assumptions; there can be no going 'back to full employment' for the simple reason that in peacetime we have never known full employment for men and women.

Beveridge's definition of full employment (without its surrounding assumptions) is entirely appropriate today. But the pattern of the jobs and vacancies which will make up full employment will vary between different people and between different stages of people's lives. There is a pressing need to make full-time jobs available to the majority of registered unemployed workers who want and need full-time employment: but policies designed purely for a world of full-time male workers will be ineffective in today's conditions.

THE CHANGING PATTERNS OF WORK

In thinking about full employment and how we achieve it, we must not underestimate the scale of the transformation which has already taken place in the organization of paid work. Figure 5.1, based on analysis of the Equal Opportunities Commission's Hours of Work survey, shows that in the early 1990s

81

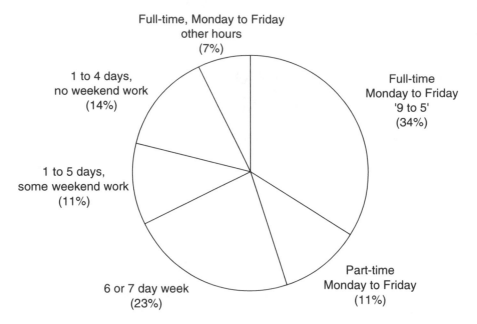

Full-time, Monday to Friday
other hours
(7%)

1 to 4 days,
no weekend work
(14%)

Full-time
Monday to Friday
'9 to 5'
(34%)

1 to 5 days,
some weekend work
(11%)

6 or 7 day week
(23%)

Part-time
Monday to Friday
(11%)

Figure 5.1 The 'normal' working week: British men and women
Source: Hewitt 1993

only one in three of the British workforce worked a standard, 9-to-5, five-day week.[1] Treating part-time employees, along with temporary and casual workers, as 'atypical' workers ignores the fact that, when it comes to the organization of working time, the 'atypical' worker is the new norm.

Part-time employees now make up one in four of the British workforce. Part-time employment remains more common among women, 45 per cent of whom work part-time, than among men (only 9 per cent). Even these 'snapshot' figures can be misleading, however: a majority of women will almost certainly spend some of their working lives in part-time employment. Furthermore, the benefits system requires unemployed claimants to accept a job offering at least 24 hours a week and, through Family Credit, tops up the wages of sole breadwinners with children working at least 16 hours a week. Furthermore, part-time employment offers students (young and mature) an opportunity to earn while they acquire skills. Thus, male part-time employment seems likely to increase. Part-time employment itself takes different forms, from zero hours contracts and casual jobs for short hours at one end of the spectrum, through to permanent, regular, part-week (or, more rarely, part-year) employment at the other. Increasingly, information technology allows employers to manage a large variety of working time contracts, matching employees' working hours to the shifting demands for product or service. In one German department store, for instance, the total number of retail hours needed is calculated each month for the month ahead;

employees then 'bid' for the hours they want. Because commission payments are higher for busy but unpopular Saturdays and lower for slack but popular early weekdays, each division of the store is able to balance staffing numbers with customer peaks and troughs. In Sweden, software is being trailed in public sector organizations which will enable completely personalized working hours to meet organizational needs while substantially recognizing employees' preferences.

How people view 'flexibility'

To the Right, 'flexibility' means the absence of labour market regulation: no minimum wages, few or no employment rights, low payroll taxes and short-lived unemployment benefit. In terms of working time, this sort of 'flexibility' means the effective right of employers to impose whatever working hours – short, long or wholly unpredictable – on their employees. But flexibility can also mean the existence of a wider range of working hours which enable different people to combine employment with family responsibilities, further education or other activities in different ways at different stages in their lives. It is particularly important to understand that most part-time employees, particularly women, do not regard part-time employment as second best. The Hours of Work survey found that:

- women working part-time were considerably more satisfied with their hours of work than either women or men working full-time (74 per cent of women part-timers rated their hours as 'very convenient' compared with 49 per cent of female and 37 per cent of male full-timers);
- women working part-time are considerably more satisfied with the time they have for their families and for themselves than full-time employees (62 per cent of women part-timers are 'extremely satisfied' with their family time, 54 per cent with their personal leisure time, compared with 29 per cent and 22 per cent respectively of the full-timers).[2]

It is certainly the case that a minority of part-time women employees, and a significant group of women who are not employed at all, would choose to work full-time if only they could make and afford child care arrangements. The General Household survey 1992 found that 64 per cent of women aged between 25 and 45 years who were not in paid employment, not registered as unemployed and had children or dependants to care for, would like employment (not all of them full-time); of those, 79 per cent said that it was 'young children' who kept them from seeking a job. Nonetheless, the most popular form of child care for women with young children is 'family friendly' working hours. According to the British Social Attitudes survey 1990, two-thirds of employed women with school-age children put 'working only while the children are at school' as their ideal form of childcare. Working hours which would allow the father to spend more time with his children was almost as popular, particularly for mothers with pre-school children.

PATRICIA HEWITT

WHO ARE THE UNEMPLOYED?

Just as old assumptions about full employment do not fit, so old definitions of unemployment fail to capture modern realities. We are all familiar with the changes to counting methods employed by the government over the last decade to soften the impact of registered unemployment. But even those who recalculate the figures to allow for these effects rarely consider the position of those who have become unwilling part-time employees. The worker who has been made redundant from a full-time job and who is looking for another is, of course, fully unemployed. But how do we treat part-time workers? The majority of part-time workers are voluntary part-time workers; in other words, they are 'fully employed' as far as they – and the government – are concerned.

At the same time, however, a minority of part-time employees are unable to find the full-time employment they want and are available for: they are in reality partly unemployed, and should be treated as such. In spring 1993, this group involved 520,000 women (10 per cent of those working part-time) and 257,000 men (29 per cent of male part-time workers), all of whom wanted a full-time job.[3] These distinctions, which may seem academic, have important practical consequences for employment policy and the social security system.

A trade union sponsored survey in the late 1980s found that a significant proportion of full-time employees – about one in three – would prefer to work shorter hours for the same pay (in other words, trading off a wage increase for increased leisure), although only one in twenty would be willing to work fewer hours for less pay. Among the over-55s, however, half wanted shorter hours and were also more likely to be willing to accept a pay reduction.[4] Full-time employees who would, if offered the choice, work fewer hours even in return for lower wages should properly be regarded as over-employed. Again, this conclusion has important implications for the approach of both employers and trade unions, particularly when redundancies are threatened.

Can cutting working hours cut unemployment?

The crisis of unemployment in the European Community has awakened interest in shorter working hours as a route to job generation. The French government has, for instance, recently proposed moving to a general four-day week; the European Commission refers to the need for working hours reduction to form part of a common programme for jobs. It is frequently argued by economists that such proposals suffer from the 'lump-of-output fallacy'; in other words, the assumption that the total amount of work to be done is fixed and that, therefore, the only way to employ more people is to share the work out more frequently. The alternative, they argue, is to increase output. There should be no doubt that the UK suffers from a demand deficit and that measures need to be taken to translate the obvious need for infrastructure investment, higher standards of care and education and so on into a demand for employment.

84

But the 'lump of output fallacy' is itself fallacious. First, it ignores the impact of productivity gains. Between 1881 and 1981, the lifetime hours worked by British men fell by nearly half (from 154,000 hours over 56 years to 88,000 over 48 years). In those sectors of the economy where technology is driving productivity upwards most rapidly, very large increases in output can be achieved with no growth in employment – or even a continuing fall. This appears to be the case in France, which has achieved very high productivity gains over the last decade, turning the economy into what the French economist, Michel Albert, has called a 'machine for unemployment'. Reductions in working hours in these sectors can moderate the loss in the number of jobs which will otherwise take place, and at the same time allow some of the benefits of productivity growth to be taken in increased leisure. In Germany, studies by both the engineering employers' association and the trade union suggest that, within the engineering industry alone, the shorter working week has increased the number of (mainly full-time) jobs by between 250,000 and 300,000.[5]

Second, the 'lump of output fallacy' argument ignores the fact that, for any given level of output and demand – and for any given level of increase in demand – the length of hours worked by each person will determine the number of people employed. The lower the average hours of full-time workers and the higher the proportion of part-time workers, the more people will be employed. The European Commission's report, *Employment in Europe* 1993, makes the point vividly when it says:

> In some countries, like Denmark or the Netherlands, a relatively high proportion of the population is engaged in work, with each person working a relatively small number of hours. In other countries in the Community, like Belgium or Italy, levels of productivity and income per head are similar to those in the Netherlands, but a much smaller proportion of the population is involved in production and their average hours worked are significantly higher. If, for example, average hours worked in Belgium were the same as in the Netherlands, and productivity remained unaffected, some 15 per cent more people could be in work – twice as many as were recorded as unemployed in 1991.[6]

Developments in the UK labour market reinforce the argument. Until the onset of the 1990s recession, overtime for male manual workers increased, reversing the trend of the previous hundred years of a steady reduction in male working hours. As the EOC survey confirmed, British men work, on average, the longest hours in the European Community, with four in ten British men working an average 46 hours or more a week in 1990. Even in 1992, manufacturing employees worked the same average hours as in the late 1970s. Thus, among men, we see very long working hours coupled with very high levels of unemployment and non-employment. Among women, on the other hand, we see a high level of part-time employment combined with a continuing growth in women's participation in the economy. On the one hand, long hours and high unemployment; on the other, short hours and high employment. The connection is not a coincidence.

Figure 5.2 shows the effect on jobs of an average decline of 4 per cent in working hours between 1983 and 1991 throughout the European Union, comparing actual changes in employment in the different countries with the number of full-time equivalent jobs. The Netherlands is particularly striking: a 13 per cent drop in working hours (about 1 per cent a year) was translated into a 30 per cent increase in the total number of people employed, but only about a 13 per cent increase in the number of full-time equivalents. In every country except the UK shorter hours and more part-time work meant that the number of new jobs outstripped the number of full-time equivalents. In Britain, however, longer working hours for full-time employees meant that fewer jobs were created than there would have been if working hours had simply remained static.

Gregg estimates that if working hours had fallen by 10 per cent between 1975 and 1990 – as they did between 1960 and 1975 – to around 36 hours per week for manual workers and 34 hours for non-manuals, the total drop in working time would have been equivalent to some 2.75 million full-time jobs.[7] Even allowing for productivity gains and other reasons why one hour released is not necessarily one hour for a new employee, Gregg estimates that if the UK had

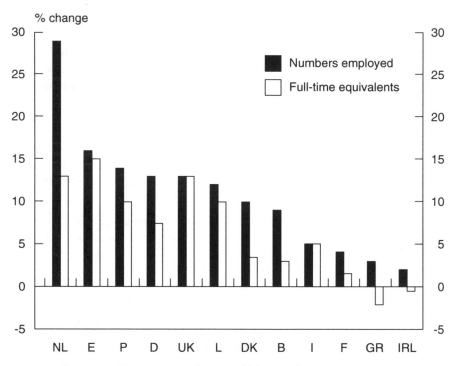

Figure 5.2 Changes in employment in the member states, 1983–91
Source: Commission of the European Community

sustained the rate of working hours cuts seen in the 1950s and 1960s, an extra one million jobs would have been generated.[8] None of this should be taken to mean that working hours could or should be cut by statute. Unlike every other EU country except Denmark (where working hours are effectively regulated by national collective bargaining) the UK has no 'normal working hours' laid down by law. Any attempt to impose a cut on long weekly hours would not only have unacceptably sudden effects on many manual workers' total wage packets, but would impose high costs on industry. Nonetheless, some action can and should be taken.

THE EU WORKING TIME DIRECTIVE

There are some advantages in the British approach to working time: the development of part-time employment has not been hindered, or pushed into the informal economy, by hostile regulation. But the disadvantages are enormous, ranging from the persistent discrimination suffered by part-time employees (lower average hourly rates of pay, less paid holiday entitlement, markedly less access to pension schemes, training and promotion, and so on) to the imposition of extremely long hours (including regular 6- and 7-day weeks) on full-time workers.

The government's opposition to any regulation of working hours reached the height of absurdity with its opposition to the proposed European Union Directive on the hours of young workers, when the Secretary of State for Employment argued that preventing 15-year-olds from working more than 40 hours a week would destroy jobs. Quite apart from any educational arguments and the scandal of very young children doing wholly inappropriate jobs often in dangerous conditions, the amount of labour supplied by three young people working 40 hours a week could also be supplied by four working 30 hours or six working 20: more, not fewer, newspaper delivery boys and girls would be employed if, in this case, working hours were regulated.

The UK government has been particularly vociferous in its objections to the European Working Time Directive which sets an average maximum working week of 48 hours. It has negotiated a ten-year 'opt out' during which workers will be allowed to volunteer for longer hours, employers will be required to maintain registers and the Health and Safety Executive will be entitled to inspect the conditions under which they are working. Nonetheless, the government remains determined to challenge the entire basis of the Directive, which has been agreed by qualified majority voting under health and safety provisions of the Single Market Act (not under the Social Chapter of the Maastricht Treaty). Despite ministerial assertions that working hours do not affect workers' health, there is ample research from different industrialized countries of the damaging effects of long hours and of variable shift patterns and night work.[9] One example illustrates the point: the independent enquiry into the Clapham Junction railway disaster in 1988, which killed 35 people, found that one reason for the faulty wiring was that the signals engineer had been working a seven-day week for the past thirteen weeks.

Instead of the highly bureaucratic procedure required under the opt-out, the UK should accept the Directive and allow it to come into effect at the same time as in the rest of the Community. The exceptions provided in the Directive, together with the averaging procedure, should meet the legitimate needs of employers to extend and vary working hours in the interests of efficiency, while providing necessary protection for employees against dangerously long working hours. Furthermore, the general exception for collectively bargained working hours would give trade unions an important bargaining counter with employers, particularly in larger organizations, who wanted variations to the shift systems permitted under the Directive. Early adoption of the 48-hour standard would provide an important signal to employers and employees of the government's commitment to a gradual reduction in working hours, while protecting individuals against employers who sought to impose intolerably long or dangerous hours.

Further reform of working time

By itself, however, the Working Time Directive will have little effect on unemployment. Apart from manual full-time employees, the group most likely to work very long hours are male managers, whose extra hours are usually unpaid and who 'choose' these hours because of pressures to compete and perform. Because of the relative autonomy which they enjoy at work, however, they are not covered by the Directive. Other measures will be required.

As indicated earlier, there is evidence of an unmet need among full-time workers for shorter working hours. By taking this factor into account, employers faced with the need to reduce their labour force – because of inadequate demand, productivity gains, or both – could avoid making even more people fully unemployed. The experience of two companies in 1993 illustrates the difference between the 'high road' and the 'low road' to flexibility. The retail chain, Burton's, made 1,000 full-time employees redundant, inviting them to apply for the 3,000 lower paid, part-time jobs which were created at the same time. Burton's were rightly – and widely – criticized for this treatment of their staff. British Airways, by contrast, also faced with the need to reduce its workforce, built upon an existing scheme by allowing full-time employees in a variety of different occupations to apply to reduce their working hours, while retaining their hourly pay rates, pension scheme membership and other terms and conditions. Those over fifty were allowed to retain full pension rights; all volunteers were offered a cash bonus in addition. BA had so many applicants that they had no trouble whatsoever in meeting their employment objectives, without resorting to costly and undesirable redundancies.

The British Airways approach should be promoted more widely, not least by trade unions. It would also be worth exploring the possibility of requiring employers, who must already in some circumstances notify and consult about redundancies in advance, to offer the option of voluntarily reduced working hours before any compulsory redundancies can be imposed. This would, of course, involve amending employment legislation.

Another example from which unions and employers could learn is the long-standing programme within the Inland Revenue, negotiated by the Inland Revenue Staff Federation, which allows full-time employees to apply to reduce their working hours, with preference given not only to parents of young children, but also to those looking after sick or elderly relatives, or approaching retirement. Over 7,000 people in a workforce of 60,000 have taken advantage of the scheme to reduce their working hours. By tackling the problem of 'over-employment' – full-time employees working longer hours than they need and want – more employment can be made available, without forcing full-time employees to take cuts in hours which they cannot afford. A further possibility, requiring government action, is to make an employment subsidy available to employers who recruit new workers (including particularly the long-term unemployed) following a reduction of working hours, including a reduction in overtime working.[10]

The legal status of part-time employment

Part-time employees are routinely discriminated against. The qualifying period for employment protection (generally, 16 hours a week for two years continuous employment, or between 8 and 16 hours a week for five years continuous employment) means that part-time employees are less likely to be protected against unfair dismissal, to qualify for redundancy pay, and so on. A recent House of Lords ruling, however, which extends protection after two years to those working below 16 hours a week, will allow many part-time employees dismissed in recent years to claim compensation. In addition, however, hourly pay rates are generally lower for part-time employees, who are also much less likely to be entitled to join an occupational pension scheme, or to receive training or promotion. The threshold for national insurance contributions provides an incentive to both employees and employers to keep working hours and/or pay below the level at which contributions will be paid.

This system of discrimination against part-time employees provides a perverse incentive to employers to organize working hours in order to avoid regulation, rather than to suit the needs of either the enterprise or the employee. The 16-hour threshold, together with the exemption of both employees and employers from national insurance contributions on earnings below the lower earnings limit (£61 a week in 1996) seems to account for the disturbing increase over the last decade in jobs offering below 16 hours a week. The taxpayer, as well as the individual employee, loses from this process. The Low Pay Network's study of job vacancies in Stirling found one employer offering 91 part-time jobs, most of them between 8 and 16 hours a week. Had all the jobs been combined into 18 full-time equivalents, the Exchequer would have received almost £42,000 in taxes and contributions; as it was, the tax bill amounted to only £1,500.[11] The easiest way of removing this perverse incentive is to convert employers' NICs into the equivalent of a payroll tax, with contributions charged from the first £1 of any employee's earnings.

It is argued by the UK Government that fair treatment of part-time employees would destroy jobs. But avoiding regulation is not the main reason for the increase in part-time and other forms of 'non-standard' employment (despite the effect of regulation on jobs offering very short hours). The real reason for the growth in flexibility, confirmed by evidence from employers in the UK and other industrialized countries, is the need to improve efficiency by matching labour supply more closely to customer demand. Any organization which operates round the clock, round the week, round the year, or something approaching it – and this includes a growing number of supermarkets and banks as well as hospitals and factories – has to mix and match different working time contracts in order to operate. As one major chain store manager said: 'If you count "full-time" as the hours our shops are open, then no one – from managers to shop assistants – works full-time in our operation.' If part-time (including part-year as well as part-week) employment is to make its full contribution to productive efficiency, then a new system of 'fair flexibility' is needed. The essential requirement is for the UK to accept the principle of equal treatment of part-time employees, on a pro rata basis with full-timers. Ideally, employment rights should apply to all employees, whatever the length or pattern of their working hours. In practice, a threshold (for instance, the 8 hours per week proposed by the European Union) will probably be needed if only to prevent industrial tribunals from being over-whelmed with small claims.

Changes in the working lifetime

Shorter working hours do not have to take the form of a shorter working week. The introduction of paid maternity leave, as well as unpaid career breaks, has opened up to women the possibility of a working lifetime which does not follow the old male model of full-time education/full-time employment/full-time retirement. A small minority of men have begun to combine part-time employment with family responsibilities in a similar way. There are sound social reasons for government to promote this greater participation of men in family life. Furthermore, as the need to re-skill the workforce grows, time for education and training (sabbatical leave) will need to become a normal part of everybody's working life.

New and more flexible working lives can give individuals greater choice about how they balance paid employment with other aspects of their lives. Breaks in employment can also provide opportunities for other people to take employment. When one employee takes maternity leave, a new employee may be required on a temporary contract to replace her; this temporary job can not only give an un-employed person a point of re-entry into employment, but normal turnover levels mean that the temporary job may be a stepping stone to long-term employment. A policy of wage subsidies for the long-term unemployed could, for instance, be applied to temporary replacements for employees on maternity or other leave, as well as to other vacancies.

An example from Denmark illustrates how education policy can interact with unemployment policies. The 'adult re-education' programme enables employees to spend up to fifty-two weeks in developing their skills and education levels; employers in a downturn can use the programme to avoid redundancies, while improving skills. It can be combined with unemployment schemes so that a company preparing for a new development – for instance, the introduction of new technology perhaps combined with an expansion of output can send some existing employees for a year's education and training, replacing them in the meantime with unemployed people who have already received the same training. The company pays half the wages for both the employee on training leave and the formerly unemployed worker, with the government making up the difference.

Time and money

The difficulty with reducing working hours in order to reduce unemployment is, of course, the effect on the incomes of those whose working hours are cut. If the original employees maintain their earnings while cutting their hours (a result which is made possible by the productivity gains which often accompany a reorganization and reduction in working hours), there is no scope left to increase employment. Alternatively, if the numbers employed are increased, wages may have to be cut. At the same time, some of those now working very long hours – particularly male manual workers – do so because basic wages are too low to provide an adequate income. Thus, shorter working hours will often be resisted unless total earnings are maintained.

First, it is essential to unpack the assumptions about a 'family wage' which often underpin objections to the growth of part-time employment and calls for the growth of 'family supporting' employment. In two-adult households, however, the norm is now for both adults to be employed. Attempts to restore the ideal of a 'family wage' risk returning women to their old position as secondary, subsidiary workers. The Family Credit system, designed for a single breadwinner, has the perverse effect of removing any incentive for the claimant's partner to take a job (except in the very rare situation where she can earn enough to take the whole family off benefits). But the longer she remains outside employment, the more difficult it becomes for the family to take the most effective path to a reasonable income, which is to have both earners employed.

The most common pattern is, of course, to have one partner working full-time, the other working part-time. The loss of income is, at least in part, compensated by not having to pay for alternative child care as well as by the gains to the parents in having at least one of them spending time with their child(ren). In practice, the full-time employee is almost always the man, the part-timer the woman, reflecting men's higher average earnings. But that could and should be changed, both as women's earning power increases (the earnings gap between young women and men before they have children is now very low indeed) and if the extension of part-time opportunities opens up well-paid, high-skilled, part-time employment to men as well as women. The 'average' family, with one full-time and one part-time earner, has an income which is 150 per cent higher than that of the single-earner family. In future it should be increasingly possible for that to be earned by two partners/parents each working 75 per cent of full-time hours.

It is, of course, much easier for single people without children (including students) or for adults with partners to make trade-offs between time and money. As Gregg and Balls have demonstrated,[12] most part-time employment in the UK is done by women whose partners are in full-time jobs. The income from a part-time job will not support a lone parent and children, or a family with only one adult available for employment. But even here a way forward can be found by reforming the social security system (together with reforms to the Child Support Agency, which could enable a growing proportion of lone parents to add maintenance to earnings and, if necessary, benefits).

Second, it should be noted that a policy of reducing wages at the bottom of the labour market – for instance, by the abolition of the wages councils – may well have the contradictory effect of increasing labour supply. Individuals and families who cannot make ends meet by earning, say, £3 an hour for a 40-hour week and who cannot obtain a better paid job may try and increase their earnings by working longer hours – either by the full-time worker taking on additional overtime if that is available, or by a second worker taking on part-time work. Lower wages, far from solving the unemployment problem, may compound it. Thus, a national minimum hourly wage has an important role to play in improving the returns to part-time and other low-paid work, and encouraging employers to improve productivity.

THE SOCIAL SECURITY SYSTEM AND UNEMPLOYMENT

Unemployed people and their families are trapped between a flexible labour market and an inflexible social security system.[13] Many of the new jobs which are being created today and will be created in future are part-week or part-year. But, instead of creating incentives, the benefits system locks claimants out of precisely those jobs which form the majority of vacancies on offer. These disincentives include the following:

- employment of 16 hours a week or more disqualifies a claimant from income support. Family Credit is only available to low-paid workers with children; it can take several weeks to establish a claim. Loss of a temporary job can mean further delays in re-establishing a claim to income support. Many low income families simply cannot risk the insecurity of low-paid, casual employment, even with the supplement of Family Credit, while people without children cannot qualify for Family Credit at all;

- if the partner of an unemployed claimant keeps or gets a job, benefit is reduced pound for pound once earnings go above the permitted threshold. This is one reason why the wives of unemployed men (or men receiving Family Credit to top up low wages) are so much less likely to be in employment than the wives of fully employed men;

- for lone parents, the same pound for pound reduction in benefit (albeit over a higher threshold), coupled with the problems of finding and financing child care, mean that part-time employment is simply not worthwhile. Lone parents are less likely to be employed than they were ten years ago; but those who are employed are more likely to work full-time than women with partners.

Instead of locking people out of part-week and part-year employment, the social security system should encourage and enable people to work part-time. In some cases, part-time employment will be the preferred option. This is particularly true for lone parents, although a significant minority of registered unemployed people are also seeking part-time work. In other cases, a part-time job may be all that is available for someone who actively wants full-time employment. Such a person should be able to combine part-time employment with part-time unemployment benefit.

The Commission on Social Justice, which was established on the instigation of the late Rt. Hon. John Smith under the auspices of the Institute for Public Policy Research, carried out a detailed study of the social security system. Options which government should consider include:

- the provision of a smooth path between out-of-work benefits (including income support) and in-work benefits (including Family Credit) in order to enable unemployed families to move more easily into part-time and/or temporary, as well as permanent and full-time, employment;

- higher thresholds for earnings and (for lone parents) maintenance before benefit is reduced, coupled with a lower withdrawal rate. In Australia, for instance, the withdrawal rate of benefits is generally 50c in the $ rather than 100 per cent;

- a disregard for child care costs, together with investment in child care facilities, which would help lone parents in particular to move towards financial independence. Development of child care facilities would generate new jobs and would, over a period, be self-financing;

- development of a part-time unemployment benefit, which would cover both part-time employees who lost their jobs and continued to look for part-time employment, and full-time employees who took part-time employment while continuing to seek a full-time job. The Belgium social security system, which includes a part-time benefit of this kind, could provide a model.

EQUAL OPPORTUNITIES

Much of the campaign for equal opportunities over the last two decades has rested upon the assumption that if women are to enjoy men's opportunities and men's pay, then they need to work men's hours. This assumption is increasingly being called into question, particularly by women who are combining employment with family. The traditional nuclear family of the 1950s, which underpinned the Beveridge view of the post-war welfare state, depended upon most men earning a family wage and most women remaining at home once they had children. The availability of men for full-time employment was not some independent, 'natural' state of affairs: it required (and at the same time made financially possible) the availability of women as full-time carers in the home. If, however, both men and women pursue the traditional male pattern of full-time employment, then a substantial gap opens up at home.

In the USA, where two parents working full-time is a common pattern, the result has been a well-documented 'parenting deficit' for children. In the UK, as the survey evidence quoted earlier shows, most women with children positively prefer to spend a significant amount of time with them when they are young. It should not be the objective of policy to demand that women see as little of their children as men traditionally have done. Instead, we should enable both women and men to pursue more flexible working lives, in which earning and caring can be shared between them.

There is a growing emphasis, at least rhetorically, upon 'family friendly' working practices. But in practice, and often in design, these are almost entirely confined to women. If, however, only women are expected and allowed to take parental leave (part-time or full-time) or to work shorter hours when their children are young, then they will continue to face the choice between working the hours they want in a lower paid and less skilled job, or getting the jobs they want at the price of seeing too little of their children. That choice is not only painful for individuals, it is extremely inefficient for the economy. Despite the Conservative government's concern with 'rigidities' in the labour market, no attention is paid to the rigidities which lock well-educated women out of senior jobs, particularly at managerial level. Whereas 60 per cent of graduate men are employed in managerial or professional jobs, 60 per cent of graduate women are working in clerical and administrative employment – further compounding the problem faced by men without degree level qualifications in obtaining any employment at all. But one of the main reasons for the under-employment of well-educated women is the absence of 'family friendly' working hours in senior posts. The objective of full and fulfilling employment, therefore, requires a more radical equal opportunities strategy which will make available to both men and women a far greater choice of working hours, in a far wider range of jobs than exists at present.

NOTES

1 P. Hewitt, *About Time: The Revolution in Work and Family Life*, London: IPPR/Rivers Oram 1993.
2 Catherine Marsh, *Hours of Work of Women and Men in Britain*, Equal Opportunities Commission, HMSO 1992, Tables 9.1 and 9.4.
3 *Social Trends* 1994, HMSO, Table 4.13.
4 P. Rathkey, *Time and Work: Employee Preferences and Policy Options*, Bradford: Jim Conway Memorial Foundation, September 1988.
5 Harmut Seifert, *Beschaftigungswirkungenen und Perspektiven der Arbeitszeitpolitik*, Berlin: March 1989.
6 *Employment in Europe 1993*, Commission of the European Communities, pp. 87–8.
7 P. Gregg, 'Share and share alike', *New Economy*, Spring 1994, 1 (1).
8 Gregg, op. cit.
9 Hewitt, op. cit., pp. 84–5.
10 Gregg, op. cit.
11 'Is part-time work the future', *Poverty*, Spring 1994, 87: 17.
12 E. Balls and P. Gregg, *Work and Welfare*, London: Commission on Social Justice Issue Paper No. 3, Institute for Public Policy Research 1993.
13 See E. McLaughlin, *Flexibility in Work and Benefits*, Commission on Social Justice Issue Paper 11, Institute for Public Policy Research 1994, for a full discussion of this problem.

6

WHY MANUFACTURING STILL MATTERS

Working with structural change

Christine Greenhalgh and Mary Gregory

INTRODUCTION

In the 1960s manufacturing industry provided over eight million jobs in Britain. Now there are barely four million. Although job destruction is a necessary part of the process of economic growth, job losses on this scale could not be offset by the contemporaneous creation of new jobs in other sectors. This loss of four million manufacturing jobs, and the pace at which it has occurred, have had a major and continuing impact on the decline from full employment. While deindustrialization is not a uniquely British phenomenon, it began earlier and has been markedly more severe in Britain than in other advanced economies. We shall argue that, in addition to its obvious impact on unemployment, this dramatic loss of manufacturing jobs also has highly damaging qualitative effects. The decline of manufacturing experienced in Britain poses a threat to economic growth and future employment prospects throughout the economy. The development of policies to promote UK industry is a necessary part of a strategy for employment and prosperity.

THE DECLINE IN BRITISH MANUFACTURING

Manufacturing employment in Britain began to decline from 1963 – the only major industrial economy to experience a reversal before the oil shock of 1973. Since then the decline has been continuous. As Table 6.1 shows, manufacturing employment has more recently begun to fall in other countries of the G5, but the decline in Britain has been of longer duration, and at a much higher rate, particularly in the 1980s. The fall by 20 per cent in British manufacturing employment in under three years in the early 1980s has no parallel among the major economies (although a few of the small OECD countries, notably New Zealand and Sweden, have recently come close).

The contribution of manufacturing to total employment has shrunk in a similar way. At the beginning of the 1970s one worker in every three was employed

Table 6.1 Growth rates of manufacturing employment in G5 countries
(average annual percentages)

	1960–68	1968–73	1973–79	1979–90	1960–90	1990–95
UK	–0.3	–1.0	–1.3	–3.1	–1.6	–4.8
USA	2.3	0.2	1.1	–0.5	0.7	–0.5
Japan	4.1	2.0	–1.3	1.1	1.6	–0.4
Germany	0.3	0.9	–1.4	–0.2	–0.2	–8.9[a]
France	0.5	2.1	–0.9	–1.7	–0.3	–0.4

Note: [a] 1991–95
Source: OECD *Historical Statistics* and *Main Economic Indicators*

in manufacturing. By the 1990s this had fallen to one worker in five, and is still falling. Again this decline has been exceptionally severe relative to other industrialized countries. In the 1960s the share of manufacturing in total employment in Britain was probably equalled only by Germany. Within the G5 Britain now occupies fourth place, behind Germany, Japan and France, and ahead only of the USA (see Figure 6.1). A further description of these developments is given in Mayes and Soteri (1994).

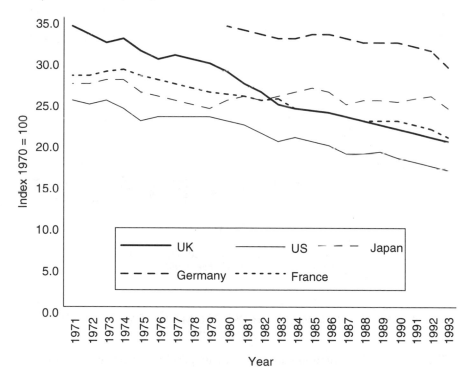

Figure 6.1 Share of manufacturing in total employment
Source: OECD *Labour Force Statistics*

How far declining employment in manufacturing should be a cause for concern depends in part on the trend in manufacturing output. Falling employment accompanied by rising output indicates labour-saving technical progress, while static or declining output indicates job shedding without expansion. For Britain the harsher interpretation of deindustrialization applies. As shown in Figure 6.2, the UK has had much the weakest growth of manufacturing output among the G5, with zero growth in the sector as a whole between 1970 and 1985, and less than 2 per cent per year on average since then, mostly achieved in the boom of the late 1980s. The USA, by contrast, has doubled its manufacturing output over the period, even with latterly declining employment. Deindustrialization in the USA is a very different phenomenon.

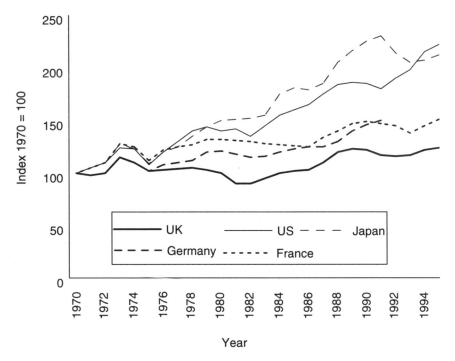

Figure 6.2 Growth of manufacturing output
Source: OECD *Main Economic Indicators*

WHY DID SO MANY JOBS IN MANUFACTURING DISAPPEAR?

What has caused the disappearance of so many jobs in manufacturing, and why have the losses been so much more severe in Britain than elsewhere? Several explanations are widely canvassed, of varying degrees of accuracy.

The first is technological change in production processes in manufacturing, the microchip revolution and increasing automation on the shop floor resulting in the shedding of labour from factories. In itself this is not necessarily an adverse development either for the individual or for the economy as a whole. If workers released from repetitive and physically hard manufacturing jobs transfer to more interesting and lighter work in services, they are gainers. Where automation brings higher productivity, output and earnings rise. How far technological change is job creating as well as job destroying is an ongoing debate. While the evidence of history is that job creation has been the more powerful element, the distribution of jobs will not remain unchanged, and manufacturing seems set to be a long-run loser. However, while the other countries of the G5 can draw some comfort from this view of declining manufacturing employment, the weak performance of manufacturing output in Britain gives the lie to such a positive interpretation. While technological change has certainly contributed, to construe Britain's high rate of job loss as reflecting the world's fastest rate of technological change in manufacturing exceeds the limits of credibility.

Britain's specific incidence of job loss is often attributed to the advent of North Sea oil. Britain became a substantial oil producer, causing a rise in the pound and adversely affecting manufacturing competitiveness – the so-called 'Dutch disease' explanation of deindustrialization. However, British manufacturing output shares at home and abroad were already showing a persistent decline in the period before North Sea oil, although the over-appreciation of sterling in the early 1980s undoubtedly did considerable damage. Moreover, an adverse impact on manufacturing from North Sea oil was by no means inevitable. Nineteenth-century Britain, the USA in the early post-war years, and currently Japan, all show that substantial trade surpluses can be maintained for significant periods. Policies to control the appreciation of the pound were available. Any consequences of North Sea oil for the exchange rate and for manufacturing derive from explicit or implicit policy choices.

The main immediate cause of job loss in British manufacturing has been the loss of market share at home and abroad. This process has two sides: import penetration reflecting the loss of domestic markets, coupled with a lack of export success. Total trade has been rising around twice as fast as world income throughout the post-war period and most economies are now trading larger shares of national output than in earlier decades. In the more successful economies, such as Germany, rising exports have either led the way or at least kept pace with the growing consumption of imports. In employment terms, the British trade deficit shows domestic expenditure generating more jobs abroad than foreign expenditure generates internally. More generally, the British trade deficit reflects the success of other advanced economies, particularly Germany within Europe, and of course Japan, in British and third country markets (see Tables 6.2, 6.3, 6.4).

Despite recent optimism about exports, the UK's balance of visible trade has been persistently negative in the 1990s. Competitiveness worsened sharply

Table 6.2 Shares in world trade in manufactures (percentages)

	1950	1960	1970	1980	1990
UK	25.5	16.5	10.8	9.1	8.6
USA	27.3	21.6	18.6	16.0	16.0
Japan	3.4	6.9	11.7	13.7	15.9
Germany	7.3	19.3	19.8	20.9	20.2
France	9.9	9.6	8.7	10.5	9.7

Source: Crafts 1991

Table 6.3 Imports as a percentage of domestic demand for manufactures

	1970	1980	1989	Average annual growth 1970–80	1980–89
UK	14.6	22.9	30.0	4.6	3.1
USA	4.4	8.7	13.9	6.9	5.4
Japan	4.0	5.5	6.3	3.3	1.5
Germany	13.4	19.8	26.8	4.0	3.5
France	14.5	21.3	29.9	3.9	3.8

Source: OECD *Industrial Policy in OECD Countries: Annual Review* 1993

Table 6.4 Export destinations and import sources of UK trade

	1970	1980	1990
Share of total exports going to:			
Western Europe	46.2	57.6	61.8
North America	15.2	11.2	14.4
Other developed countries	11.8	5.6	5.6
Rest of world	26.8	25.3	17.3
Share of total imports from:			
Western Europe	41.5	55.9	64.8
North America	20.5	15.0	13.2
Other developed countries	9.4	6.8	7.4
Rest of world	28.6	22.4	14.6

Source: OECD *Industrial Policy in OECD Countries: Annual Review* 1993

until 1992, improved with the devaluation following exit from the ERM, but subsequently deteriorated again; in the mid-1990s competitiveness was back at its 1990 level. The volume growth of exports over this period has been generated by the new projects brought into the UK by foreign multinationals, rather than by any transformation of the basic competitiveness of UK industry.

Looking forward, the picture of falling manufacturing employment seems set to continue. Clearly there is unlikely to be any respite from the impact of labour-saving technology as developments in the microchip and its application continue to forge ahead. More importantly, in spite of the job losses, technological progress cannot and should not be resisted. The emphasis must be on stemming the tide of output loss and restoring output growth. Reversing the declining market shares in manufacturing trade could be achieved over the longer term by recapturing markets at home and, particularly, abroad. But economic theory teaches us that comparative advantage is the basis for the gains from trade. Newly industrializing countries are emerging throughout East Asia, and elsewhere, with China only the largest of these. In the face of this, why, if at all, should we attempt to raise the share of manufacturing output in the British economy or support manufacturers in their attempts to regain markets?

WHY MANUFACTURING MATTERS

Manufacturing is important for the continuing prosperity of an advanced economy, for four separate reasons.

- the productivity contribution
- the jobs contribution
- the technology contribution
- the trade contribution

The productivity contribution

It is an established fact of life that rates of productivity growth in manufacturing are consistently higher than in services. Over the 1980s, for example, output per worker in British manufacturing increased at an average rate of 4 per cent per year, more than double the productivity growth rate for the economy as a whole (see Table 6.5). The implication of this general pattern is that manufacturing makes an exceptionally large contribution to economic growth.

It is particularly significant that during the period from 1985 to 1993 output

Table 6.5 Whole economy and manufacturing productivity growth in the UK, 1960–90 (average annual percentage changes)

	Whole economy			Manufacturing		
	Output	Employment	Output per worker	Output	Employment	Output per worker
1960–73	2.9	0.3	2.6	3.1	−0.5	3.6
1973–79	1.4	0.2	1.2	−0.7	−1.4	0.7
1979–90	2.1	0.4	1.8	1.0	−3.0	4.0
1990–95	1.1	−1.0	2.2	0.1	−3.5	3.7

Source: Economic Trends Annual Supplement
Note: These ratios of output per worker do not take into account changes in part-time working or hours of work. However, more sophisticated studies such as Muellbauer (1991) have confirmed these differences by sector and period.

per worker in the manufacturing sector grew very rapidly. This was a period when output growth in manufacturing began to revive, stabilizing the share of manufacturing in total output for the first time since the 1960s. In this eight-year period, manufacturing, with 20 per cent of total employment, contributed about 70 per cent of the rise in output per worker in the whole economy. It is this rapid productivity growth which permits real income per worker to rise, both through the increased wages of the smaller manufacturing workforce but also indirectly, through the effect of the falling relative price of manufactured goods, which makes all consumers better off.

Worldwide, productivity growth in manufacturing is accelerating rather than slackening. The measurement of productivity growth in the service sector is obviously more difficult because so much of the output is intangible, making adjustment for quality changes rather speculative. In the case of public sector services, output may not be marketed, precluding the measurement of output separately from expenditure on inputs. Nevertheless, it is clear that for many of the most labour intensive services, particularly personal services including health care and education, the possibilities of achieving higher productivity per worker by increasing the use of capital equipment or by reorganizing production are rather limited.

The jobs contribution

Services are always claimed to be more labour intensive than manufacturing and in an immediate sense this is true. However, the number of jobs sustained by a sector is not fully reflected by the number of people directly employed there. All industries purchase goods and services from other producers as inputs into their own production. At a minimum, these purchases will be heating, lighting and office supplies, plus the services of a bank and an accountant. At the other extreme, some manufacturing and construction operations involve a wide and complex range of requirements, stretching back across many stages of processing. Through these backward linkages production activity in one sector generates output and employment in others. The sector's total contribution to employment is the number of jobs it sustains in its own production activity, plus the number it generates through its purchases from other sectors. Conversely, when output is reduced the direct job losses are compounded by the indirect effects inflicted on suppliers.

Both the extent and the pattern of these inter-industry purchases vary widely between manufacturing and the service sector (see Table 6.6). Overall, for each £1 of gross output produced in manufacturing more output is purchased, and from a wider range of activities, than with service output. In addition, each £1 of output in manufacturing requires more output from the service sector than applies in the reverse direction, in the purchase of manufactured goods for use as intermediate inputs by services. Thus manufacturing sustains a far higher proportion of jobs at any time than is measured by its share in total

Table 6.6 Wage income generated by UK manufacturing and services

	Primary+manufacturing			Services
	Growing	*Cycling*	*Declining*	
1974	0.47	0.52	0.74	0.58
1984	0.40	0.50	0.71	0.56

Notes: These figures were computed by the authors using available UK industry input–output tables. They measure the total amount of employment income generated per unit value of final expenditure on domestic output in the named sectors, including both jobs in the same sector (direct employment) and jobs in supplying sectors (indirect employment).

Growing/Cycling/Declining refers to sub-groups of non-service industries, grouped by their output trends over the whole period 1974-89. Growing includes agriculture, North Sea oil and gas and several high technology manufacturing sectors; Declining includes coal and ships; most mature technology manufacturing appears in the Cycling category. For further details see Greenhalgh (1989).

employment. This is much more the case than with services. A change in output in manufacturing has much greater knock-on effects on other sectors than a change in output in services.

The impact of import penetration on job losses is clear in this context. Import penetration destroys both direct and indirect employment. Technical change destroys some direct employment in manufacturing plants, particularly of low-skill workers, but the inter-industry demand for different manufactures or for service inputs may well increase. Also if the new manufactured products are cheaper and better in quality the demand for them will rise, creating jobs in both sectors.

Concentrating too much on services may not be desirable or possible. If there are fewer manufacturers then the demand for such services as banking, insurance and finance is also progressively reduced. In the limit it becomes reduced to demand from personal customers. Can we imagine the City of London continuing to sell a sophisticated range of services to overseas companies if there were to be no home base of company demand? The exploitation of economies of scale and the existence of a critical mass of service suppliers with the requisite skills seems essential in the competitive world of trade in financial services.

The technology contribution

Manufacturing matters for the rest of the economy also through its forward linkages, the products it makes available to other producers as well as to consumers. An industry may be creating and supplying more than just the outputs for which it charges a price. Consider the issues of new knowledge and product innovations. These can be thought of as intellectual feedstocks which create new opportunities for profit. An example would be a work station developed by an electronics manufacturer and supplied to the banking or insurance sector.

The equipment enables the banker to offer new and improved services to his customers. The computer supplier gains the profit on his sale of equipment to the banker, but probably rather little of the extra profit obtained by the banker. In economic parlance, positive external benefits (producer–producer externalities) are created by innovations.

The manufacturing sector, particularly the engineering and chemical industries, is the dominant source of innovations, whether these are measured by patents registered or by survey records (see Table 6.7). The application of innovations, however, is widely spread across economic activities. As the domestic manufacturing sector shrinks, the fountain of domestic technology dries up and the capacity to generate innovations dwindles. It is not adequate to assert, as Brown and Julius (1993) do, that high-tech services drive research in new products. The human race has dreamed of being able to fly since Icarus, and perhaps even before. It requires an aerospace industry to convert the dream to reality. Similarly, while sickness creates the demand, only the pharmaceutical industry creates the new drugs. If technical advances are not being supported in the UK then, as new products emerge worldwide, dependence on foreign manufacturers for sophisticated products will increase and with it import penetration and the vulnerability of export market share. In an increasingly integrated world technological performance and trade are ever more closely linked.

The comparative advantage of the rich countries is continually moving towards technology-intensive goods and services as they become too costly as manufacturing sites for standard products which can be produced with well-known technology. Advanced countries like Britain have to produce high value added products and to be continually advancing the quality and design features of their output. This gives them the opportunity either to benefit from their monopoly of production or to sell their know-how via the granting of licences to other countries to produce their patented products.

In employment terms, the threat is that this kind of manufacturing has little need to employ unskilled workers for repetitive tasks. The challenge is that both the R&D process and the parallel high technology production increasingly

Table 6.7 Major innovations in UK tradable manufacturing and service sectors, 1951–83

Number and share of innovations by sector

Allocated to industry of	*Innovation producer*		*First commercial adoption*	
Growing industries	1595	(54%)	1053	(37%)
Cycling industries	772	(26%)	1071	(37%)
Declining industries	194	(7%)	171	(6%)
Services	398	(13%)	584	(20%)

Source: Calculations by Greenhalgh, using the University of Sussex Science Policy Research Unit survey data 'Innovations in the UK since 1945'. Collection of these data has been discontinued since 1983.

employ skilled workers, who operate in a multi-disciplinary environment involving frequent task changes.

The trade contribution

A final reason why manufacturing matters is in its contribution to trade. Trade allows specialization, giving rise to the well-known gains from trade. An economy producing mainly non-tradables limits its access to these gains and to the dynamic advantages which tend to follow from them. Manufacturing output is highly tradable and widely traded; although it is only around 20 per cent of UK gross domestic product it provides over 60 per cent of exports. A shrunken manufacturing sector means that the gains from trade can increasingly be realized only through the service sector.

Services are much less tradable than manufactures. The range of tradable services, and the volume of trade which they can generate are simply too small to balance our demand for imported manufactures. This issue was thoroughly investigated by the House of Commons Trade and Industry Committee, which concluded:

> Unless it can significantly increase its manufactured exports, the UK would require an almost inconceivable rate of growth in service exports to achieve a positive balance of trade . . . every 1 per cent decline in exports of manufactures requires more than a 2½% rise in exports of services to compensate. Only about 20% of service output *can* be exported . . . to balance the [trade] account would require a trebling of exports of services, which, as regards the financial sector, would be equivalent to absorbing the entire current international financial activity of New York and Tokyo.
>
> (Trade and Industry Committee, 1994, para. 21(ii))

Worse, the UK's share of world exports of services has declined faster than its share of world exports of manufactures and is now smaller than the shares of France or Germany. Moreover, a Britain heavily specialized in tradable services is at risk from this excessive concentration – having all the eggs in one basket leaves the economy vulnerable to fluctuations in world demand and supply for these items.

It has frequently been argued that UK growth has historically been constrained by the weak external performance of the economy. The constraint arises because of the high marginal propensity to import as incomes rise. There is a direct brake because imports are a drain on aggregate demand in the UK, but in addition government is forced to intervene as trade deficits cannot be financed indefinitely. With fixed exchange rates (such as Bretton Woods or the EMS) in order to reduce a deficit the government has to deflate the economy, leading to the familiar stop–go problem. With flexible exchange rates (as now and for much of the last two decades) devaluation may occur automatically, but this is not a costless solution to a deficit. A feature of sterling devaluation which is too often overlooked is that it causes a real income loss for UK residents, who have to 'sell cheap and buy dear' afterwards due to the worsened terms of trade.

POINTERS FOR A SUPPLY SIDE POLICY

A healthy manufacturing sector within the economy requires an appropriate environment within which manufacturing production and trade take place. The first requirement of all is a suitable macroeconomic environment, in terms of exchange rates and interest rates. Manufacturing above all involves exposure to trade and therefore to the exchange rate. The correct exchange rate for the economy as a whole is one which does not undermine manufacturing competitiveness. We cannot expect manufacturers to incur the costs and take the risks of entering new markets, with the long-term commitment of resources which this involves, if these efforts are to be undermined by an overvalued exchange rate. Nor are widely fluctuating exchange rates anything but damaging to business decision-making. British industry has also been handicapped by high interest rates and, more generally, a higher cost of capital than major competitors. This handicap is compounded by the variability of interest rates.

The second important policy area is that of vocational training. Both manufacturing production processes and their integral R&D activities require the number of technically trained workers to be increased; at the same time redundant workers moving to jobs in services require retraining. In addition, there is general recognition that the level of training and skills before employment begins is a major area of deficiency. There has been much talk about the extent and content of vocational training in the UK over the last decade and some reorganization of training supply. Even so, government policy is still primarily to let private markets for skills and training operate.

The government's 'Competitiveness' White Papers (DTI 1994, 1995) emphasize target setting as a centrepiece of its strategy. The original targets, however, and the initiative in setting them, derived from the CBI (1989, 1991) rather than government itself. These targets themselves fell short of what is already being achieved elsewhere, for example, in France and substantially exceeded in South Korea. The 1995 White Paper revised upwards all the training targets for the year 2000. But to make a genuine contribution target setting has to be accompanied by effective mechanisms for the delivery of the training and for its proper validation and accreditation. The level of government funding for all types of vocational training has been *falling* quite sharply in real terms since 1987. The training programmes supported by government funds are largely confined to those for youths and the unemployed. Public finances make very little contribution to training or upgrading of skills of adult workers, which are seen as a matter for workers and their employers. There is no legal requirement for firms to spend resources on training, as has existed in France for the last two decades. The government's targets are an insufficient recognition of the level of training and skills required for effective international competitiveness. The mechanisms proposed are too weak to guarantee their delivery, given that increased investment in training is dependent on employers putting their resources on the line, to become investors in people.

A final important supply side policy area is that of investment in the creation and diffusion of new technology. The positive externality of the manufacturing sector in the generation of new knowledge deserves to be recognized, and firms investing in R&D given a share in this. In other countries (e.g. the USA and France) this is achieved by giving extra tax credits to firms undertaking these activities. The UK government has, however, explicitly ruled out such a policy for the immediate future in its Technology White Paper (1993). Furthermore, the 'Competitiveness' White Paper (DTI 1995) illustrates the rapid fall in the share of business R&D expenditure funded by government, from almost one-third in 1983 to less than 15 per cent by 1992. In its own words this fall arose 'mainly because of declining defence R&D' (p.136). The key question is why was the peace dividend wasted on tax rebates rather than being devoted to continuing support of industrial R&D? Declining levels of government support for science and technology are unique to Britain among the G5 countries in this period. The recent Technology Foresight exercise aims to direct this shrinking budget towards a prioritized set of science research areas which are expected to give rise to commercial application in the medium term – back to picking winners, but now with a market gloss.

CONCLUSION

High-technology manufacturing matters for sustaining economic growth, for improving the international trade balance and for sustaining employment, including in services. Exchange rate and financial policies, the commitment to skills and the delivery of effective amounts and quality of training, and recognition and support for the contribution of R&D are all essential elements in a supply side policy. But the first precondition is the recognition that manufacturing matters.

REFERENCES

Brown, R. and Julius, D. (1993) 'Is manufacturing still special in the new world order?', *Finance and the International Economy* 7, The Amex Bank Review Prize Essays, R. O'Brien (ed.) Oxford: Oxford University Press.
Confederation of British Industry (CBI) (1989) *Towards a Skill Revolution*, London: CBI.
—— (1991) *World Class Targets*, London: CBI.
Crafts, N. (1991) 'Reversing relative economic decline? The 1980s in historical perspective', *Oxford Review of Economic Policy* 7 (3), Autumn.
Department of Trade and Industry (DTI) (1994) *Competitiveness: Helping Business to Win*, Cmnd 2563, London: HMSO.
—— (1995) *Competitiveness: Forging Ahead*, Cmnd 2867, London: HMSO.

Greenhalgh, C. (1989) *Employment and Structural Change in Britain*, London: Employment Institute.

House of Commons, Trade and Industry Committee (1994) *Competitiveness of UK Manufacturing Industry*, Second Report, House of Commons, Session 1993–94, London: HMSO.

Mayes, D. and Soteri, S. (1994), 'Does manufacturing matter?', in A. Buxton, P. Chapman and P. Temple (eds) *Britain's Economic Performance*, London: Routledge.

Muellbauer, J. (1991) 'Productivity and competitiveness', *Oxford Review of Economic Policy* 7 (3), Autumn.

UK Government (1993) *Realising our Potential: A Strategy for Science, Engineering and Technology*, Cmnd 2250, London: HMSO.

Yates, I. (1992) *Innovation, Investment and Survival*, London: Royal Academy of Engineering.

7

TECHNICAL CHANGE AND UNEMPLOYMENT[1]

Christopher Freeman

INTRODUCTION

It seems only yesterday that almost every government in the OECD area was committed to full employment as a primary objective of government economic and social policy. Unemployment levels of 2 per cent or even 1 per cent were commonplace in most European countries (see Table 7.1). At that time, in the 1950s and 1960s, it was often assumed that Keynesian theories and Keynesian policies had permanently solved the pre-war problem of persistent large-scale unemployment.

In the wake of the return to mass unemployment since the late 1970s, however, contemporary forecasts of future levels of unemployment are often pessimistic. Even those forecasts which assume a sustained recovery of production, investment and international trade over the next few years are generally cautious about any major concomitant reduction in the prevailing high levels of unemployment. Moreover, there are a number of features of the present pattern of unemployment which were described by the Secretary General of the OECD as 'disturbing, perhaps alarming' in his Report to Ministers in June 1993. Many assume a further deterioration in the situation and even permanently higher levels of unemployment (Macrae 1994). Rifkin (1995) entitled his book *The End of Work*.

ECONOMIC THEORY, TECHNICAL CHANGE AND UNEMPLOYMENT

What role has technological change played in this shift from optimism to pessimism? From a brief review of pre-classical, classical, neo-classical, Keynesian and structuralist theories of technical change and employment, it is evident that all of them actually agree that the adjustment of employment to technical change is by no means an instantaneous or automatic process. Furthermore, all of them recognize that there are periods when the problems of structural adjustment and structural unemployment are particularly acute. They differ in their assessment of the speed and smoothness of the adjustment and the relative importance of the various adjustment and compensation mechanisms.

109

CHRISTOPHER FREEMAN

Table 7.1 Unemployment in various countries 1933–94
(as % of the labour force)

Country	1933	1959–67 average	1982–92 average	1992	1993	1994 (forecast)
Belgium	10.6	2.4	11.3	10.3	12.1	13.0
Denmark	14.5	1.4	9.1	11.1	12.1	11.9
France	4.5*	0.7	9.5	10.4	11.7	12.4
Germany	14.8	1.2#	7.4#	7.7	8.9	10.1
Ireland	na	4.6	15.5	17.2	17.6	17.8
Italy	5.9	6.2	10.9	10.7	10.2	11.1
Netherlands	9.7	0.9	9.8	6.8	8.3	9.3
Spain	na	2.3	19.0	18.4	22.7	23.8
UK	13.9	1.8	9.7	10.1	10.3	10.0
Austria	16.3	1.7	3.5	3.7	4.2	5.3
Finland	6.2	1.7	4.8	13.1	18.2	19.9
Norway	9.7	2.1	3.2	5.9	6.0	5.9
Sweden	7.3	1.3	2.3	5.3	8.2	8.8
Switzerland	3.5	0.2	0.7	2.5	4.5	5.0
USA	24.7	5.3	7.1	7.4	6.9	6.5
Canada	19.3	4.9	9.6	11.3	11.2	11.0
Japan	na	1.5	2.5	2.2	2.5	2.9
Australia	17.4	2.2	7.8	10.8	10.9	10.4

Notes:
* 1936 na = not available
# The Federal Republic for the period 1959–81
Source: Maddison 1991; OECD *Employment Outlook* 1993

At one extreme is the endogenous self-adjusting, market-clearing model based on Say's Law, though as Keynes put it, neo-classicals mostly recognize that the adjustment takes place with many 'creaks and groans'. At the other extreme are political economy theories, such as those of Perez (1983) or Boyer (1988), which hold that adjustment is achieved only through social and political changes to accommodate the characteristics of radically new technologies. The theories, however, are not quite so incompatible as they appear at first sight. Many neo-classical theorists would certainly accept the importance of institutional change and some like Olson (1982) have developed a theory of institutional rigidities. Furthermore, everyone would accept that regional disparities and the complications of trade and international competition may aggravate structural problems. However, uncertainty about the speed of adjustment means that forecasts about future levels of employment and unemployment have varied a great deal: whether they are made by Keynesians, by neo-classicals or by others.

During the course of the twentieth century we have had two long swings in the conventional wisdom about unemployment: from a relatively optimistic view at the beginning of the century to deep pessimism during the 1930s; then once more to over-optimism in the 1950s and again to a deep pessimism in the 1980s and 1990s. It seems therefore that the beliefs of economists, and of the governments which they advised, were heavily influenced by the experience of the previous decade, and that their notions of the feasibility and desirability of low levels of unemployment varied accordingly. Those involved in the business of long-term forecasting will recognize this as a familiar syndrome.

Some eminent economists have explicitly assumed that growth rates will remain depressed for a long time. They frequently also did this in the 1930s and 1940s. Writing in 1981, Paul Samuelson commented:

> It is my considered guess that the final quarter of the 20th Century will fall far short of the third quarter in its achieved rate of economic progress. The dark horoscope of my old teacher Joseph Schumpeter may have particular relevance here.

Samuelson's reference to Schumpeter serves to remind us that, rather than simply to extrapolate from the experience of recent years, it may make more sense to try and understand the long-term fluctuations in the behaviour of the economic system. Indeed, this may help to explain the long-term changes in the opinions and theories of the economists themselves.

These fluctuations cannot be explained in terms of conventional business cycle analysis but need to take into account additional dimensions of analysis: the rise of new technologies, the rise and decline of industries, major new infrastructural investments, changes in the international location of industries and technological leadership. It was primarily Schumpeter, Kondratieff and other long-wave theorists who introduced these topics into the debate.

THE RISE OF NEW TECHNOLOGIES

Schumpeter (1939, 1943) emphasized the importance both of organizational innovations and of technical innovations, and of their interdependence. This combination is characteristic of a change of 'technological paradigm', such as the introduction of information and communications technology (ICT) or, in earlier times, of electrification or steam power.

As with these earlier technologies, the pervasiveness of ICT is not just a question of a few new products or industries but of a technology which affects every industry and every service, their inter-relationships and indeed, the whole way of life of industrial societies. Whereas incremental changes in existing technologies cause few problems for society, a combination of radically new technologies, such as electrification or ICT, involves many social and institutional changes, some of which are painful and difficult, including of course changes in the pattern of employment and skills.

One hundred or even fifty years ago, very few people would have imagined that most households in Western Europe would have a car, television, refrigerator, washing machine and many other appliances which we now take for granted. Nor would they have imagined that the industries which produced these goods, the services which sold, repaired and delivered them and the infrastructures which they used would employ tens of millions of people.

It is comparably hard today to imagine the future patterns of manufacturing and services in fifty or a hundred years' time. Yet only with this long-term historical perspective is it possible to avoid the poverty of imagination which sees only the contemporary job-reducing side of technical change.

In the 1950s the electronic industries generally were still 'fitting in', albeit somewhat uncomfortably, to the old world Fordist paradigm. Computers became part of the centralized, departmental, hierarchical structures of the large firms which adopted them. Their main advantages at this stage were the time savings in storing and processing of enormous volumes of information in standardized applications such as pay roll, tax, inventories, etc. They certainly did not yet revolutionize the organization of firms, for example, by making available information at all levels in all departments. Radio and television fitted in well to the old Fordist paradigm of cheap, standardized consumer durables supplied on hire purchase to every household, like washing machines, cars or refrigerators.

Although their revolutionary technical potential was already clearly visible, computers were still rather expensive, user-unfriendly items of equipment. It was widely assumed that large mainframe computers in specialized data processing departments or groups assisted by the hardware suppliers would be the normal pattern of diffusion outside scientific and military applications. IBM became by far the most profitable firm in the world industry by operating on this basis. Its own management structure differed to a relatively small extent from those of other large firms, even though it spent a great deal on training and R&D and had its own strong company traditions.

A major characteristic of the semi-conductor and computer industry from the 1960s onwards was the very rapid change in the successive generations of integrated circuits. The number of components which could be placed on one tiny chip doubled every few years until it has now reached many millions and still continues to expand. This meant that all those firms making the numerous products which used these chips were also obliged to make frequent design changes. Rapid changes in design and product mix thus became a characteristic feature of the electronics industry and they increasingly used their own technologies to meet this requirement (CAD, networks of computer terminals, integration of design, production and marketing, etc.). Speed, storage capacity, flexibility and networking thus emerged in the 1980s as strongly inter-related characteristics of the new techno-economic paradigm. Organizational and technical change became inextricably connected and there were strong pressures for greater flexibility in working hours from social changes. These interacted with the potential of ICT to deliver this flexibility.

A new style of management and a new pattern of organization within and between firms has emerged as a result. The development and diffusion of this new pattern has been and still is a long and painful process for both large and small firms since it has involved intensified competition and the displacement or reform of many old institutions and practices. We now turn to the creative side of this process of destruction.

Despite all the turbulence and restructuring, the ICT industries and services have been the fastest growing group of activities in world production, world trade and world employment. They have also shown the highest rates of productivity increase both in capital and in labour. They have been almost the only sector to make major price reductions in the 1980s and 1990s.

Many ICT companies continued to show high growth rates throughout the recession of the early 1990s, even though some of the largest companies experienced a downturn in sales of computer hardware. No fewer than thirty-eight of the one hundred fastest growing companies in the USA were ICT companies (Juliussen and Juliussen 1993). Many of them had growth rates of 50 per cent or more per annum and they included software companies, networking services, peripherals, telecommunication services, information services, disk drives and components. Even though the shift from mainframes to client-server networks and to PCs and portables caused some problems for American, European and Japanese hardware manufacturers, the software, information systems and networking services continued to show great dynamism in the whole world economy. For a small sample of the largest firms in the world industry *Datamation* (15 June 1993) estimated that revenues of firms providing software grew by more than 150 per cent between 1988 and 1992 and information service revenues by more than 70 per cent. Sales of the Japanese information service industry grew by more than 300 per cent between 1985 and 1991 (Baba *et al.* 1994). These high growth rates have continued in the 1990s even when other sectors were depressed.

We shall take the example of software employment to illustrate the general problem of assessing the future potential impact of ICT on employment growth. Employment in software and information services was one of the fastest growing categories in all OECD countries in the 1980s. In Japan employment grew from about 75,000 in 1980 to over 350,000 in 1990 (Baba *et al.* 1994). In the USA the number of employees in 'computational data processing services' grew from 304,000 in 1980 to 835,000 in 1991 (*Statistical Abstract* 1992). These official estimates understate total software employment because of the difficulties of measuring software activities in user firms both in the USA and in Japan.

The total number of people working in software activities of all kinds (i.e. the software industry, plus hardware firms, plus user firms) is two or three times as great as the official figures for the software 'industry'. In the USA where the specialized industry is strongest, there are probably now (1994) about two million people employed in software work. In Japan there are nearly a million and in Western Europe well over two million. These estimates can be cross-checked with many consultants' reports and independent industry estimates even though there are no official figures. For example, in Britain, while hardware industry and software employees with 'IT skills' were estimated at 120,000 in 1988, the number of employees with IT skills was estimated as an additional 180,000 in user industries and the growth rate of employment as 8 per cent per annum (Oakley 1990). There is thus no doubt that software and information services have been one of the fastest growing categories for new employment in the past decade and that the total employment gains were much greater than those registered in the software industry itself. Worldwide there were well over ten million people working in software activities by 1994.

Many estimates of future employment growth forecast a continuing high growth rate for software, although not quite so rapid as in the 1980s. The US Bureau of Labour (1992) in its forecasts for the year 2005 puts the projected growth for 'computer scientists and systems analysts' as 79 per cent from 1990 to 2005 and for 'computer programmers' as 56 per cent. No other occupations except 'home health aides' show such high growth.

However, some well-informed commentators have cast doubts on these estimates of future employment growth in the service industries, particularly for software. For the first time in the recession of the 1990s, there were significant redundancies among software employees and it was suggested that software employment had reached a plateau and might even decline in the future. The reasons which were sometimes advanced to justify a pessimistic forecast for future software employment were these:

1 The automation of coding and testing of new software.
2 The spread of Object-oriented Programming (OOP) and other techniques which greatly increase software labour productivity.
3 The universal availability of standard packages, many of which are user friendly, relieving the users of the need to hire specialist software personnel.
4 The improved skills of software users, many of whom no longer need 'hand-holding' support. A high proportion of graduates in many different disciplines now have computer skills, even though they are not designated as software or computer professionals.
5 Related to this, the need for mainframe data processing or specialist support groups is said to be diminishing with the shift to client-server networks.
6 The subcontracting of some software activities to Asia and to the Caribbean (and on a small scale now to Eastern Europe).

If it were true that for these reasons software employment would level off or decline in the next decade, this would be a very important change in the labour market. However, there are also some good reasons to believe that employment growth will continue at a high rate both in Europe and the USA. The main reasons for a more optimistic forecast are the following:

1 ICT will continue to diffuse at a very high rate over the next decade. There are still innumerable applications of computers, especially in multi-media, and all of these require software for their implementation.
2 Even though it is perfectly true that standard software packages have vastly improved and diffused very widely, the needs, the technology and the organization of firms are changing all the time and will continue to do so. To achieve a good 'match' between technology, organization and software is not

a matter of static 'maintenance' but a creative activity which will continue to make new demands on software skills.

3 Most large organizations have inherited a mixture of hardware and software from different suppliers. PCs and portables have proliferated at the fringes and their numbers are now very great. However, the need remains for client-server networks and for many other networks based on reliable secure communication. Despite the spread of 'open systems', much effort for the foreseeable future will continue to go into 'middleware' (i.e. software appropriate to organizations operating a variety of different equipment).

4 Parallel processing, virtual reality and multi-media are all likely to experience extraordinarily rapid growth in the next decade and will make huge new demands on software applications skills.

5 The small-scale redundancy which has been experienced, especially in the UK and the USA, is mainly associated with temporary phenomena such as defence business contraction, switching from old programming languages such as COBOL to the newer programming languages such as C and to the effects of the recession.

6 There is a vast new area of potential employment growth associated with the infrastructural investment in cable and both wired and wireless telecommunications, which is taking off in the USA, Europe and Japan. This growth will be in many new interactive services to households as well as to business. Part of it will initially be 'edu-tainment'. The demand for home education to complement the formal education system is potentially almost limitless, as is the learning capacity of most human beings. This market will be opened up by enterprising companies and educational organizations all over the world but it will require extraordinary software skills, linked to multi-media and entertainment skills. In the immediate future an even greater demand is being generated in the education system for CD-ROM packages offering new ways of learning in every discipline.

VARIOUS FORMS OF FLEXIBILITY

Almost everyone now agrees that flexibility is essential to overcome structural unemployment, but this means very different things to different people. Traditionally, classical and neo-classical economic theory placed the main emphasis on wage flexibility and the mobility of labour. According to many economic historians (e.g. Dobb 1946) the breakdown of serfdom and other feudal limitations on the movement of labour were essential to the growth of a capitalist labour market. The so-called 'second serfdom' or preservation of feudal institutions in Eastern Europe is often advanced as the main explanation for the delay in the spread of industrialization from Western Europe. Historians have also placed great emphasis on international migration as well as the migration of workers from country to towns. In Third World countries where a high proportion of the labour force is still employed in agriculture this migration is still the main source of flexibility in the supply of unskilled workers.

Recently, there has been a big change in the international division of labour with increasingly strong competition from low-wage countries where the supply of unskilled labour is still extremely flexible in the traditional sense. From this perspective the evidence presented by Wood (1994) is illustrative of the new emerging low-wage employment pressure on unskilled labour in the Northern developed countries. The pressure from the South for international downward wage equalization of the North's unskilled labour, whether through international migration or imports of goods and services is undoubtedly a new and crucial 'flexibility' pressure (for a detailed debate on this issue see Chapter 8). On the other hand, since World War II the 'participation rate' of women in the labour force has steadily grown in the industrialized countries. Of course, there are many other factors which have led to this rise in women's participation, such as the fall in family size and the change in women's attitudes, together with legislative changes but the demand from employers usually for lower cost labour has also been essential.

However, this basic type of flexibility affecting mainly the supply of unskilled workers and their wage rates is only one type of flexibility. Other equally important types of flexibility are the ways in which work is organized and the ways in which the workforce acquires new skills. Without adequate training and education no amount of unskilled labour could develop or produce many of the complex products and services of modern industrial economies. Even well-trained and educated workers could not cope with the speed of change in product mix and process technology without flexible organizations, retraining and contracting arrangements between firms and individuals. One of the main characteristics of the ICT techno-economic paradigm is flexibility in design, manufacturing, marketing and delivery of services. Moreover, ICT has the potential to reduce the need for geographical mobility. Whereas during the industrial revolution increased flexibility was achieved by switching labour from domestic 'cottage' industries to factory production systems, the reverse can often be the case now and there are strong environmental protection grounds for using and reinforcing this potential.

To achieve these other types of organizational and skill flexibility is far more difficult than to achieve traditional labour supply flexibility. The change in skill composition which is needed for the ICT paradigm is probably greater than for any other technological revolution. However, the alternative to competing in highly skilled, high value added types of manufacturing and service activities is to compete in low-skilled or unskilled labour with countries which have far lower wage rates and longer hours of work.

There are certainly many labour market economists both in North America and in Europe who would still put the main emphasis on the need to reduce relative wages (and social benefits) for less skilled workers and for young workers. In this more traditional vision much of the blame for the rise in unemployment, par-ticularly in Europe, is still put on the lack of downward wage flexibility to enlarge the employment creation potential at the low skill/low wage end. In this view, the combination of existing income tax structures and minimum wage legislation discourages the supply of low-paid work; the amount of unemployment and social assistance benefits might have removed incentives for unemployed workers to seek more actively for work.

However, the wage flexibility argument cannot be discussed purely in static economic terms. The question can be raised to what extent such immediate wage adjustments would not have severe, long-term negative consequences for both labour productivity growth and competitiveness. Whereas from a static, short-term point of view such policies might well generate low-skill employment possibilities in the non-tradable service sector – the so-called 'hamburger economy' or 'shoe-shine boy economy' – and thus reduce some of the structural long-term, low-skill unemployment, there exists a real danger that these measures could also lead to downward pressure on labour productivity with spill-overs to the tradable sectors, such as sweat shops in clothing and textiles, and a move towards long-term specialization in low-skill activities.

Paradoxically, the wage flexibility argument appears, from this perspective, rather similar to the argument for full protectionism. If there were full protectionism, for instance, at the broad level of the EU trade bloc (or even the new European economic space), low-skill employment is likely to be generated in many of the labour-intensive, low-wage sectors which would now substitute for previous imports of such commodities. The new employment created would be substantially higher than the employment decline in the EU's world export sectors and full employment would probably be quickly reinstalled. Apart from the obvious welfare losses from EU autarchy, the loss of the dynamic competitive impact of foreign imports would, however, in the long term, severely undermine the EU's growth and competitiveness. In an open world, downward wage adjustment appears to be the same type of escape from adjustment as protectionism. Introducing it as a main policy device could, from this perspective, lead to the 'import of underdevelopment': a process of a more lateral international division of labour, where wage differentials within the developed countries increasingly resemble wage differentials between countries.

From a social, from an economic and from a technological point of view the alternative path of a shift to high skill, high value added activities is greatly to be preferred to the low wage solution. In the early decades of the nineteenth century it was the British industrialist, Robert Owen, who, in his factory at New Lanark, in his writings and his political activity, most clearly provided an alternative to the prevalent pessimistic Malthusian trend in classical economics at that time. Most industrialists and economists in the early days of the industrial revolution tended to assume that population pressures and the necessity to sustain profitability would persistently drive wages down to or below subsistence level. Particularly in times of recession most industrialists and their political spokesmen insisted that social reforms, such as shorter working hours or restrictions on the employment of children, would lead to the ruin of industry because they would reduce profitability and competitiveness.

Owen maintained that better work organization, better education and training (he had his own school at New Lanark), social reforms and superior technology would together make it possible to offset such downward pressures and indeed to raise profitability. Later, Marx also recognized that the tendency to a falling rate of profit which he had identified could be offset by technical and organizational innovations and by the opening of new markets. Schumpeter followed him in his model of the profits of innovative entrepreneurs, diffused through imitation and band-wagon effects and then gradually eroded until a further set of innovations once more temporarily counteracted the tendency to diminishing returns.

There have thus been two main co-existing approaches to the restoration of profitability during cyclical downturns. The immediate response of many industrialists and bankers and the policy-makers whom they advise is to cut labour costs by reducing the labour force and ultimately by reducing wages. The latter is of course far from easy because of resistance from the workforce. For this reason policies designed to weaken the bargaining power of trade unions are characteristic of long wave downturns and have been particularly evident in the 1980s, as in the 1930s, 1880s and 1820s. Since the prevalence of mass unemployment may be insufficient, legislation to weaken trade unions or even their outright prohibition has often been a feature of these downturns.

As in Owen's day, employers and political organizations are divided in the relative emphasis which they place on different types of flexibility. While there is substance in all the various approaches, the main danger now lies in under-estimating the role of these other types of flexibility.

We indicated in our description of the development of the ICT techno-economic paradigm that among its leading characteristics are greatly increased flexibility in product mix, process change, design, manufacturing systems (FMS, etc.), marketing response to changes in consumer demand and delivery of services, including ultimately teleshopping, telebanking, teleconferencing and teleworking, all now rapidly developing. This enhanced flexibility cannot be achieved without flexibility within the firm and between firms in their sub-contracting relationships and alliances. One of the main reasons for the collapse of the militarized centrally planned economics of Eastern Europe was its inflex-ibility in all these dimensions. It actually coped quite well, relatively speaking, with the growth of heavy industry based (quite explicitly) on Fordist and Taylorist ideas of management and work organization. Economic growth in Eastern Europe in the 1950s and early 1960s was relatively strong and they were 'catching up'. But they completely lacked the flexibility to adapt to the very different needs of ICT.

Nor is this transition easy for the more flexible capitalist market economies. They too suffer from innumerable institutional rigidities in their management systems, working practices, standards, regulation systems and so forth. An impor-tant source of flexibility in market economies has always lain in subcontracting, enabling firms to adjust to the changes in the pattern and timing of their new orders, which can rarely be precisely predicted. Small firms and self-employed

118

individuals play an exceptionally important role in achieving this type of flexibility which is one reason why the centrally planned economies found it so difficult to achieve (even though they had their own semi-legal intermediaries in the system). The rapid establishment and growth of new small firms (SMEs) has been recognized everywhere as essential to renewal of employment growth and flexibility. Fluctuating and changing workloads, however, require not only flexibility in changing consortia and partnerships, but also flexibility in working time. The traditional 40- or 48-hour working week, with 2 to 4 weeks annual holiday was quite well suited to dedicated Fordist mass and flow production processes, although even there some flexibility had to be achieved by overtime arrangements, shift working, etc. The flexibility now required is far greater.

It should be as easy for a father to get time to look after a sick child as for a mother, or to meet the children after school and care for them. But in practice, it is often far more difficult for fathers even when they very much want to take this time off. Flexibility of working hours is thus increasingly important for men as well as for women and not only for 'new men', but for 'old' men too, even though simple biological differences mean that the division of labour can never be quite the same. The 'parenting deficit' identified by Etzioni (1993) and other sociologists as a key social problem can only be reduced if this type of flexibility improves.

A reduction in working hours could apply to weekly, annual and lifetime hours. Charles Handy (1989) has estimated that lifetime working hours have fallen from about 100,000 hours for his generation to 50,000 for his children, while a slightly more precise calculation by Bruce Williams (1984) estimated the decline in lifetime working hours in Britain as 42 per cent from 1881 to 1981 (from 154,000 hours to 88,000). Handy suggested that typically those who worked 100,000 hours did 47 hours a week for 47 weeks a year, for 47 years of employment, whereas today typical patterns could be for 50,000 hours made up from a 37-hour week for 37 weeks of 37 years, or 45 hours for 45 weeks for 25 years (early retirement and long education), or 25 hours for 45 weeks for 45 years (continuous part-time work). The slow decline of annual working hours continued in the 1980s but there are some slight indications of a reversal at least for some groups in the most recent period.

Hewitt (1993, see also Chapter 5) insists that there should be a very wide variety of working hours which would not necessarily conform precisely to any of the above patterns. She argues that this is the actual trend of events and not just wishful thinking. Among the various possibilities she mentions are flexitime, the 9-day fortnight, special leave for new parents (men and women), part-time working before and after retirement, job sharing, longer working day with shorter working week, weekend jobs, annual hours contracts, zero hours contracts (work 'as and when required'), individually contracted working hours, career breaks, and sabbaticals. All of these have been spreading according to the evidence which she presents. Government authorities have quite often been ready to introduce part-time working arrangements for some of their own civil servants.

119

As Hewitt recognizes, there are some dangers in the trend which she observes towards flexible part-time working. She is concerned that social security arrangements in particular are lagging behind the speed of change and that while some employers, such as B&Q, may make relatively good schemes, others may use the change simply to avoid their responsibilities to employees. The 1994 legal decision of the House of Lords on the application of EU legislation to British part-time workers may have some countervailing effects.

In the absence of a strong overall demand for labour, the spread of part-time work could be largely involuntary. The very real dangers to work morale were pointed out in an editorial in the *Economist* (17 July 1993):

> Challenged by nimbler rivals, big firms have little choice but to slim down. Many are still too bureaucratic and need to shed yet more workers. With competition increasing, firms of every size must react more quickly. But bosses are wrong to believe that the best way to do this is to tear up the implicit contract they have had with their employees. At present too many firms are trying to heap all of the uncertainty created by increased competition and technological change upon the shoulders of individual workers. There are limits to how far firms can adopt this approach if they hope to remain competitive beyond the shortest of short terms.

Raising the general universal standard of literacy and numeracy is essential to enhance flexibility, but it has to be complemented by intensive education and training for specialized skills, especially those related to ICT. Contrary to the pessimistic views sometimes put forward, there will in fact be an enormously increased need for software designers and engineers. They will be needed not least to achieve the objective of raising the quality of education and training throughout the system. But they will also be needed for numerous other applications of computer systems, such as telecommunication networks, data banks, teleconferencing, traffic control, monitoring of arms control agreements, many types of R&D, etc. However, whereas computer hardware and software professionals are at the heart of the ICT revolution, there is also a parallel though less intense need for many other professionally qualified people in natural science, engineering, social sciences, medicine, management and humanities. Although there are conflicting views and a possibility of alternative patterns of evolution in different countries, the main trend which is being driven by the ICT revolution appears to be towards a generally higher level of both specialized skills and general education with a declining share in future workforce composition both for unskilled and lower qualified workers. To some extent this evolution depends on the policies which are adopted and we have argued that for many reasons to compete with higher skills is more desirable than to adjust downwards to compete in low-skill, low-wage activities. It is to the policies needed to implement this goal that we turn in the final section.

POLICIES FOR EMPLOYMENT

Full employment, or at least the substantial reduction of unemployment, is a very important policy objective for most if not all countries. This is of course a value judgement but it is one which is professed by most governments and international organizations and (which is more important) by almost the whole population. They might differ to some degree on definitions of 'full employment' and there is sometimes a case for using the expression 'active society'. 'Full employment' is to some degree associated with the notion of adult male 16–65 employment, rather than a flexible pattern of lifetime work opportunities and education, for men and women, young and old, full-time or part-time, which should now be feasible. On the other hand there is a danger that to drop the expression 'full employment' could imply acceptance of a large amount of involuntary part-time and casual work. Whatever the precise terminology the goal should be that work or education should be available for all who seek it, including the numerous discouraged workers and involuntary part-time workers who today do not find full-time employment opportunities.

It will not be easy for Europe to generate a large number of new jobs. Nor will it be easy to retrain large numbers of people. Many new jobs will still be needed for unskilled or low-skilled people for a long time to come. It is essential to realize that, even if an optimistic scenario for ICT could be realized, only a minority of the new jobs needed would actually be in the ICT industries and services or indeed in ICT occupations in other industries and services.

However, the job creation effects would not just be felt in software occupations or even mainly in software activities. They would be felt in many other service industries as well as in the manufacture of computers, telecommunication equipment and other electronic products. The main effects would not be so much in hardware as in the area of information services, data banks, publishing, education, training and health services. However, there are important complementarities between hardware and software, manufacturing and services, and various types of services. Software professionals can seldom provide the type of interactive services which are needed except in collaboration with experienced professionals in other fields, just as they have to collaborate with engineers and managers in the design of manufacturing systems. Hybrid professionals might very well dominate in the end. 'Multi-media project coordinator' or some similar occupation might be one of the fastest growing occupations in the next decade, even though it has not yet entered the official classification. This can be seen already in the tendency for informatics to become one of the specializations for other types of engineer rather than the sole specialization. Many other skilled and less skilled workers will be needed in other industries and services, stimulated by Keynesian multiplier effects.

It is important to re-emphasize the point that ICT affects all industries and services, creating new investment opportunities everywhere. The impetus which a new techno-economic paradigm can give to the economic system lies not so much in particular products or services as in the boost it can give to investment and to consumer confidence generally. While it is very hard to predict exactly which products or services will achieve the highest growth rates or when, there can now be no doubt about the pervasive stimulus to the economy from ICT. The extent and duration of this stimulus will however depend on public policies which are adopted over the next few years.

The points already discussed lead to the following policy conclusions with respect to new employment and employment policies:

1 To realize the vast future job creation potential of ICT will require substantial further investment in the telecommunication infrastructure ('information highways and byways') and related data banks, services and buildings.
2 The transformation of the skill profile will require heavy 'intangible' investment in the education and training infrastructure.
3 The scale of the unemployment problem and the intensity of low-wage competition, especially in Europe, makes it necessary to adopt other measures to generate and sustain new employment in the medium- and long-term. These would aim to foster a 'sheltered' second-tier economy based on non-traded services, construction and environmental improvement.

Recovery has to be strong enough that total output growth exceeds the growth rate of labour productivity, as in the 1950s and 1960s. Circumstances vary in different countries, but in general it can be said that both in Europe and Japan there is a strong case for a new form of Keynesian public investment policy to provide the basic infrastructure for an ICT-based economy. The influence of an old techno-economic paradigm could still be clearly seen in the measures announced by various governments in the 1980s and early 1990s concentrating mainly on the older industries and infrastructures – road building, cars, steel, oil, construction, etc. – and with little to say about new technologies. Two exceptions were the technology policy announced in 1993 by the Clinton–Gore administration and the European Commission's (Delors) White Paper. Both envisaged a significant role for public as well as for private investment for 'information highways' and for 'wiring up' schools and hospitals. It remains to be seen how far these ambitious policy proposals will actually be carried into effect with all the various constraints in the US and European budgetary and political systems. Nevertheless, the proposed policy packages were a significant event, marking as they did the recognition of the importance of ICT infrastructure and of information technology policy issues and indicating constructive and imaginative thinking about these problems.

With the advent of 'new' growth theory (Romer 1986, 1990; Lucas 1988) there is now a renewed and much more generally accepted converging view that another of the most critical factors behind economic growth and development is, and has been, educational investment. These two types of infrastructural investment are in fact closely related.

Very many parents and grandparents must have watched with admiration and amazement as their children and grandchildren learned to excel in computer games which they could hardly tackle. Not only do many children concentrate for hours on games but they will go on day after day, even though the obsolescence rate in these games is high and fashion plays a big part. Yet the very same children will often say 'school is boring'. Here surely is a tremendous challenge to the entire education profession all over the world. Learning should be exciting and interesting, not boring, and often it should be fun.

Some enthusiasts are so impressed by the versatility and potential of ICT that they imagine that the regular educational institutions can be partly or even completely bypassed. Some commercial interests also see great possibilities in developing the home market for education while some educationists are so depressed by conditions in schools and what are seen as the contemporary failures of the system that they also flirt with the idea of 'deschooling' to a greater or lesser extent. Finally, there are people who see this as an opportunity to reduce public expenditure.

It is true that there is a greatly increased potential for people of all ages (certainly not only children) to learn all kinds of things at home and it is certainly desirable to exploit this in a variety of ways. However, the idea of displacing the formal education system is both wrong and dangerous. Certainly schools and universities can be greatly improved, more exciting, and can make far greater use of ICT than they do today but they are needed more than ever for the following reasons.

1 Although children can indeed show great concentration and determination in playing computer games and some can learn a lot at home, there are also subjects and activities which can less easily be learnt at home or not at all. Most children benefit from interacting with other children and learn from each other, as well as from media and from teachers. Most also need some personal help, care and guidance in their studies. Computer games, CD-ROM and multi-media services cannot entirely displace teachers any more than books can.

2 Schools are extremely inportant for socialization and communication. One of the major needs of the future workplace is communication skills. It is difficult, if not impossible, to acquire these in isolation or purely through ICT. Not only in work but also in social and political life, communication and socialization are extremely important. Schools have a major role in social cohesion and in national culture.

3 The home environment for many children does not facilitate home learning on any kind of regular or systematic basis. One consequence of 'deschooling' would be to divide the population into information-rich households and information-poor households. While this would not correspond exactly to income distribution, it would generally further handicap the children of less wealthy parents, who are already disadvantaged educationally in various ways. One of the major advantages of the school system is universality, providing

children from all kinds of households with opportunities to learn. While it is true that there are also some children who do not learn in the formal system but through other channels, there would almost certainly be a massive decline in the educational standards of a large number of children if deschooling was pushed a long way.

4 In addition to the social and educational reasons for improving rather than bypassing the formal eduction system, there are also strong economic reasons. Much equipment which cannot conceivably be provided to every single household can be provided at reasonable cost in educational institutions. Libraries are an obvious case and the argument applies *a fortiori* to CD-ROM libraries, video libraries, and other ICT resources and equipment, especially virtual reality equipment (VR). But the argument also applies to laboratories, art rooms, workshops, sports facilities, music rooms, theatres, and much else. It is true that many professional people may have their own libraries, including video libraries and their own workshops. It is also true that there is a tendency as incomes grow to prefer ownership to borrowing but the same people who own many books usually also make use of libraries and other collective facilities. The children of deprived households have no chance if they do not have access to public facilities. There are many indivisibilities in education as in industry and commerce and education can no more be a purely individualistic activity than production. 'Video-on-demand' (VOD) is the goal of some of the big consortia which are being formed to deliver information services and entertainment to households via cable TV networks or satellite. But even if they succeed, as they probably will, this will not be a cheap service, so that there will still be big economic advantages in providing education services through the education system.

5 Finally, schools do not only have an educational and socialization function, they also have what some people call a 'custodial' function. Even if a larger number of parents work at home they do need time to work relatively free of interruptions. Children also need time to learn free of interruptions from parents, brothers, sisters, friends, etc. Indeed, a very strong argument can be made that rather than children spending less time at school, they should spend more.

Organizations such as 'Education Extra' have been formed precisely in order to promote and extend after-school but at-school activities. Such activities have many advantages.

- They enable the community to take advantage of the public investment in buildings and other facilities, which otherwise are idle most of the time.
- They enable children to broaden their learning to a wider range of subjects, activities, societies, etc. Many of them greatly improve their communication skills, other social skills and ICT capability.
- They enable children to do their homework at school. This is exceptionally important for disadvantaged children with difficult home conditions but

more and more schools are finding that it improves the quality of after-school learning for many pupils who find it harder to work once they get home.

- They enable schools to become a focus for community life more generally. They can involve local industry and commerce, who find it much easier to interact with the school in these after-school activities and indeed to promote some of them.

- Many schools already have a wide range of activities, including self-supported studies and industry-supported studies, in what are technically after-school hours. They are often also the focus of computer-based activities. Indeed both schools and universities would become the focus of all kinds of ICT-based activities for local communities.

- The extension of these activities, together with increased provision of nursery school education, would greatly improve the possibilities for women as well as men to work more flexible hours. They would also provide new opportunities for adult education, as already indicated in the case of the Motorola experiment (Wiggenhorn 1990).

Therefore we would argue the very reverse of the deschooling argument in favour of an enhanced role for the public education system in disseminating and using ICT-based media of all kinds. In fact we would go much further and argue that it is essential for public education policy to play an active role in developing new course material in co-operation with industry. To develop new modules for new courses in every discipline and combination of disciplines and to keep them up to date is an absolutely enormous educational undertaking. It requires the active participation of the teaching profession at all levels and not just in a few specialized 'technology' schools.

At this point in the argument the objection is often raised that schools and the teachers are too conservative or even that they are Luddites. It is indeed true that the teaching profession or parts of it have not always been specially receptive to new technologies. But just as in the case of industry and commerce, where there is also often resistance to the introduction of ICT, it is necessary to understand the reasons for this suspicion or hostility. It is also essential to study the experience of successful institutional and technical change to understand why it often fails, whether in the classroom, the boardroom, the factory or the bank.

The commonest cause of failure in industrial innovation is to neglect to involve the prospective users of a new process or product in its design, development and application. Numerous case studies over the past thirty years support this generalization. There is no reason to suppose that education is any different in this respect. Originally, lack of user-friendliness was the biggest problem with computer software and computer-based innovations. Consequently it is not at all surprising that teachers, like many other people, were put off in the 1960s and 1970s by the early attempts to woo them with educational technology. They had the strong impression that they were being pressurized by people who had little knowledge of classroom activities, of education and of the specific disciplines they were teaching. They felt that they were being asked to use material that neither they nor their pupils found particularly helpful. Not surprisingly then early efforts often failed, as did similar early efforts with robotics and office computers. Most of the teachers knew little or nothing about ICT which did not help matters either.

Now the situation has changed dramatically. Not only the teachers but also the children are users of ICT in education. In Britain and in many other countries public policies have helped to achieve widespread availability of PCs in schools and even to achieve very early small-scale applications of VR and CD-Rom. Much of the software is easy to use and computer games are now so popular that they have familiarized a new generation with interactive learning. Many more of the teachers are also now computer numerate. Finally, there have been great improvements to the technology and software has improved, costs have come down so low and quality has improved so much that rapid progress is now being made.

However, every new ICT product has to be developed with care and attention to user needs. Whether considering virtual reality (VR) software for medical students or aircraft pilots, and soon for many other education and training applications, or remedial mathematics CD-ROMs for children with maths phobia, the rule is the same: user friendliness is an absolutely essential ingredient. The computer companies learnt this the hard way as the market expanded from the first patient and mathematically inclined professional scientists to the wider market in industry and goverment. Now the lesson has often to be relearnt with every new educational software package which is produced. The very long gestation period of VR also illustrates this point (Sherman and Judkins 1992).

It is quite possible that once information highways, byways and networks are established a larger proportion of teaching and learning will be on the basis of networked services. Technologies such as CD-ROMs will be rather less important, but the same considerations apply in developing networked educational services or VR techniques. Consequently, a policy for developing the use of ICT in education should be based on the following principles:

- Every multi-media team to develop a CD-ROM, CD-I, VR or other IT-based product for education or even for 'edu-tainment' should include not only a software professional but also an educational professional. In-service training should aim to provide all teachers with opportunities for temporary attachment to public or private agencies which are designing and developing the thousands of new titles which are needed. They would join a multi-media or VR team working in their own subject area.
- The education system should stimulate and assist the formation of some multi-media and VR teams in both the private and the public sector, partly through the secondment of teachers, partly through the use of educational activities for trial development and partly through such organizations as the British Centre for Education Technology (CET) and the Open University

(OU) and their equivalents in other countries. Just as war-time radar development required the co-operation of industry, government and universities, so too does this vast educational R&D activity. It needs to be promoted by a lead institution (in the British case probably the OU) which is involved in the design and development of new products, but is also a network co-ordinator and sponsor of many other projects.

- Constant updating of ICT products is necessary and it is especially important to achieve flexible adaptation to local needs. This again points to the need to involve schools and teachers.

Success in future international competition will depend very much on the effectiveness of this form of education infrastructural investment and the determination to enlist the full co-operation of the teaching profession in these changes and to raise their professional status to reflect their true importance to society. The traditional function of education in sustaining and transmitting national culture should of course never be lost sight of; it could also be revitalized by these new approaches.

CONCLUSIONS

Western Europe can remain competitive in world trade, even with a rising level of living and environmental standards, provided appropriate policies are adopted for structural competitiveness.

Those who fear competition often forget the two-edged nature of international trade. A prosperous China, a prosperous India, a prosperous Russia and a prosperous Brazil would certainly present enormous and intense competition for Western Europe: they would also present enormous opportunities for West European exports. Of course, this trade needs to be conducted fairly under agreed rules of international co-operation and regulation and it will not be easy to handle all the disputed issues which may arise. There is a strong case for wider international efforts to regulate social as well as environmental standards in world trade competition. The ILO and the UN environmental organizations have an increasingly important role to play in the family of international organizations.

'Beggar-thy-neighbour' responses to unemployment, often under the pretence of free trade, are particularly disturbing. Such policy responses represent to some extent the mirror image of the traditional protectionists. They include various attempts at reducing domestic labour costs relative to major competitors, through reductions in or even abolition of minimum social legislation, environmental rules and regulation, etc. Free trade in this social deregulation sense has undoubtedly a negative connotation. The benefits of trade should lead to better international allocation of resources, thus increasing welfare at the world level. The response of the developed countries should not be to try to adjust downwards, to reduce social achievements so as to remain competitive in sectors in which they can no longer achieve comparative advantage. Such negative adjustment trends contrast sharply with positive adjustment policy proposals aimed at helping workers, firms and sectors to adjust towards higher skills, higher value added and higher income levels. Developed countries must keep running to stay in the same place.

The impression of a much more competitive international environment is undoubtedly a reflection of the fact that the process of catching up which is taking place in countries such as those in South and East Asia has been and is being successful. This is to be welcomed and a major objective of international policy should be to enable African, Latin American and East European countries also to catch up. The rich, developed OECD economies no longer operate in an industrial vacuum, where more than 80 per cent of world production or world trade originated from within these countries. The world economy, particularly in the Asian Pacific area, and by and large outside of the OECD, has grown and is likely to continue to grow much more rapidly than the old North Atlantic US–European core base. The fact that most of the employment concerns are being voiced in Europe is from this perspective not surprising. Whether one likes it or not, it is part of a more general structural shift in the growth and employment pole from Europe–USA to Asia. Europe needs to respond to this, not by deregulating its social achievements so as to stay competitive or keep international firms located in Europe, but by investing more in education, training and its own technological and physical infrastructure.

There is also a need for a further stimulus to employment which would be less vulnerable to the shocks of international competition and the vagaries of the business cycle. In the past such a 'sheltered sector' existed in many countries in public and private service industries. In particular in Japan, for example, the retail trade sector performed this function. With the growing pressures on some service industries to be internationally competitive and the efforts to reduce central government expenditures, it has become essential to reconsider the role of the non-traded sector of the economy specifically with respect to employment.

The fastest growing occupations are in four categories (see Table 7.2):

• ICT occupations
• Education
• Caring personal services
• Repair and maintenance.

Tax arrangements vary in different countries and there is also variation between central, regional and local government finance. But in many cases the decision to avoid VAT (and the ease of doing so) leads to many of the third and fourth categories being performed largely in the 'black' informal economy. For this reason proposals for VAT exemption and other tax changes appear eminently sensible. They would also lead to more accurate statistics of employment and unemployment and to the entry of new firms into the area of personal services. Considerable ingenuity will be needed in tax reform but the general objective is clear. The decentralized local government role is very important and there is

Table 7.2 Occupational employment forecasts (USA) percentage increase
1990–2005

Home health aides	+91.7
Systems analysts and computer scientists	+78.9
Computer programmers	+56.1
Child care workers	+48.8
Information clerks	+46.9
Registered nurses	+44.4
Nursing aides	+43.4
Cooks	+41.8
Gardeners	+39.8
Lawyers	+35.1
Accountants	+34.5
Secondary school teachers	+34.2
Educational assistants	+34.4
Food counter	+34.2
Guards	+33.7
Food preparation	+31.6

Source: US Bureau of Labor Statistics 1992

ample scope for the expansion of local government personal services for the aged, the sick and the needy. Local authorities are far better able to organize and supervise these services than central government, but in some countries centralization of finance and political power does not permit them to do so. There is a need for 're-inventing government' so as to strengthen decentralized institutions, public enterprise and voluntary services as well as market-based services.

Just as the whole area of personal services is in need of rejuvenation and reform, so too in the environmental sphere. The investments required in waste and water management, emissions control equipment, alternative low emission transport systems and in recyclable material are substantial in almost every country. Many of these environmental needs will require local investments and are likely, at least in the short run, to generate new employment opportunities. The clean up of industrial dereliction caused by earlier phases of industrialization is already an important source of employment in some localities, but of course will usually be accompanied by environmental improvement, including new parks, nature reserves and leisure facilities as well as new public infrastructure. Continuous environmental improvement and personal services could thus constitute the twin supporting pillars of a sheltered economy offering a wide variety of new employment opportunities, related to local needs and circumstances.

A return to full employment is a difficult but by no means an impossible task. It requires an imaginative combination of public and private investment. Nightmare scenarios of total dehumanizing computerization are often misconceived, although the humanization of work remains an extremely important social objective. ICT-based services will not (indeed cannot) replace personal caring services, including most health and education. What they can do is to improve and enhance these services and in some cases to make them more accessible to people who could otherwise not enjoy them. Second, the growth in demand for education, health and many other personal caring services can indeed also generate a great increase in employment, including professional ICT-related employment, as well as educationists and health professionals who are also skilled in ICT.

These expanding services can of course vary greatly in quality and in the skill with which they use ICT. The response from consumers will depend very much on these factors. Clearly there is an extremely important role for public policy in setting and achieving high standards in health and education. There is also a major role for public policy in stimulating research, development and demonstration. The combination of jobs which are created may be a high proportion of low pay and low quality jobs or a high proportion of high value added and higher quality jobs.

Advocates of reduction in wages and social provisions for unskilled workers in Europe believe that this is necessary to generate employment more quickly, as they believe has already occurred in the USA. However, as the OECD (1993) Interim Report points out, there is a danger of being caught up in a low wage trap on a long-term basis. To avoid this danger of a permanent, large, low-wage, low-skill underclass, it is essential to press forward with policies for training and high quality services, so that more highly skilled jobs become a steadily larger proportion of the total. The diffusion of ICT can contribute a great deal to this process.

NOTE

1 I am grateful to my friend and colleague, Luc Soete, who collaborated with me in much of the research on which this chapter is based (see Freeman and Soete 1994).

REFERENCES

Baba, Y., Takai, S. and Mizuta, Y. (1994) 'The evolution of the software industry in Japan: a comprehensive analysis', in D Mowery (ed.) *The International Computer Software Industry*, Oxford: Oxford University Press.
Boyer, R. (1988) 'Technical change and the theory of regulation', in G. Dosi *et al.* (eds) *Technical Change and Economic Theory*, London: Pinter.
Datamation (1990, 1991, 1992, 1993) 'The Datamation 100'.
Dobb, M. (1946) *Studies in the Development of Capitalism*, London: Routledge.
Economist (1993) Editorial, *Economist*, 17 July.
Etzioni, A. (1993) *The Parenting Deficit*, London: DEMOS.
Freeman, C. and Soete, L. (1994) *Work for All or Mass Unemployment?*, London: Pinter.
Handy, C. (1989) *The Age of Unreason*, London: Century Hutchinson.
Hewitt, P. (1993) *About Time: the Revolution in Work and Family Life*, London: IPPR/Rivers Oram Press.

Juliussen, K. P. and Juliussen, E. (1993) *The 6th Annual Computer Industry Almanac*, Austin, Texas: Reference Press.

Lucas, R. F. B. (1988) 'On the mechamisms of economic development', *Journal of Monetary Economics* 22: 3–42.

Macrae, N. (1994) 'The Jolly Roger flies for full employment', *Sunday Times*, 20 March.

Maddison, A. (1991) *Dynamic Forces in Capitalist Development, a Long-run Comparative View*, Oxford: Oxford University Press.

Oakley, B. (1990) 'Trends in the European IT skills scene', Pergamon Infotech, London, Conference on Human Resource Development in IT, 19–21 February.

Olson, M. (1982) *The Rise and Decline of Nations*, New Haven: Yale University Press.

Organization for Economic Co-operation and Developoment (OECD) (1990, 1992, 1993, 1994) *Employment Outlook*, Paris: OECD.

Perez, C. (1983) 'Structural change and the assimilation of new technologies in the economic and social system', *Futures* 15 (5): 357–75.

Rifkin, J. (1995) *The End of Work*, New York: GP Putnam.

Romer, P. M. (1986) 'Increasing returns and long-run growth', *Journal of Political Economy* 94: 1002–37.

—— (1990) 'Endogenous technological change', *Journal of Political Economy* 98, S71–S102.

Samuelson, P. A. (1981) 'The world economy at century's end', *Japan Economic Journal*, 10 March: 20.

Schumpeter, J. (1939) *Business Cycles: A Theoretical, Historical and Statistical Analysis*, New York: McGraw Hill.

—— (1943) *Capitalism, Socialism and Democracy*, 6th edn, 1987, London: Unwin Paperbacks.

Sherman, B. and Judkins, P. (1992) *Glimpses of Heaven, Visions of Hell: Virtual Reality and its Implications*, London: Hodder and Stoughton.

Statistical Abstract (1992) Washington DC: United States Government Printing Office.

United States Bureau of Labor Statistics (1992) *Outlook 1990–2005. Projections of US Labour Force Occupations*, Bulletin 2402, Washington DC: US Government Printing Office

Wiggenhorn, W. (1990) 'Motorola University: when training becomes education', *Harvard Business Review* 68 (4), July–August.

Williams, B. (1984) *Shorter Hours, Increased Employment* (Three Banks Review, September), reprint of OECD Conference Paper, Paris: OECD.

Wood, A. (1994) *North–South Trade Employment and Inequality, Changing Fortunes in a Skill-driven World*, Oxford: Clarendon Press.

131

8

DOES GLOBLIZATION THREATEN LOW-SKILLED WESTERN WORKERS?

Richard B. Freeman

INTRODUCTION

During the past two decades the economic position of low-skilled workers in Western countries has deteriorated sharply. In the USA this has taken the form of a huge drop in the real earnings of less-educated men, particularly young men. In much of Western Europe, it has taken the form of high rates of unemployment among less skilled and young workers. In the UK the relative earnings of the less skilled have fallen, though their real earnings have risen somewhat, but their unemployment is high. Over the same period trade has expanded, particularly with less-developed countries (LDCs), and immigration from LDCs has accelerated.

Are these developments causally related? Are trade, immigration and related globalization trends, such as transfer of technology and capital flows, immiserating low-skill workers? Or is the tendency for the economic outcomes (earnings or chances of employment) of workers with similar skills to move toward similar levels across countries in an open economy vastly exaggerated?

There are three possible answers to the question of whether globalization is harming the economic position of low-skilled Western workers: 'No' and 'Yes' and the ever-popular 'Up to a point'. In this chapter I review the arguments and evidence for these responses, grouping often disparate studies into the camp in which they fit best. Since the sensible response to almost any social science question is 'up to a point', my categorization and discussion asks whether analyses are closer to 'no' or to 'yes'.

I wish to stress from the outset that there is no link between the answer to the question posed above and any particular chosen stance on trade. In Europe, there has been longstanding concern over possible 'social dumping', in which the low wages or labour standards in poorer countries reduce the well-being of those in advanced countries. The French, in particular, have worried about the effects of trade with less-developed Asian countries on European wages and labour standards. Debate over the North American Free Trade Agreement (NAFTA) brought the issue of what globalization does to wages and employment into the policy arena in the USA, with a resultant simplification and hardening of positions on the factual question under consideration here.

Supporters of NAFTA seem to feel impelled to answer the title question 'no', while opponents feel impelled to answer 'yes'. If you want free trade, downplay any problems it may create and sell it as a cure-all. If you favour protection, blame the nation's ills on trade (and those nefarious foreign lobbyists in Washington DC, or supporters of GATT). However, the logic of the case does not dictate such. There is nothing inconsistent between concluding that globalization did not harm low-skill Western workers in the 1980s and endorsing protectionism as a way to raise their income in the 1990s. Nor is a free trade stance inconsistent with the belief that globalization has harmed low-skill workers: the increased national income due to lower trade barriers could be re-distributed through other policies to the low skilled. Knowing that development X causes problem Y does not mean that removing X is the best way to remedy Y. My colleagues who believe that technological change underlies the deteriorating economic position of less-skilled Americans do not endorse Luddite policies to help them. Adrian Wood, who has made the strongest case that trade with LDCs is harmful to less-skilled workers in the West, is a free trader (see Wood 1994). Jagdish Bagwati, who stands in the 'no' camp, favours redistributive policies to aid less-skilled workers (Bhagwati 1993). In any case, I consider what globalization does to the less skilled not in terms of political debate over trade and immigration policies, but as a factual matter orthogonal to those debates.

SOME BASIC FACTS

The natural place to begin is with the two trends of concern: (a) the declining position of low-skilled workers in advanced economies and (b) the globalization of the economy.

The economic problems of low-skilled workers

Europeans know well the economic problems of low-skilled workers, particularly the young: high levels of unemployment and spells that last for long periods of time. There is a plethora of studies of European unemployment and a wide set of proposed policy solutions, many espousing US-style labour market flexibility and deregulation as the cure-all to joblessness. Rather than dwell on the European unemployment problem, I want to stress that a parallel economic disaster has befallen low-skilled Americans, especially young men, in the form of rising wage inequality, skill differentials and continued high unemployment among the less skilled. The drop in the relative position of the less skilled in the USA has four dimensions:

1 It shows up in the hourly earnings of workers with specified skills. The college/high school wage premium doubled for young workers in the 1980s

as the weekly wages of young male college graduates increased by some 30 per cent relative to those of young males with twelve or fewer years of school-ing (see Figure 8.1a). In addition, among workers without college degrees the wages of older workers rose relative to those of younger workers (see Figure 8.1b). The earnings of blue-collar workers grew much less rapidly than those of managers or professionals.

2 It shows up in widened earnings distribution for workers (see Figure 8.1c). The hourly earnings of a full-time worker in the ninetieth percentile of the US earnings distribution (someone whose earnings exceeded those of 90 per cent of all workers) relative to a worker in the tenth percentile (someone whose earnings exceeded those of just 10 per cent of all workers) grew by 20 per cent for men and 25 per cent for women from 1979 to 1989. Much of this increase took the form of greater wage differentials for similar workers across establishments in the same industry.

3 It shows up in the employment opportunities of low-skill workers. While job-lessness among white-collar workers increased in the early 1990s, the longer term trend in the USA (and elsewhere) has been for reduced work from the lower skilled workers whose earnings have been falling. Some interpret this as normal labour supply response to changes in economic incentives. Others view it as reflecting more constrained labour market behaviour: the low skilled want to work, even at low wages, but cannot get jobs at those wages. Whatever the precise mechanism, the reduction in their earnings has not created a plethora of jobs for the low skilled.

4 It shows up in the real compensation – fringe benefits as well as earnings – of low-wage Americans. If the American earnings distribution widened in an era of rapidly increasing real earnings, so that the living standards of low-skill workers increased a trifle, or even fell a trifle, American economists would not be ringing alarm bells. An increase in the skill premium, due largely to higher real earnings of the skilled, might upset egalitarian fetishists but not mainstream economists. But that is not what occurred in the past decade or two. The rise in earnings inequality did not take the form of improved real earnings for the higher paid but reduced real earnings of the lower paid. Rising inequality was accompanied by sluggish growth in real earnings, so that the economic position of low-skilled men, especially younger men, fell by staggering amounts. Most striking, the real hourly wages of young males with twelve or fewer years of schooling dropped by some 20 per cent from 1979 to 1989. The real hourly earnings of all men in the bottom decile of the earnings distribution have fallen by comparable amounts since the early or mid-1970s.

One result of widening inequality and poor growth of real wages in the USA is that low-paid Americans have much lower levels of real earnings than similarly situated low-paid workers in Europe or Japan. Using current exchange rates, American workers in manufacturing are paid considerably less than the workers

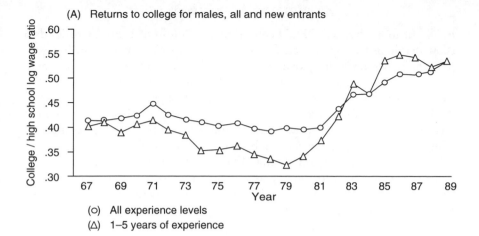

(A) Returns to college for males, all and new entrants

(○) All experience levels
(△) 1–5 years of experience

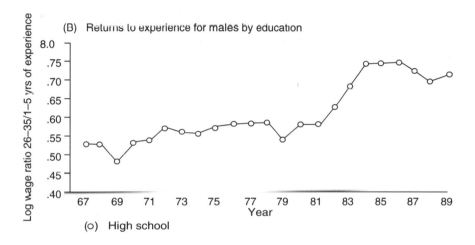

(B) Returns to experience for males by education

(○) High school

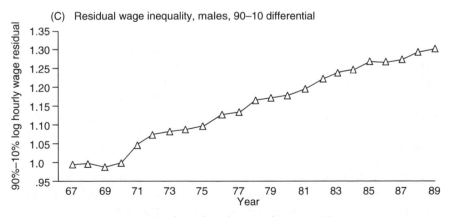

(C) Residual wage inequality, males, 90–10 differential

Figure 8.1 US relative hourly wage changes, 1967–89

in all but four advanced OECD countries: US Bureau of Labor Statistics data show that hourly compensation for production workers in manufacturing is 60 per cent higher in Germany than in the USA; 44 per cent higher in Switzerland, 22 per cent higher in Austria, for example (US Bureau of Labor Statistics 1993). But wage comparisons based on exchange rates are a poor guide to living standards across countries: exchange rates fluctuate wildly and bear only a modest relation to differences in price levels. Purchasing power parity price indices, which contrast the cost of a comparable basket of commodities across countries, offer a better way to compare earnings. On a purchasing power basis, the average American worker is paid roughly as much as the average worker in Western Europe. But given this, the fact that low-paid American workers are much further below the average than low-paid workers in other countries implies that low-paid Americans have lower earnings and living standards than low-paid workers in those countries.

I estimate that among men in the bottom decile, Americans earn roughly 45 per cent as much as Germans, 54 per cent as much as Norwegians, half as much as Italians, for example (Freeman 1994). Scaling bottom decile workers in the USA at 100, the earnings of bottom decile Europeans is 144 and those of bottom decile Japanese is 106 (see Figure 8.2). Moreover, with the greater social safety net in Europe than in the USA – more generous unemployment benefits, national health insurance, and the like – unemployed workers in advanced European countries have living standards above those of full-time, year-round, low decile US workers.

In short, something big happened in the US labour market in the 1980s (or earlier): immiseration of low-skilled male workers that parallels and perhaps exceeds the something big that happened in European labour markets in the 1980s: the rise in unemployment. The economic troubles that afflicted low-skilled European and American workers cries out for explanation. What was different about these decades than previous decades?

The globalization of the economy

One thing that distinguishes the past two decades from earlier periods is that the economies of the USA and the rest of the West became increasingly global. Between 1960 and 1990 exports plus imports over gross domestic product (GDP) more than doubled in most advanced countries. Investments expanded overseas. European and Japanese investments in the USA increased more rapidly than did US investments overseas, so that foreign assets in the USA exceeded in value US assets abroad (US Bureau of the Census 1993). By 1989, 9.3 per cent of manufacturing employment was in foreign-owned firms. There was a huge rise in immigration, largely from Third World countries into advanced OECD countries. In the USA immigration rose from 373,000 legal immigrants in 1970 (1.8 persons per thousand US population) to 643,000 in 1988 (2.6 persons per thousand). Illegal immigration was also substantial over this period, as

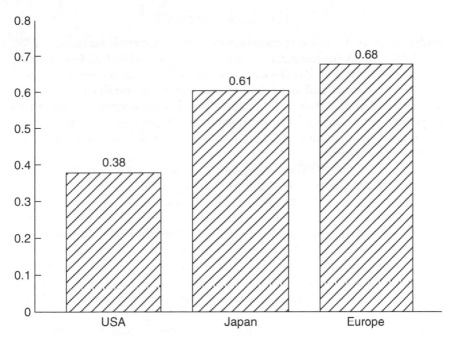

Figure 8.2(a) Pay of low-wage workers vs median earners

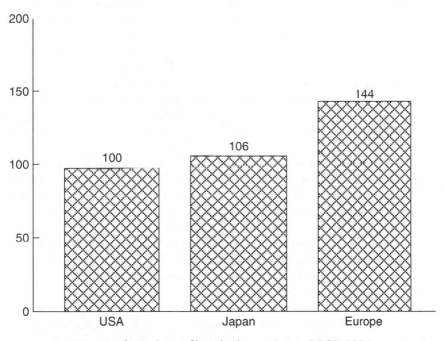

Figure 8.2(b) Real pay of low decile men (using OECD PPPs)
Sources: Calculated from OECD 1993, table 5.2, with Europe estimated as weighted
average using 1988 employment for weights, from OECD, 1990

evidenced by the 1.2 million persons granted permanant residence status in 1989 and 1990 through the Immigration and Control Act of 1986 (US Bureau of the Census 1993, Table 6). But the USA was not the leader in immigrants received per person. Canada had more immigrants and many continental European countries had sizeable growth of immigrant populations, ranging from Sweden to Germany. The collapse of the Soviet bloc and the ease of movement among European Union countries brought fears of increased immigration to many advanced EU countries.

To the extent that the West's comparative advantage lies with skilled labour – college graduates, scientists, engineers, and the like – globalization of the economy might be expected to benefit those workers relative to the less skilled. Exports would be labour-skill intensive. Imports would be unskilled-work intensive. Foreign capital investments would use Western skilled workers. Investments overseas would employ less-skilled foreign workers. Brain drain concerns notwithstanding, most immigrants would be less skilled. The bottom line would be a change in the West's implicit factor proportions favouring the more skilled, which would raise their relative earnings and reduce the real earnings of the less skilled.

There is evidence that globalization in fact operates in just such Heckscher–Ohlin ways to augment the USA's implicit relative supply of less-skilled workers. American exports are labour-skill intensive. Imports are intensive in less-skilled labour. Imports from less developed countries (LDCs), which are presumably more intensive in less-skilled labour than those from developed countries, increased as a ratio to GDP from 0.01 in 1960 to 0.03 in 1990. By contrast, US firms invest overseas in part to hire less-skilled, low-paid workers. The average education of immigrants has fallen compared to that of Americans and the earnings gap between natives and immigrants in the US job market has widened (Borjas 1992). Immigrants who work in manufacturing are over-represented in import-intensive sectors, not in export-intensive sectors (Abowd and Freeman 1991).

I have not made comparable estimates for European countries, but I would wager that the results would be quite similar. Indeed, according to Wood's (1994) calculations, North–South (i.e. advanced OECD countries and LDCs) trade has increased immensely. Exports of manufactures from the South to the North rose at 15 per cent per year in real terms from the 1950s through to the 1980s. In 1989, 53 per cent of Southern exports consisted of (light) manufacturing goods compared to 5 per cent in 1955. The factor content of exports and imports in both the North and South is consistent with trade based largely on differences in the skill mix of the work force (i.e. the North imports goods made with less-skilled labour and exports goods made with skilled labour).

What caused the increase in manufacturing imports from LDCs? Reductions in trade barriers on the part of countries contributed. So too did the shift in LDC development strategies from import substitution to export promotion. Perhaps World Bank and IMF pressures on LDCs to export to pay off debts played a part as well. Another factor is the population induced increase in the supply of (less-skilled) labour in LDCs: the LDC share of the world labour force increased from 69 per cent in 1965 to 75 per cent in 1990. In addition, the education of workers in LDCs increased substantially – in 1960, the mean years of schooling in the LDC world was 2.4 years; in 1986 it was 5.3 years. An increasing proportion of LDC workers thus have the basic skills necessary for industrial jobs, and the LDC share of world manufacturing employment grew from 40 per cent to 53 per cent from 1960 to 1986. Finally, the diffusion of technology due in part to multinational firms has put advanced countries on roughly similar production frontiers and brought modern production techniques to many LDCs as well.

But the timing and magnitude of globalization of the Western labour markets is not fully consistent with the notion that trade and immigration underlie the economic troubles of low-skilled Americans. Most trade is among developed countries, whose skilled/unskilled labour factor proportions are not particularly different. The *bête noire* of protectionist sentiment in the USA is Japan, not China or Sri Lanka; it is the loss of employment in automobiles, not in manufactures of cheap children's toys, that worries union leaders. The increase in manufacturing imports from LDCs and the rise in inequality in the USA is, moreover, not all that highly correlated. Imports from LDCs per US worker rose during the 1980s when American earnings inequality increased and the ratio of LDC imports to GDP actually fell in the decade. Estimates of the implicit labour supply in exports and imports suggest that trade shifted implicit factor proportions in the 1980s only modestly (Borjas *et al.* 1992). For Europe, the rise in unemployment and imports from LDCs seems to be more closely aligned (Wood 1994), though it does not appear that the countries with the greatest increase in joblessness, such as Spain, have experienced extraordinary trade flows.

In short, globalization of the Western economies and increased linkages with the economies of LDCs may have contributed to the economic woes of low-skill Western workers. But the gap between 'may have' and 'has' or 'is' is large, and not bridgeable with aggregate statistics on globalization and inequality. The bridging is a job for professional economists.

THEORY VS EVIDENCE

The original draft of this chapter was prepared for a conference in Washington DC held on the day Congress voted on NAFTA. At the time I thought the effect of globalization on the well-being of Western workers was one of theory vs evidence. The relevant trade theory – factor price equalization – makes a powerful case that globalization must be lurking somewhere as a major element in the travails of low-skill Western workers. By contrast, evidence based on analyses of the labour skill content of export and import sectors for the USA (Borjas *et al.* 1992) suggested only modest globalization effects in the 1970s and

1980s. Theory – yes. Evidence – up to a point, but a point closer to no than to yes. Organizing the issue in this way was, I subsequently discovered, incorrect. Trade theory offers many empty boxes in which to put one's hat; and some theorists dismiss factor price equalization as 'inherently implausible . . . an inadequate guide to reality' (Bhagwati 1993). On the empirical side, Wood (1994) presents evidence that trade with LDCs is at the core of the labour market problems of Europe and the USA. Since both the 'yes' and 'no' cases marshal theory and evidence on their behalf, it is necessary to examine the full cases that they present.

The 'yes' case – globalization lowers demand for low-skill Westerners

As the billion of people who live in East Asia and Latin America qualify for good, modern jobs, the half billion Europeans and North Americans who used to tower over the rest of the world will find their upward progress in living standards encountering tough resistance.

(Paul Samuelson, quoted in Bhagwati 1993: 7)

The argument that globalization harms low-skilled workers in the West has a common-sense appeal as well as a grounding in theory. If I can hire an LDC worker at $0.50 an hour to do the same work that a low-skill Westerner (LSW) does for $10.00 an hour, the LSW is in trouble. Whether the LDC worker is an immigrant to the West or works in my overseas plant is irrelevant: factor mobility and trade are substitute ways of getting the job done – bringing effective factor proportions and relative earnings into alignment across countries. Indeed, it is not even necessary that there be any trade or immigration: I threaten to move the plant to an LDC or to import LDC immigrants to take LSW's job unless he takes a cut in pay. In the USA such threats have been sufficiently numerous in collective bargaining to have contributed to the opposition of unionists to NAFTA. If the LSW agrees to the pay cut, presto; the invisible hand has done its job, invisibly. No trade, no immigration, but immiseration of low-skilled workers due to the threat of globalization.

There is, I want to stress, nothing peculiar about the notion that immigration and trade (or almost any other economic change that may increase GDP) harms some people. Not even manna from heaven benefits everyone – think of the poor matzoh maker whose market manna took. This point can be seen more readily in the case of immigration than trade (where we need two sectors and factors). Immigrants increase an economy's labour supply. In a two factor (capital and labour) aggregate production function world, this drives down the marginal product of labour (= wage), while increasing the marginal product of capital. With constant returns to scale the gain to capital exceeds the loss to native labour, because part of the fall in the wage is borne by the immigrants. Any change that increases the effective supply of a given factor will, all else the same, reduce its rewards. Factor price equalization implies that globalization which increases the

140

nation's effective supply of less-skilled labour reduces the incomes of the less skilled.

Is there any presumption that globalization is tending to equalize wages around the world, as suggested by Samuelson? Trade experts are divided. Jagdish Bhagwati regards factor price equalization as a theoretical curiosity, based on unrealistic assumptions. Many other trade analysts have a similar point of view, given the prima facie huge differences between wages across countries. But Leamer (1991) and Sachs and Shatz (1994) take the likelihood of factor price equalization seriously, as, apparently, does Samuelson.

There is some evidence against dismissing out of hand the proposition that an open economy creates a tendency for equalization of factor prices, at least of relative factor prices. Studies which show that differences in the human capital of the workforce across countries account for a sizeable fraction of differences in labour productivity imply some rough equalization of marginal products (at least in relative terms) and thus in rates of pay. The closer human capital comes to explaining differences in output across countries, the greater is the plausibility that wages are not all that different for similar workers (Kreuger 1968). Davis (1992) has presented evidence that trade has reduced the dispersion of industry wage differentials, suggesting that trade affects the industry rents that end up in workers' pockets. The rapid development of Korea has been accompanied by declining educational premiums which have brought wage differentials and real wages closer to those in developed countries (Kim and Topel 1994).

All of this is suggestive, not compelling. Can we do better? Start with the difference in manufacturing wages between the USA and seven LDCs that are part of the world trading community, Mexico, Korea, Hong Kong, Singapore, Brazil, the Philippines and Thailand. At current exchange rates, the ratio of wages or labour costs in these countries to the US wages in manufacturing for the median country (Brazil) is 17 per cent. But purchasing power parity price (PPP) indices show that GNP in PPP in Brazil is 1.78 times GNP in exchange rate units (World Bank 1993). In PPP terms, the wage in Brazil was 30 per cent of the US wage.

How much of this 70 percentage point difference can possibly be attributed to differences in human capital? The two biggest measurable factors are education and age. Roughly, a worker in an LDC is a 30-year-old person with 6 years of schooling, whereas the typical worker in the USA is a 40-year-old with 12 to 13 years of schooling. A 25- to 34-year-old American male with less than 8 years of schooling earned $7.64 per hour in 1990, whereas a 35- to 44-year-old with 12 years of schooling earned $13.91. One in the 35- to 44-year-old group with one to three years of college earned $17.39 (based on US Bureau of the Census 1993). Thus, Americans might be expected to earn twice as much as workers in LDCs on the basis of greater age and education. In the case of Brazil, this would double the PPP unit wage ratio from 0.30 to 0.60. Thus, 43 per cent (= 0.30/0.70) of the US–Brazil gap in earnings adjusted for purchasing power is attributable to differences in measured human capital. The results are similar for most of the other countries. For example, the ratio of manufacturing wages in Mexico to those in the USA of 0.15 rises to 0.36 using the World Bank's purchasing power adjustment; differences in educational attainment between the countries can explain roughly half of this.

There are problems with the calculations underlying this stylized contrast. Education figures for LDCs are crude; Behrman and Rosenzweig (1994) have pointed out differences in educational compositions of populations across data sets. At this stage of the analysis, the education and age data are for countries, not for manufacturing workers. The wage data are also far from ideal; manufacturing wages are based on establishment reports, which exclude small informal sector firms. They refer to all production workers, a category that includes everything from highly skilled mechanics to knitters. Purchasing power parity indices are also crude and problematic: they differ depending on source and years reported. Still, these calculations go some way towards dispelling the view that the real wages of comparably skilled workers are so different between the leading industrial country and important LDCs as to make the notion of a trend toward equalization nonsensical.

But, it might be contended, does this not run counter to direct observation? I think not, at least for the urban areas which are part of the world economy. Perhaps it is naive but when I first visited LDCs what struck me was that the upper- and middle-class persons with skills comparable to mine had more or less comparable living standards. American inner cities do not look all that different from many Third World cities; living standards of the urban poor seem more aligned around the world than they did, say, in the 1950s. Europe may have avoided this outcome through its higher social safety net, which can be viewed as a tax on highly skilled labour to maintain the living standards of less skilled labour. Moreover, given differences in infrastructure capital, including well-established rules of business operation, and in capital–labour ratios between developed and less-developed countries, there have to be substantial differences in real pay across countries. But a sizeable proportion may very well be due to differences in labour skills, which are immense. Barro and Lee (1991) estimate that roughly half of the population in developing countries have had no schooling. Perhaps differences in the real earnings of people across countries have fallen with globalization.

Until 1994 there was no serious empirical study that tried to prove that globalization is immiserating low-skill workers; then came the major study by Wood (1994). At the minimum, Wood shows what 'yes' requires to make its case. One can summarize Wood's analysis in five propositions:

1 North–South trade consists largely of manufactured goods, the basis of which are differences in the ratios of more-skilled to less-skilled labour, not differences in capital, which is completely mobile. The real value of Southern exports grew largely in the 1980s when less-skilled workers faced large drops in labour demand.

2 Declining barriers to trade, exogenous to the labour market, underlie trade flows between LDCs and the West. This means that one can take changes in trade flows as an explanatory variable for labour market developments.

3 Estimates of the factor content of trade based on sectoral labour usage in developed countries understate the effect of LDC trade on labour, because LDCs export different and non-competing goods within sectors. The 'right' counterfactual labour skill coefficients are those in developing countries, adjusted for labour demand responses to higher wages in the North. These estimates give reductions in labour demand due to imports of manufactures 'ten times the conventional ones' – suggesting a loss in economy-wide demand for unskilled labor of 5 per cent.

4 Trade with LDCs has induced substantial labour-saving innovation in the traded goods sector, that shows up in part in falling production worker shares of employment in those sectors. This has further reduced economy-wide demand for unskilled labour by 5 per cent.

Similar effects occurred in traded services and, through demand for intermediate goods, on non-traded sectors. These effects reduced economy-wide demand for unskilled labour by an additional 10 per cent.

5 The sum of all these effects is a 20 per cent fall in demand for unskilled labour, which can account for the rise of inequality in the USA and of unskilled unemployment in Europe. The growth in LDC imports in the 1980s and cross-country differences in the problems of less-skilled workers – bigger in the USA than in Japan – are consistent with the huge globalization effect.

The heart of Wood's (1994) empirical analysis is proposition (3). Using Western input ratios to measure the effect of LDC trade on demand for less-skilled labour shows only a modest effect (Borjas *et al.* 1992). But using LDC input ratios adjusted for the higher wage of unskilled workers in the North, Wood generates large effects. If the UK did not import children's toys from China, how many less-skilled workers would we use to produce those toys – as few as suggested by input coefficients in the current UK toy industry or many more? Wood opts for the latter and shows that the change in coefficients has an order of magnitude effect on the calculations.

The claims made in proposition (4) are the most problematic. Wood readily admits that they are based on a mixture of 'calculation and guesswork', with a greater weight on the latter. It is possible that employers introduced labour-saving technologies in response to competition from low-wage employers overseas, but I am more impressed by the fact that most technological advances have occurred in sectors that use skilled labour. Imports had nothing to do with the huge productivity advance in the sector that made greatest use of less-skilled workers, the coal industry, where some 50,000 miners produce as much today as 500,000 miners in the 1950s.

Wood's bottom-line proposition (5) shows that, recognizing (1) and (2), and making adjustments in (3) and (4), you indeed reach the strong 'yes' conclusion. Does Wood's book make a compelling case for yes? You should read it yourself and decide. To me it does not. Rather, what the book does is lay out the path one must follow to attribute all of the immiseration of the less-skilled to globalization. Some of the steps along the way are problematic (of which Wood is fully aware), but they are laid out sufficiently clearly that you can choose the point at which to demand more evidence or to decide for the contrary position.

The 'no' case: globalization does not harm low-skill Westerners

The most direct response to the 'yes' case is to invoke the presumption of innocent until proven guilty and then point to the gaping holes in that case. First, recall that factor content analyses of imports and exports based on extant skill coefficients show only modest effects of balanced trade on demand for labour by skill class. Wood (1994) had to use entirely different production coefficients to get a sizeable impact of trade on demand (which he then had to blow up further). There is no compelling reason to accept the adjusted coefficients over the observed coefficients. Second, the evidence from these analyses is, trade experts tell us, incomplete: if trade is causing the fall in wages of the less skilled, prices in unskilled intensive sectors should be falling (Bhagwati 1993; Leamer 1991; Lawrence and Slaughter 1993). Univariate correlations between the proportion of workers who are unskilled and price changes by sector do not show such a pattern (Lawrence and Slaughter 1993). Price determination models that take account of technological changes (faster in sectors with skilled labour) may very well find this to be the case, but so far the evidence is not there.

I am uneasy about this counter-argument, for it raises doubts not only about how trade effects relative prices, but also how technology and other factors do so. In a competitive market, declining wages (due to any possible cause) which reduce the cost of the goods they produce will, other things being equal, reduce the price of those goods relative to other goods as well. Any failure of the prices in unskilled-labour-intensive industries to drop despite falling real wages challenges not only the factor price equalization story but any other competitive market based story of the fall in demand for the less skilled, including one of the trade story's main competitors, that exogenous technology has lowered demand for less-skilled labour. My guess is that a properly specified price model would show that, controlling for technological change (which reduces the prices of goods in some skilled-labour-intensive industries such as personal computers) and for shifts in product demands, the fall in the real wages of the less skilled is associated with falls in the relative prices of the sectors which employ them. Parenthetically, the absence of such connection raises doubts not only about factor price equalization effects but also about the gains from trade as well. What is the benefit of importing children's toys from China if the price of those toys (produced by unskilled labour) is not lower than they would be in the absence of trade?

Consistent with my scepticism of these analyses, moreover, Sachs and Shatz (1994) have examined the underlying data for Lawrence and Slaughter and found significant problems. They find that trade has some effect on the demand for less-skilled labour, but not the overwhelming effect that a 'yes' response requires. In addition, the geographically concentrated aspect of globalization – immigration – is not associated with geographical differences in the well-being of less-skilled Westerners. Throughout the West immigrants are concentrated in immigrant gateway cities or areas (New York, Houston or Miami in the USA) but studies have not found that less-skilled natives do worse in those areas than in others with little immigrant flows (Altonji and Card 1991; Lalonde and Topel 1991; Card 1990, for the USA; Hunt 1992, for France). It is difficult to accept the globalization story for the entire economy without explaining this seemingly contrary cross-area evidence.

Magnitudes

Granting that 'yes' has not yet made its case, is it plausible to think that it could do so? The argument that it could not rests on the potential magnitude that even sizeable trade effects could plausibly have in a largely service sector economy.

If a large increasing proportion of Western workforces was employed in traded goods, one might expect trade patterns to have a massive effect on the relative demand for less-skilled labour. But the share of workers in traded goods has trended down as manufacturing productivity has outpaced expansion of output. I am not sure at what point one should dismiss out of hand globalization stories based on spill-overs from one sector to the aggregate workforce, but the 'yes' story has a bit of the flavour of the tail wagging the dog. If 20 to 30 per cent of the workforce is in traded goods, it is difficult to see how even large changes in that sector can drive the entire job market. Indeed, Wood (1994) had to blow up the effects of imported manufactures to the whole economy to get his bottom line 20 per cent reduction in labour demand. There has certainly been increasing trade in services, and tourism is an important component of the global economy and major employer of less-skilled workers. However, my sense is that Wood's 'blow-up' factor is too large here. I would look more for the cause of the problems of low-skill workers in the non-traded goods sector, where so many of them are employed, than in traded manufacturers. Moreover, it is hard to believe that in the future the traded goods sector can have as large an effect on the aggregate labour market as it might have had in the past.

That trade-induced shifts in demand against less-skilled workers would have to be of magnitudes greater than they appear to be in order to drive the immiseration of the less skilled can be seen in other ways. Consider displaced workers, many of whom suffer huge losses in real earnings as a result of being in the wrong job at the wrong time. Is the vast bulk of these workers displaced because of trade? No. Do those who are displaced because of foreign competition suffer more in the job market than others? Kruse (1990) shows that in fact they do, but not in sufficient magnitude to make trade-displaced labour the key economic loser in the economy. Freeman and Katz (1990) show that the effects of trade-induced changes in output on employment are no different from the effects of domestic demand induced changes in output, and the latter are far greater than the former. Finally, the first order effect of globalization is presumably on gross domestic product. The effects on relative factor incomes are second order changes in marginal products. If we observed large first order effects from changes in trade regimes, we might expect sizeable second order effects. But analyses of wildly heralded changes, such as the US–Canadian trade agreement or the Common Market, show that other factors have dwarfed their putative effects on the economy. Computable general equilibrium and related analyses of the Canadian-American free trade agreement predicted gains in employment and wages in its aftermath.

In fact Canada suffered a huge depression after the free trade agreement. This was not because of the agreement (although it did lead to manufacturing shutdowns) but because other economic forces were far more important in determining economic outcomes (Stanford 1993). The same can be said about the benefits of the Common Market, which was supposed to produce a substantial boom in Europe but which obviously did not do so. Indeed, in an autumn 1993 survey 80 per cent of businessmen in Europe responded to the question: 'Has the single market brought noticeable benefits to your company?' with a resounding No (*The Financial Times*, 9 November 1993). German reunification and policies towards the former East Germany, the collapse of the economies in transition, Bundesbank interest rate policies and many other factors seem to overwhelm the benefits of the Common Market. If changes in trade policy are not the driving force in the world economy, at least over the medium term, they are surely unlikely to be the driving force in changes in demand for less-skilled labour over the same time period.

The benefits of trade

Assume that your mandate as a policy-maker was to increase the quality of jobs in the West: more good jobs, fewer low-wage, 'bad' jobs. What might you do? Reduce trade barriers and let globalization shift the demand for workers from low-skill industries to the high-skill industries in which the Western economies have a comparative advantage? Let Mexicans, Chinese, etc., produce children's toys and let Westerners work in higher skill (value added) activities? Is not the great benefit of trade or immigration to Western workers that it creates demand or incentives for them to upgrade their skills? If it harms unskilled labour, so what? Turn them into skilled workers and they can all eat cake.

The issue hinges on how easy it is for people with limited education and blue-collar job skills to transform themselves into workers with largely white-collar (computer-oriented?) skills. If unskilled labour is highly malleable, so that the less-skilled Westerner (LSW) can compete with the less-developed country

146

(LDC) worker by upping his skills in a short time-span (whereas the LDC, who still trails the American in years of schooling by substantial amounts, cannot do so), the 'globalization leads to immiseration' argument has got it all wrong. Perhaps there is a temporary adjustment problem, but as labour supply adjusts, the net effect of trade will be to move workers from less-skilled jobs to more-skilled jobs. If, on the other hand, unskilled labor is not readily malleable – if a large proportion of the population does not have the capacity to obtain the white-collar, college-type skills that seem necessary for good jobs – the supply side solution will not work. Elasticities of supply to college and specific occupations tend to be high among young people (my stylized elasticity is 2), suggesting at the minimum that this argument has some merit over the long run. But among older workers, the record in training those displaced from blue-collar jobs for better jobs is rather poor.

There is another benefit of globalization to low-skilled workers that has not been factored into the analysis: the reduced price of commodities and higher quality or variety of goods available to them from an open economy. Before Samuelson developed the factor price theorem, Ohlin argued that the economy-wide gains from trade might in fact make the scarce factor better off (see Wood 1994). While this is not true in the usual static trade model, surely the low-skilled workers enjoy some of the benefits from trade, and the usual model could readily understate the offsetting gains if they buy 'cheap imports' more than do high-skill workers (which seems plausible). There is, finally, the possibility that greater globalization will kick off a growth spurt which benefits everyone. The power of this argument is not that we know that globalization will induce growth – even for the LDCs where an export strategy is associated with a growth spurt, no one has a clean neo-classical story as to why – but that a more rapid growth rate is probably the best cure for all economic ills. If, by some Schumpeterian creation and destruction process, or some Kreugerian–Olsonian elimination of rent-seeking behaviour, or by defensive technological progress à la Wood, globalization sparks growth, the net gain may be positive even to the less skilled who otherwise might lose.

Are the 'no' arguments compelling? If one applies the innocent until proven guilty test, I think they carry the day. But if one asks instead the betting question of whether they make the odds on 'no' exceed the equiprobable 50–50, I think not. At this level I do not find the 'no' arguments any more compelling than the 'yes' arguments.

CONCLUSION: IN LIEU OF A COMPELLING ANSWER

So I end up perplexed. In an ivory tower it is legitimate to say one is perplexed and to ask for more time or money to work out the solution, but that would be a cowardly evasion of a conclusion. So, without much confidence, let me state my current view: that globalization has probably been and will be more impor-tant in harming the position of less-skilled Americans than labour economists (myself included) have estimated. There is too much sense in the notion that globalization creates one big labour market (through factor price equalization or capital and labour mobility) and enough glimmers of evidence for me to buy the 'no' case at this time. My suspicion is that additional work on both the trade and immigration effects will lend increasing support to the 'yes' case. But, having said that, I feel the urge to backtrack – to reiterate the weaknesses of the 'yes' case. . . . But I will leave that to you, if you are so inclined.

My perplexity ends when it comes to assessing what the existing labour market situation of less-skilled workers means for Western economies. Whether the answer to the globalization question is 'yes' or 'no', the fact is that European unemployment and the falling real earnings of the low paid and the growing inequality in the USA are social disasters. Whether it is worse to have long-term unemployment among a large proportion of the population or for them to receive poverty wages I leave to your judgement. When I visited Venezuela and Columbia in the early 1970s I was shocked at the gap between rich and poor: the wealthy in their apartment buildings protected by guards carrying sub-machine guns; and the poor living a few blocks away in shanty-towns. The USA, I remember telling my South American friends, is nothing like this; doormen in the upper East Side of New York or at the Watergate in Washington DC do not carry guns. But today no American tourist would be shocked at the inequality in Caracas or Bogotá: the tourist might even ask, where are all the homeless folk, as they went from historical site to historical site?

When there is a big fire, the key thing is to put it out. Determining the causes of the conflagration is interesting and important, but should not interfere with the fire brigade pouring water on the blaze. To maintain a decent society, we have to find policies that redistribute income or jobs to our low-skilled brethren (policies that enhance the skills of the less educated can help but will hardly be adequate), regardless of what caused their economic problems. This will require policies whose first priority is job creation and economic growth rather than maintaining low rates of inflation – but that is the subject of another even more controversial chapter.

NOTE

I have benefited from the comments of Adrian Wood and Lawrence Katz. This is a modified version of a paper given at the Urban Institute Session on Policy Responses to an International Labor Market on 17 November 1993, entitled 'Is Globalization Impoverishing Low-Skill Americans?'.

REFERENCES

Abowd, J. and Freeman, R. (1991) 'Internationalization of the U.S. labor market', in J. Abowd and R. Freeman (eds) *Immigration, Trade and the Labor Market*, Chicago: University of Chicago Press for NBER.
Altonji, J. and Card, D. (1991) 'The Effects of immigration on the labor market

outcomes of less-skilled natives', in J. Abowd and R. Freeman (eds) *Immigration, Trade and the Labor Market*, Chicago: University of Chicago Press for NBER.

Barro, R. and Lee, J.-W. (1991) 'International comparisons of educational attainment', NBER Working Paper 4349, New York: NBER.

Behrman, J. R. and Rosenzweig, M. R. (1994) 'Caveat emptor: cross-country data on education and the labor force', *Journal of Development Economics* 44 (1), June: 147–72.

Berman, E., Bound, J. and Griliches, Z. (1992) 'Changes in the demand for skilled labor within U.S. manufacturing industries: evidence from the annual survey of manufacturing', unpublished paper, July, New York: NBER.

Bhagwati, J. (1993) 'Trade and wages of the unskilled: is Marx striking again?', conference paper, American Enterprise Institute, 10 September.

Blackburn, M., Bloom, D. and Freeman, R. (1990) 'The declining position of less-skilled American males', in G. Burtless (ed.) *A Future of Lousy Jobs?*, Washington DC: Brookings Institution.

—— (1992) *Changes in Earnings Differentials in the 1980s: Concordance, Convergence, Causes and Consequences*, NBER Working Paper 3901, November, New York: NBER.

Borjas, G. (1992) 'National origins and the skills of immigrants', in G. Borjas and R. Freeman (eds) *Immigration and the Work Force*, Chicago: University of Chicago and NBER.

Borjas, G., Freeman, R. and Katz, L. (1992) 'On the labor market effects of immigration and trade', in G. Borjas and R. Freeman (eds) *Immigration and the Work Force*, Chicago: University of Chicago and NBER.

Bound, J. and Johnson, G. (1992) 'Changes in the structure of wages in the 1980s: an evaluation of alternative explanations', *American Economic Review* 82, June: 371–92.

Card, D. (1990) 'The impact of the Mariel boatlift of the Miami labor market', *Industrial and Labor Relations Review* 43, January: 245–57.

Davis, S. J. (1992) 'Cross-country patterns of change in relative wages', *NBER Macroeconomics Annual*, New York: NBER.

Davis, S. J. and Haltiwanger, J. (1991) 'Wage dispersion within and between manufacturing plants', *Brookings Papers on Economic Activity: Microeconomics* 115–80.

Deardorff, A. and Hakura, D. (1993) 'Trade and wages: what are the questions?', American Enterprise Institute mimeo, 10 September.

Filer, R. (1992) 'Immigrant arrivals and the migratory patterns of native workers', in G. Borjas and R. Freeman (eds) *Immigration and the Work Force*, Chicago: University of Chicago and NBER.

Freeman, R. (1994) 'How labor fares in advanced economies', in R. Freeman (ed.) *Working Under Different Rules*, Washington DC: Russell Sage Foundation for NBER.

Freeman, R. and Katz, L. (1990) 'Industrial wage and employment determination in an open economy', in J. Abowd and R. Freeman *Immigration, Trade and the Labor Market*, Chicago: University of Chicago Press for NBER.

Hunt, J. (1992) 'The impact of the 1962 repatriates from Algeria on the French labor market', *Industrial and Labor Relations Review* 45, April: 3.

Katz, L. F. and Murphy, K. M. (1992) 'Changes in relative wages, 1963–1987: supply and demand factors', *Quarterly Journal of Economics* 107, February: 35–78.

Kim, D.-I. and Topel, R. (1994) 'Labor markets and economic growth: lessons from Korea's industrialisation, 1970–90', in R. Freeman and L. Katz (eds) *Differences and Changes in Wage Structures*, Chicago: University of Chicago Press for NBER.

Kreuger, A. (1968) 'Factor endowments and per capita income differences among countries', *Economic Journal*, September: 641–57.

Kruse, D. (1990) 'International trade and the labor market experience of displaced workers', *Industrial and Labor Relations Review* 41 (3), April: 402–17.

LaLonde, R. J. and Topel, R. H. (1991) 'Labor market adjustments to increased immigration', in J. Abowd and R. Freeman (eds) *Immigration, Trade and the Labor Market*, Chicago: University of Chicago and NBER.

Lawrence, R. and Slaughter, M. (1993) 'Trade and U.S. wages: great sucking sound or small hiccup?', MICRO–BPEA meeting, 10–11 June.

Leamer, E. (1991) *Wage Effects of a U.S.–Mexican Free Trade Agreement*, NBER Working Paper 3991, New York: NBER.

Levy, F. and Murnane, R. (1992) 'U.S. earnings levels and earnings inequality: a review of recent trends and proposed explanations', *Journal of Economic Literature*, September.

Mishel, L. and Bernstein, J. (1993) *The Joyless Recovery*, Economic Policy Institute Briefing Paper 200, Washington DC: Economic Policy Institute.

Murphy, K. M. and Welch, F. (1992) 'The structure of wages', *Quarterly Journal of Economics* 107, February: 285–326.

OECD (1990) *Employment Outlook*, Paris: OECD.

—— (1993) *Employment Outlook*, Paris: OECD.

Sachs, J. D. and Shatz, H. J. (1994) 'Trade and jobs in U.S. manufacturing', *Brookings Papers on Economic Activity* 1: 1–84.

Schmidt, J. (1995) 'The changing structure of male earnings in Britain, 1974–1988', in R. Freeman and L. Katz (eds) *Differences and Changes in Wage Structures*, Chicago: University of Chicago Press for NBER.

Stanford, J. (1993) 'Continental economic integration: modeling the impact on labor', *Annals of the American Academy of Political and Social Science*, March.

US Bureau of the Census (1993) *Statistical Abstract 1992*, Washington DC: USGPO.

US Bureau of Labor Statistics (1993) *International Comparisons of Hourly Compensation Costs for Production Workers in Manufacturing*, Washington DC: USGPO, June.

Wood, A. (1994) *North–South Trade, Employment and Inequality*, Oxford: Clarendon Press.

World Bank (1993) *World Development Report*, Washington, DC: World Bank, Tables 1 and 30.

9

CAN ECONOMICS SOLVE THE PROBLEM OF UNEMPLOYMENT?

Paul Ormerod

INTRODUCTION

Unemployment has re-emerged as a major policy issue in the Western world. Yet as I point out in my book, *The Death of Economics* (1994), conventional economics has little to offer in terms of understanding and solving the problem.

The free market, competitive model of microeconomic theory faces formidable theoretical and empirical problems. Yet proposals which call for deregulation and flexibility in labour markets are based on a belief in this model as a good approximation to reality. A familiar mode of discourse in economic debate is for a set of policies to be 'tested' by examining their impact in one of the various large-scale macroeconomic models which exist, such as the publicly available version of the Treasury model in the UK. But, whatever the economic nuance of any particular model, whether monetarist or Keynesian, such models are deeply flawed. They are unable to generate the most salient features of developed economies, namely that they grow over time. Their forecasting record, even in the very short-term, is abysmal, and the various models are still unable to agree on the effects even of simple policy changes.

A great deal of the debate on economic policy takes place around ideas and policy packages whose purpose is essentially counter-cyclical in nature. In other words, their aim is to move the economy from the recessionary to the expansionary phase of the cycle. However, as I discuss in this chapter, such policies are conceptually quite distinct from those which might generate and sustain full employment. The correlation which exists in all developed countries between growth and employment/unemployment over the course of the cycle misleads people into believing that it persists over the course of several cycles. But it does not. Unemployment in the medium and longer term essentially depends upon the social values, institutions and history of a country, and not upon technical aspects of economic policy.

PAUL ORMEROD

THE FAILURE OF CONVENTIONAL MACROECONOMIC MODELLING

The performance of contemporary macro models in understanding the behaviour of developed economies is similar to that of the seventeenth century 'science' of numerology in ascertaining whether or not Anti-Christ had arrived on earth. Totally frustrated by decades of learned effort which had made no scientific progress whatsoever, in 1690, John Owen, Chancellor of Oxford University, went so far as to state: 'Take heed of computation! How woefully and wretchedly we have been misled by it!'. This could serve as the epitaph for the discipline of economics in its current state, and an epitaph in particular for contemporary macroeconomic modelling and forecasting.

But, despite the problems, there is a large number of macroeconomic models in regular use around the world, in treasuries, central banks and in large commercial companies, almost all of which are based upon the general, shared theoretical framework of macroeconomic behaviour. The models differ in the strengths of their various linkages, which are still the source of endless discussion among applied econometricians, but the underlying approach is common to all.

A substantial amount of resources has been devoted in the past twenty years to developing and refining these models. In Europe, this has been mainly at the expense of the taxpayer, although in the USA commercial funding of the models has become the norm. But despite this effort and attention, the performance of the models is sadly lacking.

The conventional reply to this criticism is that the models are only meant to serve a short-run purpose, whether in understanding the effects of policies or in forecasting. But even on their own short-run terms, there are two major problems with conventional models. First, despite the enormous amount of resources devoted to them over the years, the different models are still unable to agree on the effects of even the simplest policy changes. Second, their short-run forecasting record is abysmal.

As an example of their use to assess the impact of policy changes, Value Added Tax (VAT) is levied on most items of consumer spending in the countries of the European Community. Macro models can be used to supply answers to the question: what would happen if the rate of VAT were changed? This very question was actually asked of the six leading macro models in Britain in an exercise to compare their structures carried out in the summer of 1993 (Church *et al.* 1993). For the purposes of the exercise, VAT was assumed to be reduced by one percentage point.

In the first instance, it seems logical that a reduction in the rate of tax on spending would lead to some reduction in the average price at which goods and services across the economy are sold. Indeed, all six models agreed that initially this would happen, but in varying degrees. A couple of models thought that average prices would fall at once by 0.6 per cent, while at the other extreme another model gave the answer that prices would hardly fall at all, by just 0.1 per cent. So the six models differed in their account of what would happen to prices as soon as the rate of VAT was changed. But at least they all agreed that prices would fall. An even bigger disagreement arises when the models trace through the consequences of a change in VAT over a period of three or four years. After four years, two of the models continue to give the answer that prices would fall, and by amounts greater than the initial impact. But one model said that by then prices would not have altered at all, while the other three answered that a reduction in VAT now would actually lead to higher prices in four years' time.

In other words, a finance minister trying to decide whether or not actually to change VAT, or a managing director trying to understand the consequences for his or her business of such a change, would be given quite different answers depending on which particular model were selected to tackle the question. In the immortal words of the salesman: ' You pays your money, and you takes your choice.'

Such disagreements among models about the empirical consequences of practical policy changes are widespread and other examples could be readily supplied, both from models of the British and of other economies. The differences in the answers provided arise from the cumulative effect of what are often small and apparently insignificant differences in the various linkages within the models. Providing a full account of the reasons for such differences can be a challenging job for the model operators in the same way that, for example, tracing connections on a complicated electrical switchboard requires skill.

In terms of forecasting accuracy, the models have a very bad track record. For example, during 1992 and 1993 alone big errors were made in forecasts. The Japanese recession, by far the deepest since the war, was not predicted. The strength of the recovery in America in 1993 was not really anticipated. In Europe, neither the turmoil in the Exchange Rate Mechanism (ERM), nor the depth of the recession in Germany were foreseen by the models.

A survey published by the Paris-based international body the Organization for Economic Co-operation and Development (OECD) in June 1993 illustrates the problem quite clearly. The forecasting records of the two major publicly funded international bodies, the OECD and the IMF, and of the national governments were compared. For the seven major world economies, the forecasts for the next year for output growth and inflation were examined. The benchmark for comparison was the naive projection that the next year's growth of output or inflation would simply be equal to this year's. In other words, this benchmark requires no knowledge of economics to produce and a forecast could be made with it by anyone who understands the elementary arithmetic of percentage changes.

Over the period 1987–92, this extremely simple rule performed at least as well as the professional forecasters in projecting the next year's economic growth rate. In terms of inflation, the rule performed as well as the OECD and IMF and slightly better than the national governments. In other words, the combined might of the macroeconomic models and the intellectual power of their operators, whether based in national governments or installed in tax-free splendour at public expense in Paris or in the IMF in Washington, could not perform any better than the simplest possible rule which could be used to make a forecast.

The record of forecasting is poor whatever the theoretical nuance of the model concerned, whether it leans towards monetarist or Keynesian properties. A survey of the accuracy of British economic forecasts, for example, carried out by the London Business School in 1993 concluded that differences over time between the predictions from the various schools of thought are very small. The striking fact to emerge from the study is that errors in forecasts are much greater than the differences between the apparently contending schools of thought. This is by no means a new discovery, but it represents valuable confirmation of previous studies over the years which have come to the same conclusion.

The best recipe for forecasting success, conclude the London Business School researchers, displaying a welcome degree of irony rare amongst economists, is to 'forecast often and forecast late'. In other words, the more forecasts which one makes during the course of the year, the greater the chance that, purely at random, one of them will prove to be reasonably accurate. By forecasting as close as possible in time to the actual period being forecast, much more information becomes available about what is likely to happen. Of course, this information is not confined by some secret code to economic forecasters. It is information in the public domain, available to anyone wishing to make an informed guess about the prospects in the immediate future.

All the problems of macroeconomic models, for example, the contradictory short-run answers different models give to the same question, the poor short-run forecasting record, the inability to trust a model on its own, exist despite the effort devoted to their maintenance and construction. And they exist despite the fact that model builders and operators, particularly in Europe where a greater proportion of their work is funded by grants from the taxpayer than in the USA, pride themselves on incorporating the latest nuances of macro-economic theory into the specification of their models.

A PERSPECTIVE ON UNEMPLOYMENT IN BRITAIN AND THE EU

Unemployment in developed economies, when examined over long periods of time, shows a number of distinct characteristics. It shows regular fluctuations, but the size of the fluctuations and the average level of unemployment around which such movements take place vary in different periods. Established patterns of behaviour can, when shocked, shift rapidly and following the shock behaviour remain irregular for some years.

These key characteristics of unemployment are seen in many data series from disciplines other than that of economics. In epidemiology, for example, epidemics such as measles and rubella often show similar features. In physiology, the initial symptoms of many acute diseases show themselves in marked changes and irregularities in previously regular rhythms of breathing. Patterns of river flows, which are crucial for agriculture in many developing economies, exhibit similar characteristics. In climatology, careful reconstructions of the earth's climate are showing a history which has the pattern of periods of stable behaviour, with fluctuations of reasonable regularity, punctuated by irregularities before a new, stable pattern emerges.

The understanding of the behaviour of such data in these scientific disciplines has been increased substantially in the past ten to fifteen years by the application of a particular analytical technique – namely, the use of very small systems of non-linear equations to comprehend the essential properties of the data being examined. (An interesting collection of such papers is available, for example, in *The Nature of Chaos*, Mullin 1993.) The realization that the underlying structure of apparently complex systems can be better understood through the application of non-linear mathematical techniques is perhaps the single most important scientific advance of the latter decades of the twentieth century. A simple graphical technique is often used in non-linear systems analysis, before any mathematics is used at all. This technique gives insights into the current problem of unemployment which faces most Western economies.

The usual way of presenting graphically the movement of a series such as unemployment over time is in a simple plot of the data (see Figure 9.1). An alternative way is to use a connected scatter plot. Figures 9.2, 9.3 and 9.4 construct a scatter plot of unemployment in any particular year against unemployment in the previous year. The resulting points are then connected together in sequence. For example, the points which link unemployment in 1992 and 1991, and 1991 and 1990 are marked on the chart, and then connected together. Such charts can provide three technical pieces of information:

- Whether the data tend to exhibit cycles over time – if so, the data in a connected scatter plot will appear in the shape of an ellipse.
- The average value around which the series fluctuates. This is the point in the centre of any ellipse which, applying technical jargon, we can call the 'attractor point' of the data. The data in the series is attracted around this point.
- The magnitude of the cycles around the attractor point – an ellipse which was very tightly drawn, for example, would imply that the data showed only small fluctuations over time.

The detection of attractor points in a rigorous way can be a difficult task involving some advanced mathematics, and it is a task which is further complicated in economics both by the relatively small number of observations which is available, and by a higher level of noise in the data than is usual in, say, the physical sciences. But presenting the data in this way can give a fresh perspective on the behaviour of a series. For example, the important role which the institutions and values of a society play in reacting to major economic shocks can be illustrated by

155

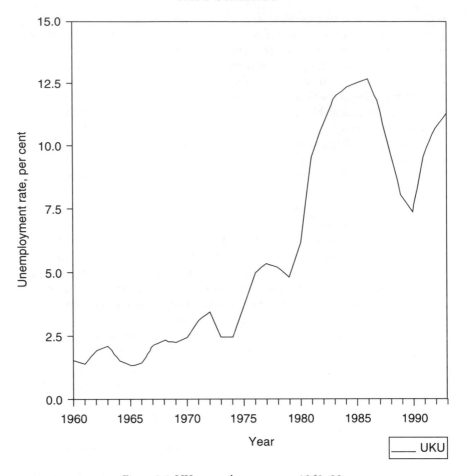

Figure 9.1 UK unemployment rate, 1960–93

presenting the data on unemployment over time in a different way than how it is usually seen.

Figure 9.1 plots the unemployment rate in the UK – defined by the official statistics – in the standard way over the period 1960 to 1993. As can be seen, unemployment was very low during the 1960s and early 1970s. The rate doubled very rapidly in the mid-1970s and then stabilized for a few years. In the early 1980s the rate once again rose rapidly and strongly, while since the middle of the 1980s unemployment has shown very marked fluctuations around a high average level.

Figure 9.2 plots these same data as a connected scatter plot. The chart is drawn up in two stages. First, unemployment in each year is plotted against unemployment in the previous year and the point is marked on the chart. For example, the point labelled 1975 on the chart tells us two things. By reading

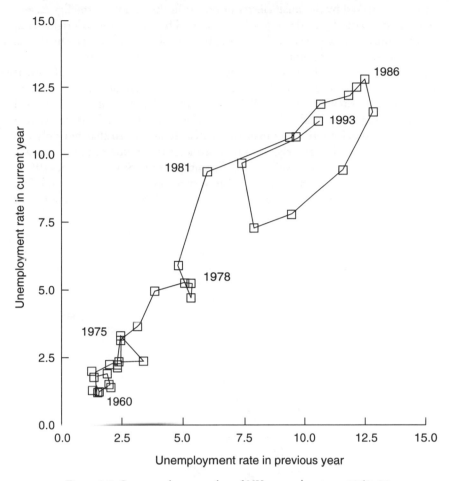

Figure 9.2 Connected scatter plot of UK unemployment, 1960–93

across the left-hand axis of the graph, we can see that unemployment in 1975 averaged around 4 per cent. Then, by reading down to the bottom axis, we see that in the year previous to 1975, in other words 1974, unemployment averaged around 2.5 per cent.

The next step to produce the graph is to connect the points together in sequence. A number of individual years are marked for convenience and arrows are used to indicate the direction of change from one point on the graph to the next.

Figure 9.2 shows that the period began with the economy moving around a low level of unemployment, marked by the points in the bottom left-hand corner. But the impact on the economy of the oil price rise of 1973–4, and the specific reactions to it, pushed unemployment higher. It began to stabilize at the end of the 1970s, marked by the small cluster of points in the middle of the figure, and then rose dramatically in the 1980–1 recession. The data at the top right-hand corner of the chart, however, are beginning to show signs of moving in an ellipse, centred on an attractor point of around 10 per cent unemployment.

For interest, Figures 9.3 and 9.4 plot West German and French unemployment in the same way and over the same period. In Germany as in Britain, unemployment was very low in the 1960s and early 1970s. The oil shock increased unemployment to around 4 per cent. But the German social market system absorbed the shock more easily than the British economy, so that not only did unemployment rise less quickly, but a new attractor point emerged more rapidly.

French unemployment exhibits a different pattern. Since the mid-1960s, unemployment rose almost inexorably. But, just recently, as in the rest of the EC, an attractor point is beginning to emerge around a high level of unemployment with large fluctuations around it.

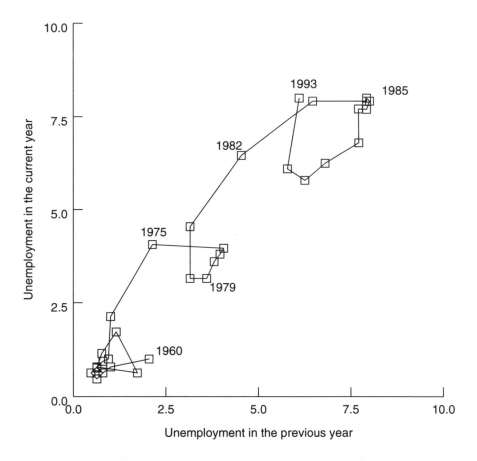

Figure 9.3 Connected scatter plot of German unemployment, 1960–93

158

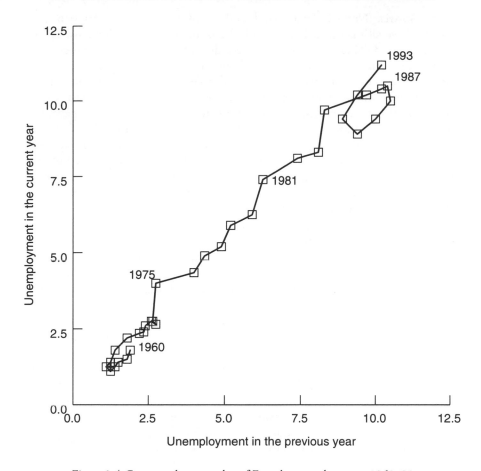

Figure 9.4 Connected scatter plot of French unemployment, 1960–93

THE ABSORPTION OF SHOCKS AND LOW UNEMPLOYMENT

The graphical approach used above highlights the facts that unemployment usually settles into periods of regular cyclical behaviour, but that it is subject to sharp shocks, following which there is no tendency for it to revert to its previous pattern of behaviour. Non-linear mathematical models can be used to describe the behaviour of an economy during periods of regular behaviour – how growth is generated and the interaction of the growth process with short-term cycles. But the response of any particular economy to shocks very much depends upon the shape of its institutions, its social values and its history.

A number of economies have preserved low levels of unemployment, not just in the 1950s and 1960s but after the 1973–4 oil shock until the present day.

159

Japan, Austria, Norway, Switzerland and, until very recently, Sweden and Finland, have all maintained very low levels of unemployment for most of the post-war period. These countries are a very diverse group in terms of their economic and social policies and are typically governed by parties of quite different ideologies. But each of them has kept unemployment low by maintaining a sector of the economy that effectively functions as the employer of last resort, which absorbs the shocks which occur from time to time and more generally makes employment available to the less skilled, the less qualified.

In Japan, the shock absorber has been the domestic service sector. Japanese manufacturing, competing in world markets, is formidably efficient, but the domestic service sector – travel, restaurants, leisure activities, and so on – employs far more people than comparable companies elsewhere in the West. The cost of the employees carrying out apparently trivial or pointless roles in restaurants, for example, appears on the customer's bill. The private service sector in Japan is by Western standards very inefficient, but it serves a valuable role for society as a whole. In the smaller European economies which have maintained low unemployment, the function of 'employer of last resort' has been carried out by the public service sector, the costs of which appear less in the expenses of private consumption than in high levels of taxation. But in both these cases, though by very different means, the electorates have been willing to pay for high employment by tolerating sectors of the economy which by the narrow standards of free market theory are inefficient.

The overall efficiency and performance of such economies has not been handicapped at all by paying the cost of their various types of social values. Japan, of course, has outstripped every other developed country in terms of growth, and the smaller European countries outside the EC – some now within the EU – have generated growth rates at least equal to those within the Community. The power of markets has been harnessed to the wider benefit of society.

ECONOMIC GROWTH, EMPLOYMENT AND UNEMPLOYMENT

The importance of a country's institutions and social values in determining the rate of unemployment can be seen not just in the different ways in which economies respond to shocks, but in the ways in which the benefits of economic growth are distributed within the economy.

Contrary to received wisdom, both of policy-makers and of orthodox economics of whatever nuance, there is little connection over time between the rate of economic growth and either the growth in employment or the rate of unemployment. Most emphatically, this does not mean that governments should cease to promote growth. But it must be recognized that growth is not necessarily a solution to unemployment. The connection between movements in output and employment over the course of the economic cycle misleads people into believing that this relationship necessarily persists over the course of several cycles. In most European countries, the proceeds of economic growth in the past twenty years have not been used to generate new jobs (in net terms), but have been appropriated by those who have remained in employment

The Spanish economy provides the most striking example of this. Since 1970, in real terms Spanish output has virtually doubled in size. Yet employment is actually lower now than it was over twenty years ago. Figure 9.5 shows the total output growth in a number of Western economies since 1970 and the corresponding change in employment. It is clear that there is no connection between economic growth and employment growth over this time scale.

The lack of connection between output growth and the labour market extends to unemployment as well. The growth rate in many Western economies from the late 1970s, once the initial impact of the oil price shock had been absorbed, has been very similar, at an average of around 2 per cent a year. Yet against this background of similar growth rates over a period of some fifteen years, unemployment rates vary very substantially across countries. France, Germany (Western), Italy, Austria and Spain all grew at an average annual rate of some 2¼ per cent in the past fifteen years. Yet unemployment averaged 9 per

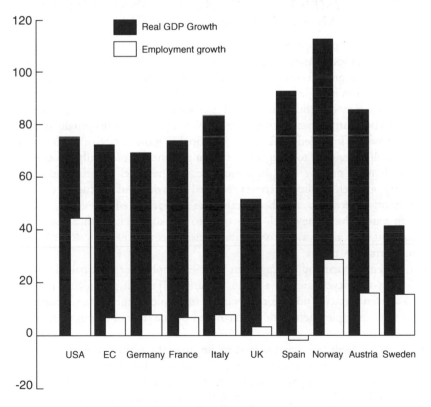

Figure 9.5 Growth and employment since 1970

161

cent in France, 6 per cent in West Germany, 9 per cent in Italy, only 3 per cent in Austria and 16 per cent in Spain.

Britain, Sweden and Switzerland – countries with governments of quite diverse attitudes to economic policy – all grew at just under 2 per cent over the same period. Unemployment averaged 9 per cent in Britain, almost 3 per cent in Sweden, and less than 1 per cent in Switzerland.

The experience of the twenty-odd years immediately following World War II misled people into believing that a rapid rate of growth is necessary to bring about low unemployment. During this period, growth was higher and unemployment lower than in the two decades following the 1973–4 oil price shock. But even in the earlier period, very low unemployment was preserved with markedly different growth rates in a number of countries. For example, unemployment averaged around 2 per cent in Germany, Norway and Britain and average annual output growth was, respectively, 5.5, 4, and 3 per cent; while despite an average growth rate of 3.5 per cent, the USA experienced an average of almost 5 per cent unemployment.

UNEMPLOYMENT AND CONVENTIONAL DEMAND AND SUPPLY SIDE POLICIES

One of the few – perhaps the only – genuine contributions made to human knowledge by orthodox macroeconomic theory is the distinction between cyclical movements in the growth of an economy and the underlying rate of growth itself. Yet this distinction is neglected in a great deal of economic policy debate.

Conventional macroeconomic demand management policy is almost invariably intended to be counter-cyclical in nature. But such policy is conceptually distinct both from policy intended to raise the sustainable growth rate of an economy and from policy designed to bring about full employment. Potentially, a successful policy of demand management, or more precisely the belief that the authorities could carry out such a policy whenever required so to do, could influence the state of long-term expectations and hence raise the proportion of any given share of profits in national income which is devoted to investment in both physical and human capital. In this way, demand management could theoretically influence the long-term growth rate.

But, in general, demand management policies simply alter the particular shape of the short-term cycle around a given underlying growth path of output and around a given attractor point for the rate of unemployment. In the medium to longer term, unemployment is not determined by the state of aggregate demand in an economy.

Newly fashionable policies designed to improve the supply side performance of the economy and, in particular, the quality of the labour force through education and training, form part of almost every goverment's plans. But it does not necessarily follow that such policies, even if successful, will succeed in reducing the average level of unemployment in any particular economy over time. Any single individual can increase his or her prospects of employment, whether moving from one job to another at a higher real wage or becoming employed in the first place, by appropriate training. But it is a fallacy of composition to suppose that such an effect will necessarily take place in aggregate if either all or even a large number of individuals increase the value of their human capital through training and education.

Successful supply side policies of this kind will increase the underlying rate of growth in the economy which is sustainable in the medium to longer term and it may therefore be sensible to try to implement such policies. They may also succeed in reducing unemployment, but whether they do or not will depend upon the effect in aggregate of the response of other individuals already in employment. The empirical evidence shows that there is no necessary connection between the longer term rate of growth of an economy and either the rate of job creation or the rate of unemployment. Given the state of long-term expectations and the associated 'animal spirits' of entrepreneurs, a certain share of profits in national income will be required in order to validate a particular path of underlying economic growth.

But the division of the resulting share of wages among the population of working age who wish to participate in the labour force, as between the employed and the unemployed, is a separate and distinct question. It is entirely possible, as the experience of Western Europe over the past twenty years shows, for the employed to operate in aggregate as a cartel and to appropriate the entire proceeds of economic growth, to the exclusion of the unemployed. Of course, in practice there are not two homogeneous groups, the employed and the unemployed, and individuals do move between the two, but it is helpful in terms of an analytical framework to interpret the European experience in this way.

EUROPE, THE USA AND FLEXIBILITY

It is perhaps appropriate at this stage to comment on the different experiences of Europe and the USA in the past twenty years. At first sight the US labour market appears to have performed better than such markets in the countries of the EU. Figure 9.5, for example, shows that over the course of the past two decades, while the total numbers in employment in the EU have risen by only 7 per cent, in the USA the corresponding increase has been no less than 45 per cent. At present, the measured rate of unemployment in the USA is below 7 per cent, while in Europe it is over 10 per cent.

An important debate at present in Europe about employment centres on the desirability or otherwise of deregulating labour markets and reducing the level of involvement by the state. Much of the conventional wisdom of economics ascribes the apparently poor European performance to a lack of flexibility in the labour market, particularly with respect to wages, and to a lack of incentive to move out of unemployment caused by both the level of benefits relative to wages and to the length of time for which unemployment benefit is paid.

In a very limited sense, conventional economics has moved on from the last period of high unemployment, the 1930s. Then, the orthodox had a stronger belief that the self-adjusting tendencies – whatever they might be – were already sufficiently powerful to guarantee that full employment would eventually be restored in the absence of government intervention.

In the 1990s the solution offered is one of the state intervening in order to remove obstacles to the workings of the free market. Economics has a strong faith that if the market economies of Europe can be moved closer to the ideal world described in free market theory, unemployment will fall. (This is not the place to discuss the very serious problems which exist with the free market theoretical model itself. These are discussed, for example, in Ormerod 1994 and in an article by Arrow 1994, who did more than anyone to establish a more mathematically rigorous theoretical foundation for orthodox competitive theory in the 1950s.)

The contrast between the USA and Europe is held to be a vindication of this latter point. The American economy has indeed created many more jobs than the EU economies, but it has needed to do so because the supply of labour has expanded more rapidly.

These two points are in fact linked analytically. Essentially, the USA operates a policy of open borders for the migration of labour. From time to time the authorities attempt with varying degrees of effort to keep out immigrants, but for all practical purposes anyone who wishes to enter the USA to work can do so. The Clinton administration has recently, for example, offered to regularize the status of millions of illegal residents. Almost all the inflow of labour into the USA is from Third World economies – indeed the USA has a major border with Mexico which is a Third World economy. Such people are willing to work for what are, by Western standards, very low wages. This low wage employment makes up most of the increase in employment in the USA.

A byproduct of this situation has been that many unskilled Americans have rejected the low wages which are on offer and have chosen crime as a career instead. But the main point of relevance here is that American labour markets have been flexible because of the supply of millions of workers from Third World countries. Arguments about the Social Chapter in Europe are very much a second order issue in terms of the flexibility of labour markets. By far the most effective way to bring about flexibility in the American sense to the labour markets of Western Europe would be to open the borders to migration from Eastern Europe and North Africa. Without such a policy, European labour markets, even in Britain, will remain qualitatively different from those in the USA. However, whatever judgement is formed on the desirability or otherwise of the economic effects, it is highly unlikely that an open border policy would command the support of West European electorates and is hence not a practical option.

Overall, the contrasts between the American and European labour markets reflect the different social values of the two systems to a far greater extent than does the organization of markets for goods and services. As John Hicks recognized in his last work (1969), in which he recanted many free market views, labour markets are different in principle from those markets he describes as belonging to the 'mercantile economy'. The labour market is fundamentally hierarchical: 'a relation based partly on force, but partly upon its own variety of ethical sentiment, loyalty on the one side, responsibility on the other'.

CONCLUSION

A system of economic relationships has been built up in many Western economies, deriving from the response of social institutions and of the general social fabric to major economic shocks, which now prevents the achievement of full employment through conventional economic policies, whether Keynesian, monetarist, or supply side.

Conventional economics, in so far as the effects of its policy prescriptions are understood – which given the record of macroeconomic models is at the very least debatable – is essentially concerned with policies which are counter-cyclical in nature. These are conceptually different from policies for sustainable full employment. The real challenge facing policy-makers is not to move the economy around the present attractor points of unemployment which exist in Europe. It is to shift the attractor points themselves sharply downwards.

The average rate of unemployment in the long run – the attractor point in the figures – is ultimately not a question of technical economic policy, but of social values. Japan and some of the smaller European economies have succeeded in maintaining low unemployment because of their willingness to pay the costs associated with a sector of employment of last resort, be it public or private. Whatever the motives of individuals in employment in the EU, their behaviour in aggregate has meant that they form a cartel which excludes the unemployed from the benefits of economic growth. It is this cultural attitude which must shift if unemployment is to be lowered permanently.

Economic policy-makers have become accustomed to being presented with detailed checklists of policies of the form: 'change taxes by x per cent, public spending by y per cent, interest rates by z per cent', and so on. While it is important to avoid serious mistakes in the design of such polices, they are essentially counter-cyclical rather than policies for full employment.

Policy-makers have far less control over the social attitudes and values which are so important to the creation and preservation of low unemployment. But encouragement can be given to the revival of the long-run trend expressed by Western Europeans over many decades, temporarily halted in the 1980s, towards substituting leisure for work. This is the direction which is required for full employment.

REFERENCES

Arrow, K. (1994) 'Problems mount in application of free market theory', *Guardian*, London, 3 January.

Church, K. B. *et al.* (1993) 'Comparative properties of models of the UK economy', *NIESR Review*, August.

Hicks, J. (1969) *A Theory of Economic History*, Oxford: Clarendon Press.

Mullin, T. (ed.) (1993) *The Nature of Chaos*, Oxford: Clarendon Press.

Organization for Economic Co-operation and Development (OECD) (1993) *Economic Outlook*, June, Paris: OECD.

Ormerod, P. (1994) *The Death of Economics*, London: Faber and Faber.

10

BUILDING FULL EMPLOYMENT WITHOUT LOW PAY

Chris Pond

INTRODUCTION

Throughout most of the past fifteen years, the prevailing wisdom has been that there is a cruel but inevitable trade-off between the quality and the quantity of jobs that an economy can generate. The higher the wage offered and the more generous the conditions of employment, the fewer jobs that will exist. This has been the underlying justification presented by ministers in Conservative government in the 1980s and 1990s for a systematic policy of reductions in pay and conditions of employment. The policy has resulted in a sharp increase in the numbers earning low wages and in a growth of wage inequality which, it has been asserted, is the major cause of the increase in relative poverty during the 1980s (Goodman and Webb 1994).

Although this justification for low-wage employment has seeped into the public consciousness as an irrefutable fact, it is a relatively recent historical phenomenon. The original constitution of the ILO, formulated three-quarters of a century ago, included among its principle objectives 'the prevention of unemployment (and) the provision of an adequate living wage' (ILO Constitution, Versailles, 1919). The notion of a quality/quantity trade-off in employment is historically, ideologically and geographically specific, as this chapter will demonstrate. It is also mistaken.

EMPLOYMENT POLICY: THE CURRENT DEBATE

The 1994 and 1996 Jobs Summit in Detroit and Lille respectively, provided a forum for debate about the very different approaches to future employment policy. On one side of the debate are most members of the European Union (EU), together with Japan, arguing that social protection and fair employment measures are essential prerequisites for economic prosperity. On the other, somewhat isolated, is the UK government which believes that deregulation is necessary to ensure the dynamism and flexibility that will create employment. Their erstwhile allies, the Americans, under the Clinton administration moved from the deregulationist camp closer to the European approach, believing in a partnership between economic and social progress.

Although the USA has created proportionately far more jobs than the EU in recent years, there is now recognition that this growth is the result of almost zero productivity increase and that the jobs created are generally poorly paid and insecure, 'lousy jobs' as some US economists describe them. Speaking at a European Commission Conference on Employment in autumn 1993, US Labour Secretary Robert Reich reported that the USA now faced two jobs crises: the first was the quality of jobs; the second the quantity. The American people's traditional confidence in progress, he explained, had been damaged by the experience of the 1980s, making them less willing to accept change, to take risks or to exhibit the flexibility that modern economies require. He raised the question in Detroit: 'Are the citizens of advanced economies condemned to choose between, on the one hand, more jobs which pay less and less, or good jobs but high levels of unemployment accompanying those good jobs?'

This view was echoed by Howard Davies, then Director General of the CBI, in a lecture to the Manchester Business School, in which he warned about the consequences of the widening divisions within the labour market and society. He pointed out that the incomes of the poorest households had declined by 14 per cent during the 1980s, while those of the highest income groups had increased by 62 per cent and suggested that government and industry needed to rethink their attitudes to training, child care, benefits and working practices.

THE EUROPEAN MODEL VS DEREGULATION

Throughout the 1990s the USA and the UK both pursued, with some vigour, the policy of labour market deregulation, arguing that 'the upward trend in EC unemployment . . . is evidence of inflexibility in and over regulation of, labour markets' (HM Treasury/Department of Employment 1993).

As a result the UK is now the least regulated economy in the EU. With the abolition of the wages councils in August 1993, Britain is the only country in Europe without legal pay protection for the poorest and the only country in the EU without legal limits to working hours and without a statutory right to paid holidays for employees. British employees have less protection against unfair dismissal and fewer rights in redundancy than citizens of any other European country. Expenditure on social protection is lower, as proportion of GDP, than in most other member states (Low Pay Unit 1993).

The impact of this policy of deregulation is evident. Britain has a higher proportion of its workforce earning less than the Council of Europe's 'Decency Threshold' than any other EU member state. The pay gap between men and women is wider in Britain than in most other EU countries and is expected to widen further since the abolition of the wages councils. Britain has longer working hours for full-timers than any other member state, as well as the highest proportion of the workforce working part-time (with the exception of the Netherlands). Although the UK was the only country to argue against Commission proposals for the protection of children and young people at work, one-third of the EC's working children are UK citizens. Low Pay Unit research suggests that three-quarters of those children in Britain are employed illegally (Pond and Searle 1990).

Some other member states within the EU have accused the UK of pursuing a strategy of 'social devaluation' through these policies, seeking to increase competitive advantage by reducing the living standards of its own citizens. Indeed, the Department of Trade and Industry has been advertising in the news-papers of other member states, encouraging firms to take advantage of Britain's low wages by investing in the UK. Although the widening disparity in incomes makes comparisons of averages hazardous, a recent European Commission Report suggested that average wealth per head was lower in the UK than the Community average, despite longer working hours and a higher workforce participation rate. The European Commission has concluded that the UK is now one of 'the poorer countries of the Community', alongside Portugal, Greece, Spain and Ireland (1991). Britain now accounts for one-quarter of all the European Community's poor. Deregulation has also left the UK as one of the lowest paid economics within Europe. According, again, to the Commission:

> Average labour costs in manufacturing in the highest cost UK region, the South East, were some 35 per cent below the average level in Germany in 1988 and around 15 per cent below the level in Northern Italy or France, outside Paris.
>
> This means that the level was similar to that in the South of Italy. Labour costs in most other parts of the UK were therefore significantly lower than in the Southern Italian regions – in Northern Ireland some 30 per cent lower.

> (European Commission 1993a)

THE COST OF THE DEREGULATION STRATEGY

Despite the low level of wages, Britain is relatively uncompetitive. This is because productivity is low, pushing unit labour costs (the amount of labour cost for each unit of production) in the UK to a level very much higher than the EC average. As the EC (1993b) Delors White Paper explains: 'Unit labour costs depend on wage and non-wage costs compared with labour productivity. Such high labour costs can be compensated for by high productivity to maintain competitive advantage.' Conversely: 'Poor education, lower skill levels, lower levels of capital investment overall and inadequate infrastructure can all offset the possible advantage to be derived from low wages.'

In part, Britain's low level of productivity is a result of long working hours and poor conditions of employment. Staff turnover and absenteeism are high by European standards and training is poor. These factors are directly related to the low wages themselves: the undervaluation of any factor of production will lead to its inefficient use. Employers have no incentive to invest in training if labour is cheap and readily available. Indeed, any firm that attempts to pursue a high training–high investment strategy risks being undercut by others seeking short-term competitive advantage by cost cutting.

As a result, despite the low level of wages and poorly regulated labour market in the UK, the male unemployment rate is amongst the highest in the EU, albeit disguised by a high female part-time participation rate. The record on job creation has not been impressive, as the Delors White Paper demonstrated: between 1970 and 1992 the UK saw employment growth of only 3 per cent. Germany created 11 per cent more jobs over the period, proportionately almost four times as many as the UK, while France created 6 per cent more jobs, twice as many as the UK. Italy created 18 per cent more jobs, six times as many as the UK. Deregulation has not allowed Britain to create employment and it has certainly not delivered prosperity. It has helped create a situation in which 40 per cent or more of the UK workforce are employed on a part-time, temporary or casual basis, or are classed as freelance or self-employed. Consumer confidence, essential for economic recovery, is one of the first casualties of such uncertainty. The policy of labour market deregulation has left the British economy in a fragile and unstable condition which has reduced its ability to recover from recession.

ECONOMIC SUCCESS AND FAIR EMPLOYMENT

The philosophy of deregulation is a relatively recent economic phenomenom. Winston Churchill established Britain's minimum wage system, which was finally abolished in 1993: 'We believe that decent conditions make for industrial efficiency and increase rather than decrease competitive power' (Churchill 1909). He also argued that, without minimum wage regulation 'the good employer is undercut by the bad and the bad employer is undercut by the worst' (House of Commons 1909).

Harold Macmillan (later Lord Stockton) was leader of the Conservative Party in 1966 when he welcomed the passing of a 'fair wages provision' as 'the protector, certainly of the standard of living of the workers, but also the standards of competence and honour of industry as a whole'. In a phraseology that might seem rather relevant in today's debates, Macmillan went on: 'There was a time when the Treasury forced so stringent an economy upon Departments that it was the Departments which were seeking always to find the little undercutting employer as a contractor . . . it was the people inside the Treasury who were always scrapping to see whether they could obtain some small advantage by placing their contracts at some slightly lower price with second or third rate contractors' (Rt Hon. Harold Macmillan MP, House of Commons 1946).

By contrast, the approach of the present government is to assume a trade-off between social justice and economic prosperity. Yet the argument at a European level and now implicitly accepted by most members of the G7, is that the quality of employment is almost as important as the quantity. Indeed, the argument runs that employment conditions and social protection are an essential pre-requisite for economic prosperity and sustainable employment growth. The arguments are based on sound economic principles:

1 Inequality is not only socially divisive but economically wasteful. It prevents many citizens from fulfilling their potential or making a full contribution.
2 Short-term competition based on cost cutting undermines investment and training or better techniques of production, damaging productivity, raising unit labour costs and reducing competitiveness.
3 Social expenditure is also a form of social investment, enhancing the stock of human capital and creating a climate of stability.
4 Partnership and solidarity improve productivity by reducing conflict and tensions within industry and the wider economy.
5 Uncertainty is the enemy of flexibility. Without protection for their employment and living standards, people are less willing to take risks and accept change.

From the point of view of the individual firm, an environment of decent employment conditions, encouraging partnership and co-operation, makes good business sense. Many of the arguments that apply at the macroeconomic level also apply at the level of the individual firm. Productivity is enhanced, not least by a reduction in staff turnover and absenteeism, in firms where staff feel valued and enjoy security and comfortably adequate living standards. As Peter Brannen, London Director of the ILO, pointed out: 'The poor are neither good producers, nor good consumers' (1994).

Flexibility is essential in the modern dynamic and very competitive economic environment. On this the G7 agree. However, flexibility requires that employees have sufficient security and certainty to accept the changes that are inevitably necessary to meet the challenges of this competitive environment. Flexibility which is based solely on the employer's terms is unlikely to encourage such will-ingness to accept change. Moreover, as the Japanese warned in their presentation to the 1994 G7 Jobs Summit: 'excessive mobility of workers discourages incentives to enhance human resource development by enterprises'.

As some firms are beginning to realize, quality employment also gives them a competitive advantage. During the 1980s, many firms recognized that identification with environmental issues contributed to their commercial success. In the 1990s the emphasis appears to be changing towards an awareness of the importance of fair employment practices as a means both of enhancing corporate image and gaining competitive advantage. This development seems to have taken place despite, or perhaps because of, central government moves towards labour market deregulation. It appears that not all firms are comfortable with an environment in which competition is solely based on cost. Productivity, customer service, quality and delivery all seem to enter the equation. These factors are inextricably linked with the conditions of employment. It may be that during the 1990s we shall see the development of 'social consumerism'. For many

171

years, consumers have expressed their views about Third World issues (South African grapes, Chilean oranges, carpets made using child labour). This trend now seems to be developing a domestic dimension. Those firms who can show themselves to be treating their employees well may see this reflected not only in the quality of service to customers, but in customer loyalty in return.

THE CASE FOR A MINIMUM WAGE

Individual firms may decide to pursue a quality employment strategy in order to enhance their own competitive position. The ILO's original constitution of 1919 called for an adequate living wage and a limit to working hours. Paradoxically, this limit was set at 48 hours a week, the number proposed by the European Commission but still opposed by the UK government as unrealistic three-quarters of a century later. Yet both the EC and the ILO were preceded by an individual employer, Henry Ford, who in 1914 introduced a maximum 48-hour working week in his own plants, while increasing the minimum wage to an unprecedented $5 (£1) a day (quoted in Quennell and Quennell 1934).

Firms who are in a powerful position, having some control over both the labour and product markets in which they operate, may be able to maintain a quality employment strategy. Yet Churchill's warning that, without some element of regulation, 'the good employer is undercut by the bad and the bad employer is undercut by the worst' remains potent. Smaller firms, or those in a highly competitive market position, may be forced by circumstance to pursue a short-term, cost-cutting approach (for a fuller explanation see Craig *et al.* 1982).

One of the principle arguments for a national minimum wage is asserted in the UN Universal Declaration of Human Rights (Article 23 (3)): 'everyone who works has the right to just and favourable remuneration ensuring . . . an existence worthy of human dignity'. In this sense a minimum wage is a means of ensuring the provision of a basic human right, which might not otherwise be delivered through an unregulated labour market. The Council of Europe's Social Charter (which the UK signed in 1965 and which must be distinguished from the EU Social Charter which the UK has never signed) provides for all citizens the right to 'fair remuneration'.

A minimum wage could also fulfil an important role in tackling poverty. As a recent study by the Institute for Fiscal Studies has pointed out: 'The gap between those who earn the most and those who earn least in the UK is growing rapidly and in 1992 was higher than it had been at any time this century. It is one of the major factors underlying the rise in inequality of household income and in poverty levels' (IFS 1994).

However, a minimum wage should also be seen as an instrument of economic policy, helping to achieve not only social justice but also prosperity. It is the centrepiece of a re-regulation strategy. In consideration of full employment, the inevitable question is whether a national minimum wage would create or destroy jobs.

WOULD THE MINIMUM WAGE COST JOBS?

The government has argued that a minimum wage would result in the loss of up to two million jobs, thirteen times as many as that predicted by the CBI. However, an internal Treasury document warned that this estimate was based on assumptions that were 'wholly arbitrary' and 'without empirical basis' (see Pond 1985). Overall, a minimum wage set at half average earnings would add less than 1 per cent to the nation's wage bill. Before the 1992 General Election, Industrial Relations Services (IRS) carried out a survey of 527 firms, asking them the likely impact of a minimum wage set at £3.40 (the previous figure equivalent to half average earnings):

- nearly two-thirds (60.7 per cent) said there would be no increase in their organization's pay bill;
- almost a third (30.2 per cent) said that it would add less than 5 per cent to their pay bill;
- almost two-thirds predicted no impact on differentials, while a fifth anticipated only a limited impact;
- of the firms surveyed 85.7 per cent did not foresee their organization reducing the numbers employed.

No one denies that firms who currently muddle along, surviving only by paying poverty wages to their staff, may find it difficult to meet the costs of the minimum wage in the short term, but as IRS concluded, on the basis of their survey: 'Although some job losses would result from the proposal to introduce a minimum wage at £3.40 an hour, they are unlikely to be large scale and will probably be far more limited than government predictions would suggest' (IRS 1992).

The National Institute of Economic and Social Research estimated before the last election that the loss might be limited to just 4,000 jobs, but more recent evidence suggests that the minimum wage could, in fact, create jobs: 'Minimum wages significantly compress the distribution of earnings and, contrary to conventional economic wisdom but in line with several recent US studies, do not have a negative impact on employment. If anything, the relationship between minimum wages and employment is positive' (Dickens et al. 1993). The 'recent US studies' referred to have shown that minimum wages either have insignificant negative or substantial positive effects on employment. Indeed, the substantial drop in the value of the US minimum wage during the 1980s was accompanied by a rise in unemployment among the unskilled.

HOW CAN WE COMPETE WITH THE NEW TIGERS?

Despite powerful evidence to the contrary, ministers continue to assert that Britain and Europe must accept a lowering of wages and social standards in order to compete with the newly industrializing economies of the Pacific Rim and Eastern Europe. Such an approach is devastating in its potential social consequences and misguided in its approach to economics. An analysis published in the *New York Times* (1993) showed the hourly cost to employers per industrial worker, including wages, benefits and taxes in the main industrialized countries in 1992:

- Germany was at the head of the chart, with labour costs of $26.90 an hour;
- Sweden followed with $24.6, followed by the Netherlands at $21.64;
- Japan and Italy, each at around $4.19 per hour, were followed by France at $17.79;
- the USA was a little ahead of Spain, with respective costs of $15.89 and $14.70;
- Britain lagged just below Spain at $14.61 an hour;
- Taiwan and South Korea followed, with $5.19 and $4.93 respectively.

Although the data for Taiwan and South Korea, drawn from a separate survey, are not strictly comparable with the other data, the scale of the gap between the UK as the lowest cost nation in the older industrialized world and the newly industrializing countries is clear. To compete on the basis of low wages alone would mean cutting UK labour costs to nearly one-third of their present level. As the European Commission White Paper pointed out:

> Compared with newly industrialising countries, particularly those just entering that path such as China, the differential in labour cost is too great for any significant employment gains to be made in Europe from wage reductions in manufacturing industry. Only high productivity and superior products will enable Europe to maintain a competitive advantage
>
> (European Commission 1993c)

Moreover, the argument that Europe must somehow defeat attempts by the newly industrializing nations to grow by trying to undercut them on wage costs ignores both the theory of comparative advantage and the lessons of economic history. Such development creates enormous opportunities for trade and increases in global economic activity. Even if Europe's share of world trade and income diminishes, the absolute level will inevitably increase, as the White Paper acknowledges: 'The presence of new vibrant economies in Asia and, soon, in eastern Europe constitutes a huge opportunity and not a threat to our standard of living.'

The argument has also been put effectively by Professor the Lord Desai (1993):

> Although wage levels are very much the object of attention, they are not of central importance. A pair of trainers carrying a label known world-wide and manufactured in East Asia which retails in our high streets has wage costs in manufacture which represent less than 10 per cent of their price. The original designer, perhaps of European origin, commands a

comparative proportion of that price. The product is made in East Asia but is created in Europe and it is creativity where Europe has the advantage.

A STRATEGY FOR GOOD JOBS

Employment policy debate during the 1980s and the first half of the 1990s has been dominated by the assertion that job creation depended on a reduction in the real and relative level of pay, especially for low-skilled groups of workers. While the UK government's enthusiasm for labour market deregulation has been mildly infectious, the concept has failed to persuade the great majority of European partners. As the European Commission's Green Paper on Social Policy (1993c) emphasized:

> It is important to underline that high standards of social protection have been a contributory factor in Europe's economic success in the past. Many would argue that high social standards should not be seen as an optional extra, or a luxury which can be done without once times get hard, but rather as an integral part of a competitive economic model. The debate between this view and those who argue that Europe's present level of social standards have become unaffordable goes to the heart of the issue.

The argument is not confined to the twelve economies of the European Union. The G7 Jobs Summit of Spring 1994 reflected the general belief that social justice was a prerequisite to economic prosperity, not an alternative to it. Similarly, pressures are mounting for the implementation of a social clause in the current round of GATT negotiations to ensure that standards of employment and social protection are enhanced by world trade, rather than diminished by it. Although sometimes presented as a form of hidden protectionism, the purpose is to ensure fair competition between nations and to use trading relationships to exert upward pressure on social standards, thereby increasing the overall level of economic efficiency.

By contrast, the UK's Conservative government continues to argue the case for labour market deregulation, a policy it would happily export to Eastern Europe and the former Soviet Union, despite the sad and sorry experience of this policy in Britain itself. Our partners in Europe, meanwhile, perceive this as a policy of social devaluation, seeking to compete by reducing the wages and living standards of UK citizens.

There is an alternative: it is to pursue a strategy designed to create quality employment, with economic activity based on high wages and high productivity, a partnership approach to industry and the provision of secure and well-rewarded jobs that encourage flexibility and willingness to adapt to the changing circumstances of a modern economy. As part of an overall strategy to create full employment, such a policy could deliver both economic prosperity and social justice.

175

REFERENCES

Brannen, P. (1994) *Mobile Capital, Unfree Labour: Economic Development and Social Justice – an ILO Perspective*, London: Policy Studies Institute, 25 May.

Churchill, W. (1909) *Liberalism and the Social Problem*, London: Hodder & Stoughton.

Craig, C., Jamling, R., Rubery, J. and Wilkinson, F. (1982) *Labour Market Structure, Industrial Organization and Low Pay*, Cambridge: Cambridge University Press.

Desai, Lord (1993) *The Independent*, 24 June.

Dickens, R., Machin, S. and Manning, A. (1993) *The Effects of Minimum Wages on Employment: Theory and Evidence from Britain*, London: London School of Economics, Centre for Economic Performance.

European Commission (1991) *Final Report of the Second Poverty Programme*, Brussels: EC.

—— (1993a) *Employment in Europe*, Brussels: EC.

—— (1993b) *Growth, Competitiveness and Employment*, Delors White Paper, Brussels: EC.

—— (1993c) *European Social Policy: Options for the Union*, Green Paper on Social Policy, Brussels: EC, November.

Goodman, A. and Webb, S. (1994) *For Richer, For Poorer: The Changing Distribution of Income in the United Kingdom, 1961–1991*, London: Institute for Fiscal Studies, June.

HM Treasury/Department of Employment (1993) *Growth Competitiveness and Employment in the European Community*, London: HMSO, September.

House of Commons (1909) *Hansard*, October.

—— (1946) *Hansard*, May.

Industrial Relations Services (IRS) (1992) *Pay and Conditions Survey*, London: IRS, 25 March.

Institute for Fiscal Studies (IFS) (1994) *What's Happened to Wages?*, London: Institute for Fiscal Studies, June.

Low Pay Unit (1993) *Deregulation: Britain Pays the Price*, London: Low Pay Unit.

New York Times (1993), 9 August.

Quennell, M. and Quennell, C. H. B. (1934) *A History of Everyday Things: 1851– 1934*, London: Batsford.

Pond, C. (1985) *No Return to Sweatshops*, London: Low Pay Unit.

Pond, C. and Searle, A. (1990) *The Hidden Army*, London: Low Pay Unit.

11

REGULATION VS DEREGULATION

Which route for Europe's labour markets?

David Marsden

INTRODUCTION

It is widely argued that one of the main causes of the current high levels of persistent unemployment, especially in the European Union, lies in excessive regulation of labour markets. Much of the debate about labour market regulation is made unduly confusing because the main arguments and policies proposed are more relevant to some sections of the labour force than to others. To help cut through the confusion, I propose to divide the active labour force into three main groups, roughly according to their level of pay. The first consists of a low-wage, and mostly low-skill and low-productivity section; the second of skilled blue-collar and junior professional workers on middle pay levels; and the third, of managerial and higher professional workers on higher incomes. Indeed, this might be illustrated by a rather simplified diagram, dividing the labour force into three income levels, A to C (see Figure 11.1).

All three sections are relevant to the jobs debate. Section A concerns employment of low-productivity, low-skilled workers. Section B is often thought of as the critical section of the labour force (skilled and professional) because its productivity, quality, skills, and innovation are the key to firms' international competitiveness, and thus to jobs overall in the economy. In section C, that of managerial and higher professional groups, incentives may be important to encourage initiative and risk-taking.

There is inevitably some over-simplification in this picture. For example, for some groups low pay is the result of discrimination rather than low skill, and many groups may span two sections. However, the primary aim is to classify the employment effects of the deregulation and regulation approaches.

This chapter tries to assess the implications of deregulation for incentives for each group. It also contrasts the individualistic approach to incentives of the 'deregulation school' with the problems of promoting co-operative work relations and information sharing. A contrast is drawn between the British and German/Dutch models, arguing that the latter achieve better co-operation in

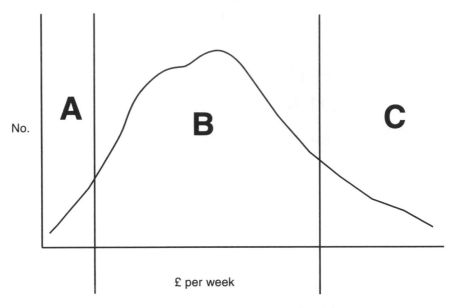

Figure 11.1 Three broad, schematic 'sections' of the labour market

the workplace, and that both have more flexibility to respond to economic shocks than is widely supposed by the deregulators. Nevertheless, not all labour market regulations are good for jobs in either the short or the long run, and a framework is needed in which change can be discussed and agreed.

THE ARGUMENTS FOR DEREGULATION

The impact on low-paid workers

A great many of the unemployed lack vocational training and skills (Pencavel 1994) and are especially vulnerable to being priced out of work by minimum wages or collective agreements, which set pay at too high a level for them to be attractive to employers. Workers at any level of skill can price themselves out of work, but the problem is more acute for the low skilled. Employers can more easily find ready substitutes for their labour as the unskilled tasks can more easily be reallocated to skilled workers than the reverse and it is easier to substitute machines for simple tasks than those requiring judgement and discretion (for a review of the empirical evidence, see Hamermesh 1993).

Apart from the low skilled, many low-paid workers are young and receiving some kind of training, often largely at the employer's expense. Such training is costly: even 'sitting by Nelly' will distract her from her own work while she instructs a new recruit. Thus the employment costs of trainees usually well exceed their earnings, especially early on. For skills which are easily transferable to other firms, employers face the risk of losing their investment should the trainee leave. According to Becker (1975) under competitive conditions firms will be more ready to provide such transferable training the more trainees share the cost, which is normally in the form of a low rate of pay, such as that of apprentices. However, the more external regulations push up trainee pay levels, the more costly training is to employers, making them less willing to hire school leavers and other trainees.

Restrictions on firms' ability to lay off workers may also discourage them from hiring. This argument is of greatest relevance to the lower paid since it is among them that jobs tend to be of shortest duration. Many lower paid jobs emerge in response to transient demand and do not involve large investments in skill development. Firms looking for short-term labour to deal with fluctuating markets often take on less-skilled workers on a short-term basis, but on the expectation that they can lay them off later. Such short-term jobs have often been used by young people moving between school and permanent work (Osterman 1980; Marsden and Germe 1991). Restrictions on lay-offs and on temporary work could close off this area of employment.

During the 1980s the USA and Britain led the way in fostering employment at the lower end of the earnings distribution (OECD 1993, Ch. 5) by means of deregulatory policies. However, the jobs are mostly low productivity ones, and although they can be of value to many on a temporary basis, and arguably preferable to the stigma of unemployment, they do not offer a solution for anyone on a long-term basis. The emergence of a group of 'working poor', that is people in work but unable to earn enough to escape conditions of poverty, now recognized in the USA, cannot be an acceptable solution.

The impact on the overall competitiveness of the economy of deregulation at this end of the market is likely to be indirect and fairly small. Most low-paid jobs are not in the internationally traded sectors, with the possible exception of tourism, and only indirectly affect the input costs of traded sectors. Thus, while policies to remove or reduce restrictions on minimum pay rates and on lay-offs may help boost jobs, the overall contribution to material prosperity and economic growth will be fairly small.

The impact on the skilled workforce

The impact of labour market deregulatory policies on raising productivity among the middle group of workers is less clear and more indirect. Most are not directly affected by changes in minimum wages. Usually employers hire such workers on a fairly long-term basis, so legal or agreed restrictions on lay-offs are less relevant. Indeed, even without restrictions, lay-offs can be costly to employers since the announcement of impending job cuts is likely to create uncertainty, damage morale and encourage those with the best external job prospects to leave.

The main effect of deregulatory policies is likely to come with measures designed to reduce the power of organized workers to resist management

179

attempts to raise productivity by reorganizing work or introducing new equipment. Although unions clearly provide them with a vehicle for bargaining and for discussing change with management, it is not so obvious that unions greatly increase their bargaining power. Such workers already have a good deal of individual bargaining leverage by virtue of their power to resign and get a job elsewhere. The employer then has the expense of finding a replacement. For workers with transferable abilities such as craft and professional skills which are widely recognized by other employers, outside job prospects are mostly fairly good. For those with firm-specific skills, built upon long experience, the cost of leaving may be higher than for those with craft and professional skills, but the employer's difficulty of finding a replacement is also greater. The cost of replacing leavers also diminishes employers' power to threaten workers with dismissal for disciplinary reasons. A number of sociological studies, such as those of Crozier (1963), testify to the considerable bargaining power of small groups within organizations even where formal union organization is extremely weak.

For these reasons, it was perhaps not surprising that Brown and Wadhwani (1990) found that Mrs Thatcher's trade union legislation had had relatively little effect upon productivity. Much more important had been the dire commercial straits of many large, unionized firms and the recognition by both workers and management that fundamental changes were needed simply in order to survive, as occurred in the car industry during the early 1980s (Marsden *et al.* 1985). The most significant change, which lay outside the labour market, was probably the government making it clear that it would no longer act as 'employer of last resort'.

The impact on higher paid professionals and managers

In the 1970s earnings inequalities declined in many Western European countries, partly as a result of union bargaining policies and partly because of government incomes policies. In Britain and Italy, and to a lesser extent France, such policies limited the freedom of firms to reward their managerial and higher professional staff, and it was widely believed that incentives suffered. Apart from any effect on higher paid workers, it can be argued that their high pay helps motivate those who are still seeking promotion and who thus hope to become highly paid in the future. Stimulation of competition among less senior managers encourages them to take initiative and to assume responsibility for their decisions, rather than opt for a quiet life.

Government deregulatory policies may not have a great deal of direct influence on remuneration policies of private firms, but they may use a number of signals. Reducing marginal tax rates on higher salaries makes higher pay worth more to those getting it. Changing employment contracts of public service managers and raising their pay is another signal.

A low wage sector 'pour encourager les autres'?

A final effect of deregulatory policies could be to increase the cost to workers of losing good jobs. If the pay of the least skilled jobs is allowed to fall, then the potential cost of losing a well-paid job is increased. This could strengthen the sanctions of employers over dissident or less co-operative workers. Thus a low-wage sector could have the effect of encouraging higher paid workers to be more compliant.

The essence of the deregulatory case hinges largely on incentives for workers and on costs to employers. The general evidence available suggests that employers' hiring decisions are sensitive to relative wage levels, particularly for categories of lower paid workers such as women, young and unskilled workers. In contrast, measuring the productivity effects of wage incentives is very difficult and, although the arguments are plausible, good evidence is hard to come by and controversial.

DEREGULATION AND CO-OPERATIVE WORK RELATIONS

Co-operation and productivity within the skilled group

The middle section of the labour force is the most important one for the achievement of international competitiveness and long-run employment levels. The efficiency with which it works, the skills applied and the general quality of the work done are critical to the production of goods and services which can be traded internationally and hold their ground in domestic markets that are increasingly open to international trade. Success in this area then generates the incomes to pay for other locally based economic activities.

Co-operative exchange between skilled and professional workers and their employers is critical to achieving high productivity levels and good quality output. Two elements in particular stand out: flexible working and effective information sharing. Both contribute to high levels of resource utilization and the latter especially to continuous incremental improvement. It is almost a truism that rigid working patterns make it hard for firms to use resources efficiently. Product market pressures are ever changing and require continuous adaptation from firms. If they cannot redeploy staff to meet new and varying needs, the only way they can meet variable sales demands is by hiring more labour than they need for most of the time. Job demarcations have their justification: qualified and properly trained people are needed to undertake particular jobs. But there are often pieces of related work, bits of preventive maintenance and minor trouble-shooting, for example, which can be done by others provided they are given some basic instruction.

Effective information sharing between groups of workers and between workers and management has also been shown to be central to achieving continuous improvement and innovation (Koike and Inoki 1990). Bits of information gleaned from contact with customers can give vital leads to product improvement. Gaining an overview of the whole process of production or service provision can reveal weaknesses in the organization which make providing a reliable and good quality service difficult to sustain.

Nevertheless, because both flexible working and information sharing are essential ingredients in power relations among groups in all organizations, they are hard to achieve in practice. They depend upon co-operative exchange and thus on the ability of the different groups involved to trust each other. In entering a co-operative relationship one is usually exposing oneself to possible exploitation by others. For example, skilled workers who teach their semi-skilled colleagues how to do some preventive maintenance share knowledge which they might otherwise use to protect themselves against possible job cuts. Indeed, many skilled and professional job demarcations originally developed in order to protect workers' job opportunities. By adopting a co-operative stance, the skilled workers in this example expose themselves to possible exploitation by both the semi-skilled and management. Equally, management might offer great employment security in return for job flexibility. It might demonstrate its good faith by keeping more people on in a recession, whereas the workers' promise of job flexibility might not be tested until the following upswing.

In the past management has been able to minimize the need for co-operative exchange in the workplace by using Taylorist patterns of work organization, with narrowly defined jobs, tight management control and little individual discretion. In practice, it did not avoid the problems of small group power relations. Because it cannot predict all eventualities and organize for them, inevitably unforeseen circumstances arise which create bottlenecks in the flow of resources within the organization. These then become a source of power for the small groups which control information and the flow of resources at these points. Again, Crozier's (1963) study of the problems of bureaucratic management control highlights many examples. Management often responds to these problems by issuing new instructions or rules, which themselves become new sources of organizational rigidity: Crozier's 'vicious circle' of bureaucracy. Dissatisfaction with boring jobs has also contributed to poor worker motivation in this kind of model.

More recently, the emergence of 'lean production' in manufacturing and its equivalent forms in the services have achieved greater levels of efficiency as compared with the older 'mass production' management methods (Womack et al. 1990). By eliminating buffer stocks, firms with lean production have developed a powerful means of searching out organizational inefficiencies, but they have also placed a premium on co-operative exchange. Information sharing about potential improvements is at the heart of this process. Equally, by removing buffer stocks, the power of discontented workers to disrupt production is greatly enhanced.

What conditions are necessary for co-operative exchange to occur? The biggest obstacle was the fear that the other party would not reciprocate and would seek to take advantage of the first party's co-operative stance by grasping all the fruits. Recent work in game theory suggests that it is very difficult to achieve mutual co-operation without the presence of trust, which we might define here as a mutual expectation of co-operative behaviour, and without some social or institutional framework to sustain that trust. This is where the problem of deregulation emerges.

It is hard to achieve a co-operative outcome among individual groups unless there is some higher level institution to police grievances and to prevent small group power relations from degenerating into a kind of guerilla war within the firm. Such institutions provide a degree of countervailing power to underwrite co-operation with management. They also provide a means of prioritizing the claims among different groups of workers, deciding which should be pursued and in which cases groups were just being opportunistic. In Britain, Brown's (1973) study of piecework bargaining showed shop stewards playing just this role. In Germany and the Netherlands, works councils play a central role in the same process. However, the more encompassing nature of works councils, representing practically all the employees in a given firm, enables them to take a broader view of the problems of co-operation and, at the same time, the legal status of their election helps to protect individual works councillors from being too strongly identified with particular work groups.

Apart from sanctions against possible non-cooperative action, the institutional framework provides a means of communication. Because the pressures on firms are constantly changing and, as a result, so are management's demands of its workforce, reciprocity cannot always be guaranteed. Both sides know this, but there is a problem of recognizing genuine cases of 'force majeure'. These can really only be judged when there is regular and open communication among the different groups and management.

Multi-employer organizations and industry-wide unions also have a role to play in underwriting enterprise level co-operation. Should co-operation break down at the enterprise level because one party seeks to exploit the other, then the higher level organization provides additional support. The possibility of escalating the conflict can deter some attempts by one party to exploit the other and the costs of such conflict encourage both industry level organizations to develop effective means of policing their own sides.

Wage incentives and co-operation

It is notable in the countries in which co-operative exchange has developed most fully in the workplace that occupational wage differentials tend to be somewhat smaller than in countries where this is not the case. This suggests that wage incentives may work in a different way in the two kinds of environment.

If one thinks of organizations with a strong management role and a heavy emphasis on individual managers' responsibility, then it seems reasonable that high wage incentives could induce better performance. However, the essence of more co-operative structures is that the managerial role is more diffused among a larger number of people who take responsibility. A striking illustration of this is that the highly trained and qualified skilled workers and middle managers in Germany should enjoy a smaller differential over semi-skilled workers than their counterparts in France, whose training is less good and whose relative skill advantage is smaller. The greater diffusion of authority and the greater responsibility assumed by skilled workers in German firms contrasts with the concentration of decision-making within the managerial hierarchy in French firms (Maurice et al. 1986). Similarly, in Japanese firms, where management authority is widely diffused among jobs and decision-making is of a more consensual nature than in many Western firms, there is less focus on management rewards as a key to motivation and performance (see Lam 1994; Nohara 1994). There are, of course, major differences between the organization of German and Japanese firms, but in both cases the greater use of co-operative exchange implies more information sharing. This in turn implies a lesser role for managers as key individuals. Not only may the co-operative model not require such large pay differentials, but it is likely that they would be harmful as they imply a concentration of rewards on key individuals.

A second influence on rewards associated with the co-operative model arises from the role of encompassing representative organizations. Dutch and German works councils and Dutch, German and Swedish industry unions belong to this category as they generally represent all the workers in their respective constituencies. Japanese enterprise unions play a similar role in their firms. Such organizations have an inherent tendency to promote reduced pay inequalities among their members. The reason is that their more powerful members could usually do better by going it alone, so that in terms of their own selfish group interest they are getting a bad deal. Hence there is the need for some moral or ideological goal to motivate them, such as wage solidarity or greater equality.

Thus, policies designed to promote greater wage inequalities in order to increase incentives for individuals could be counter-productive if, at the same time, they undermine the basis for co-operation.

IS REGULATED CO-OPERATION IN GERMANY LESS FLEXIBLE THAN THE DEREGULATED UK

It is worth contrasting some elements of more regulated systems with those of the more deregulated ones and focusing the contrast around Germany and Britain. A number of features of co-operative work relations would appear, at first sight, to inhibit swift economic adjustment. A rapid look at the experience of some of the countries known to have more co-operative systems in comparison with some of those with more deregulated systems suggests that the appearance may be deceptive.

Long job tenures could be regarded as a sign that firms are slow to adjust employment to changes in output and thus that they face formal and informal obstacles. A recent survey of job tenures across several economies in about 1990 showed that Germany and Japan had among the highest, with approximately 60 per cent of workers with five or more years' tenure. In contrast, the equivalent figures for the UK and the USA were respectively 45 per cent and 38 per cent (OECD 1993: 121). On the other hand, estimates for the 1980s of the short-run sensitivity of employment levels to changes in output for Germany were similar and if anything slightly greater than for the UK. In Japan, employment was a little less sensitive, although in the USA it was about twice as sensitive as in the other three countries (OECD 1989: 43–4). Thus, a greater degree of employment security does not necessarily prevent firms from making employment adjustments when needed.

It is often suggested that industry-wide bargaining which sets minimum rates of pay for different grades of skills across a whole industry prevents individual firms from adjusting to market pressures. Thus, encouraging enterprise bargaining and discouraging industry-wide bargaining has been a part of the deregulation agenda. Nevertheless, German industry bargaining in fact offers a good deal of pay flexibility at enterprise level. While some firms pay just above the minimum, others might pay as much as 40 per cent above as a result of negotiations between company management and works councils (see Teschner 1977; Meyer 1991). Employer representatives at the industry level know that there will be further negotiations at company level and allow for this in calculating what concessions to make.

One considerable advantage that the articulated system of bargaining has in Germany is that industry unions know they will have to live with the macro-economic consequences of the pay settlements they reach and so have a strong incentive to pay moderation. Because the works councils and company management have, by law, to reach agreement within the framework set at the industry level, there is little danger of 'leap-frogging' of the kind that has bedevilled local bargaining in the UK.

A third example is the quasi veto power vested in German works councils over a whole range of employment-related issues. Employers and works councils are obliged to reach agreement on a wide range of questions such as training, redundancies and redeployment of staff. There is also a considerable spill-over effect from these issues. Although a works council could not legally threaten to block a redundancy plan until it obtained satisfaction on, say, new patterns of work organization, management knows the works council can make its life more difficult or easier depending on its attitude to the questions which it finds important. Although some works councils have used their veto powers to gain advantages on related issues, nevertheless, reports such as that of the 1970 parliamentary commission chaired by the Christian Democrat senator, Biedenkopf, found that, in general, the powers of co-determination were used co-operatively.

In addition, the powers given to workers through their works councils have generally meant that skilled workers, unlike their British and US counterparts, have not had to rely upon skill demarcations and seniority rules to defend their skills (Jürgens *et al.* 1993).

A fourth illustration that regulation does not need to conflict with high productivity concerns vocational training. In Germany, trainee and apprentice allowances are fixed in industry agreements, the employment status of apprentices is strictly maintained. Training is undertaken according to industry-wide standards and not according to the requirements of individual enterprises. This would seem to be a recipe for a high cost and inflexible training system causing employers to cut their training intakes. Yet, generally, German employers have proved more willing to pay for the training of large numbers of apprentices than their British counterparts. Marsden and Ryan (1990) argue this is because the industry-wide and firm level structures facilitate wider acceptance of cost-sharing between workers and employers, trainees contributing to the cost of their training by means of low trainee allowances. In a low-trust environment, such trainees are always a potential threat to the status of skilled workers, especially in the latter years of their apprenticeship when they can undertake a good deal of skilled work. Similarly, because apprenticeship-based skills are transferable among firms, employers always face the risk that others will poach their expensively trained workers. The strong powers of German works councils over training provide a good deal of protection against trainees being used as cheap substitutes for skilled workers. The broadly based membership of industry employer organizations and local chambers of industry and commerce provide powerful channels for peer group pressures against employers who do not train.

Thus, what at first sight looks like a cumbersome regulatory apparatus in fact provides the basis for a strong, high quality training system. Because individual workers gain a good deal of protection from this, they do not need to develop rules which restrict job flexibility of the kind found in British, French or US firms.

Finally, the weakening of workers' collective institutions in Britain and the encouragement of a more enterprise focused system of employee relations does not appear to have generated greater identification with the goals of the enterprise. A recent review of the effects of a number of new management practices on workers' attitudes in Britain showed they did little to reduce 'them and us' attitudes (Kelly and Kelly 1991). The deregulatory environment in the UK, on this evidence, appears to have done little to increase trust and co-operative exchange, but then the deregulatory path relies on a different set of incentives.

CONCLUSIONS

The deregulatory model places primary emphasis on conquering unemployment by ensuring that the price of different categories of labour corresponds to the competitive value of their output. Once the price mechanism functions properly, average productivity may rise because of a better allocation of resources and better incentives. The model also places a very heavy emphasis on the incentive for and decisions by individual economic actors, be they workers or firms. The co-operative model, with which it has been contrasted, offers a less direct route to full employment, but one which can be achieved with less over-all pay inequality and with high levels of productivity. The route to high productivity relies less on incentives for individual performance than on those for co-operation in flexible working in the work place. The rise of 'lean production' and similar concepts in employee and production management places a new emphasis upon flexible working and information sharing. The automobile industry study of Womack *et al.* (1990) provides detailed evidence of the considerable productivity advantage of 'lean production' over the older 'mass production' model in that sector. However, the co-operative model has a number of potential drawbacks which could harm the employment of certain groups unless they are resolved.

The long-run dependency of co-operation on the support of strong workplace and higher level institutions can be problematic. Potentially, these have two faces: the capacity to underwrite workplace co-operation, but also that to block change in pursuit of individual group interests. They also have an inherent tendency towards reducing the inequality of rewards because of the need for an ideology to cement a coalition of many different occupational groups within the same bargaining alliance. If self-interest were the sole factor, the more skilled groups would usually do better to bargain alone. Solidary wage policies both reduce incentives for the otherwise higher paid and limit job openings for the low skilled. Finally, the quality of co-operation may depend partly also on long job tenures as these enable the development and testing of trust relations. This may encourage employers to segment their workforces into a stable group of 'insiders' and a less stable one of 'outsiders' more exposed to periodic spells of unemployment. Three solutions to these potential adverse side effects enhance the attractiveness of the co-operative approach.

First, the potential for the 'monopolistic' face of collective institutions to prevail can be greatly limited by ensuring high levels of competition in product markets. An example is provided by the turn-around of the British car industry during the 1980s. By the late 1970s, erosion of domestic market shares and loss of export markets left the British-based producers in a very weak position. Increased competition from UK entry into the EEC and from the rise of the Japanese car producers forced the UK-based management to press for change. Equally, on the employee side, realization that firms as large and as important to their local economies as British Leyland could go out of business began to change attitudes on the employee side (Marsden *et al.* 1985). Similar pressures lay behind the wave of flexibility agreements in the early to mid-1980s. Looking at the British economy more generally, Brown and Wadhwani (1990) concluded that product market changes had contributed more than the industrial relations law reforms to the productivity increase of the 1980s.

The second problem, that of reduced pay differentials, can be tackled on two fronts. The co-operative model places less emphasis on key individuals and so is less dependent upon strong financial incentives for individual performance. The relative over-pricing of low-skilled labour is a more difficult problem and can be tackled in the longer term by wider access to training to enable them to provide services that others wish to buy. In the short run, a number of policies are available to reduce the employment cost of these workers, such as reduced employers' social charges on low-paid labour.

Some of these policies are also relevant to reducing polarization between insiders and outsiders. More competitive product markets mean it is easier for new firms to enter and with that to hire able workers who might otherwise be excluded. Widely available training and retraining facilities both improve access to insider status and facilitate entry by new firms into established markets.

The labour market deregulation and the co-operative paths to high employment are largely irreconcileable as they stress incompatible incentives. In comparison with the deregulatory path, the co-operative one seems better adapted to emerging patterns of high performance workplaces in which co-operation and flexible working are essential. However, if it is to provide a path to full employment as well as one to islands of high productivity, it must also tackle some of its side effects on employment.

REFERENCES

Becker, G. S. (1975) *Human Capital: A Theoretical and Empirical Analysis, with Special Reference to Education*, Chicago: University of Chicago Press.

Brown, W. E. (1973) *Piecework Bargaining*, London: Heinemann.

Brown, W. and Wadhwani, S. (1990) 'The economic effects of industrial relations legislation since 1979', *National Institute Economic Review* 131, February: 57–70.

Crozier, M. (1963) *Le phénomène bureaucratique*, Paris: Seuil.

Hamermesh, D. (1993) *Labor Demand*, Princeton, New Jersey: Princeton University Press.

Jürgens, U., Malsch, T. and Dohse, K. (1993) *Breaking from Taylorism: Changing Forms of Work in the Automobile Industry*, Cambridge: Cambridge University Press.

Kelly, J. and Kelly, C. (1991) '"Them and us": social psychology and "the New Industrial Relations"', *British Journal of Industrial Relations* 29 (1), March: 25–48.

Koike, K. and Inoki, T. (eds) (1990) *Skill Formation in Japan and Southeast Asia*, Tokyo: University of Tokyo Press.

Lam, A. (1994) 'The utilisation of human resources: a comparative study of British and Japanese engineers in the electronics industries', *Human Resource Management Journal* 4 (3), Spring: 20–22.

Marsden, D. W, and Germe, J-F. (1991) 'Young people and entry paths to long-term jobs in France and Great Britain', in P. Ryan, P. Garonna and R. Edwards (eds) *The Problem of Youth: The Regulation of Youth Employment and Training in Advanced Economies*, London: Macmillan.

Marsden, D. W. and Ryan, P. (1990) 'Institutional aspects of youth employment and training policy in Britain', *British Journal of Industrial Relations* 28 (3), November: 351–70.

Marsden, D., Morris, T., Willman, P. and Wood, S. (1985) *The Car Industry: Labour Relations and Industrial Adjustment*, London: Tavistock.

Maurice, M., Sellier, F. and Silvestre, J. J. (1986) *The Social Foundations of Industrial Power: A Comparison of France and Germany*, Cambridge, Mass: MIT Press.

Meyer, F. (1991) *La contrattazione salariale in Germania. ASAP, 1991 Rapporto sui salari*, Milano: Franco Angeli.

Nohara, H. (1994) 'Structure de salaires dans l'industrie: essai d'une comparaison France-Japon', in H. Nadel (ed.) *Emploi et relations industrielles au Japon*, Paris: Editions l'Harmattan: 211–34.

Organization for Economic Co-operation and Development (OECD) (1989) *Employment Outlook 1989*, Paris: OECD.

—— (1993) *Employment Outlook 1993*, Paris: OECD.

Osterman, P. (1980) *Getting Started: The Youth Labor Market*, Cambridge, Mass: MIT Press.

Pencavel, J. (1994) 'British unemployment: letter from America', *Economic Journal* 104 (424), May: 621–32.

Teschner, E. (1977) *Lohnpolitik im Betrieb: eine empirische Untersuchung in der Metall-, Chemie-, Textil-, und Tabakindustrie*, Frankfurt: Campus Verlag.

Womack, J., Jones, D. T. and Roos, D. (1990) *The Machine that Changed the World*, New York: Rawson Associates.

12

PREVENTING LONG-TERM UNEMPLOYMENT

Richard Layard

INTRODUCTION[1]

Unemployment is one of the major sources of misery in our society. When people record their sense of well-being, it is found that being unemployed makes a person much more unhappy than being poor.[2] So a civilized society should not tolerate our present levels of unemployment. The European Union's member governments have called for unemployment to be reduced to 5 per cent. Is it possible? If we seriously want a big cut in unemployment, we should focus sharply on those policies which stand a good chance of having a really big effect. It is not true that all policies which are good in general are good for unemployment. There are in fact very few policies where the evidence points to any large unambiguous effect on unemployment and I list in Annex 1 some widely advocated policies for which there is little clear evidence.

There is, however, one issue on which there is almost universal agreement, but so far little radical action in Europe. This is the issue of long-term unemployment (LTU) where it is quite clear what could be done to reduce it. At present nearly half of Europe's unemployed have been out of work for over a year (in Britain the proportion is around 40 per cent). I believe that to prevent long-term unemployment would be one of the most significant supply side improvements which could be made in Europe. I shall therefore concentrate on this issue, and offer eleven points for Britain and other European governments to consider, if they seriously want a large and permanent cut in unemployment.

LONG-TERM UNEMPLOYMENT IS AN ALMOST TOTAL WASTE

In any economy there has to be some short-term unemployment to ease mobility and to restrain wage pressure by providing employers with a pool of workers able to fill vacancies. But long-term unemployment appears to be largely useless, since it exerts very little downward pressure on inflation. This is because employers are generally unenthusiastic about long-term unemployed people as potential fillers of vacancies. Whether this reaction is justified (by the demoralization and deskilling of the workers) or not justified is unimportant.

190

The fact is that unemployed people in Europe have a declining chance of leaving unemployment the longer they have been unemployed. This is illustrated for Britain in Figure 12.1. As a result, it is perfectly possible for employers to experience labour shortages even when there are millions of long-term unemployed. This, more than anything else, makes it impossible without new labour market policies to reduce European unemployment below around 9 per cent of the workforce without inflation rising. The secret of good employment policy is to identify those types of unemployment which can be reduced without rekindling inflation. The prime candidate here is long-term unemployment and I would urge the governments of Europe to focus much more heavily on this issue, which is such a massive fiscal burden, rather than dispersing their anti-unemployment measures over too wide a front and in the end achieving little.

EUROPEAN LTU IS DUE TO HOW WE TREAT UNEMPLOYED PEOPLE

As everybody knows, the proportion of the labour force who are long-term unemployed is much higher in the EU than in the USA, Canada, Japan, Sweden and Norway (see Table 12.1).[3] Why is this? The main reason is almost incontrovertible: it is the long duration for which unemployment benefits are payable. This is illustrated in Figure 12.3, which shows on the vertical axis the maximum duration of benefit and on the horizontal axis the percentage of unemployed people in long-term unemployment (over a year). In countries like Japan, USA, Canada and Sweden benefits run out within a year or so and unemployment lasting more than a year is rare. By contrast in the main EU countries benefits have typically been available indefinitely or for a long period and long-term unemployment is high.

The relationship shown in Figure 12.3 is of course a partial correlation. But if one allows for multiple causation, the effect of benefit duration upon the aggregate unemployment rate remains strong and clear.[4] It is interesting to note from Table 12.1 that short-term unemployment differs very much less between countries than long-term unemployment, because some short-term unemployment is inevitable in any system in which unemployment benefits are available for some period. But long-term unemployment differs sharply according to how unemployed people are treated. It is in some ways an 'optional extra' which can be easily accommodated according to the social institutions of a country.

The effect of unemployment benefit availability upon unemployment is not unforeseen. Unemployment benefits are a subsidy to inactivity and it should not be surprising if they lead to an increase in inactivity. In principle, of course, the benefits are meant to protect individuals against an exogenous misfortune and there is meant to be a test of willingness to work. But in practice it is impossible to operate such a test without offering actual work. So after a period of disheartening job search, unemployed individuals often adjust to unemployment as a different lifestyle.

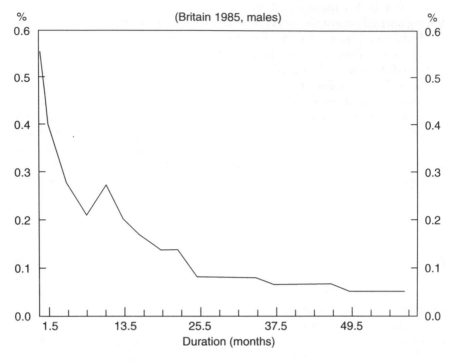

Figure 12.1 Percentage of unemployed people leaving unemployment in next three
months: by duration of unemployment experienced so far
Source: These data relate to registered (claimant) unemployment and come from the
Employment Gazette

WE DO NOT WANT A EUROPEAN UNDERCLASS

So what should we do? One possibility would be to reduce the duration of benefits
to, say, one year and put nothing else in its place. This would be the American-
style solution. But we know this only produces extra employment because people
thrown onto the labour market accept an ever-widening inequality of wages. A
much better approach would be to help people to be more employable so that
they would justify a higher wage. This leads to my central proposal.

STOP SUBSIDIZING INACTIVITY AND SUBSIDIZE
WORK INSTEAD

After twelve months the state should accept a responsibility to find people work
for at least six months.[5] That should become the method through which it sup-
ports their income. In return the individual would recognize that if he wishes to
receive income, he must accept one of a few reasonable offers. These offers
would be guaranteed by the state paying to any employer for six months the

Table 12.1 Short-term and long-term unemployment as percentage of labour force (1980s average)

	Long-term	Short-term	Total
Australia	1.9	5.5	7.4
Belgium	8.0	3.0	11.1
Canada	0.8	8.4	9.2
Denmark	2.4	5.6	8.0
Finland	0.7	4.1	4.8
France	3.9	5.0	9.0
Germany	3.0	3.6	6.7
Greece	2.9	3.6	6.6
Ireland	8.1	6.1	14.2
Italy	6.4	3.4	9.9
Japan	0.4	2.0	2.4
Netherlands	4.7	5.0	9.7
New Zealand	0.4	4.1	4.5
Norway	0.2	2.5	2.7
Portugal	2.5	4.7	7.3
Spain	10.1	7.4	17.5
Sweden	0.2	2.2	2.4
UK	4.2	5.2	9.5
USA	0.6	6.5	7.1

Sources: OECD *Employment Outlook*, OECD *Labour Force Survey*

benefit to which the unemployed individual would otherwise have been entitled. This system would have huge advantages:

- At the twelfth month it would relieve the public finances of any responsibility for people who are already in work. It is very difficult to prevent fraud without being able to offer full-time work.
- Between months twelve and eighteen, people would be producing something rather than nothing. How much would depend on the type of jobs offered.
- But the biggest effect would come after the eighteenth month. Provided the work had been real work with regular employers, unemployed people would have reacquired work habits plus the ability to prove their working capacity. They would have a regular employer who could provide a reference or (even better) retain the individual on a permanent basis. The main justification for the proposal is not that it employs people on a subsidized basis but that, by doing so, it restores them to the universe of employable people. This is an investment in Europe's human capital.

JOBS SHOULD BE WITH REGULAR EMPLOYERS

This is the central objective of the exercise. Job creation schemes in the past have often failed because the jobs have been marginal and have failed to make the

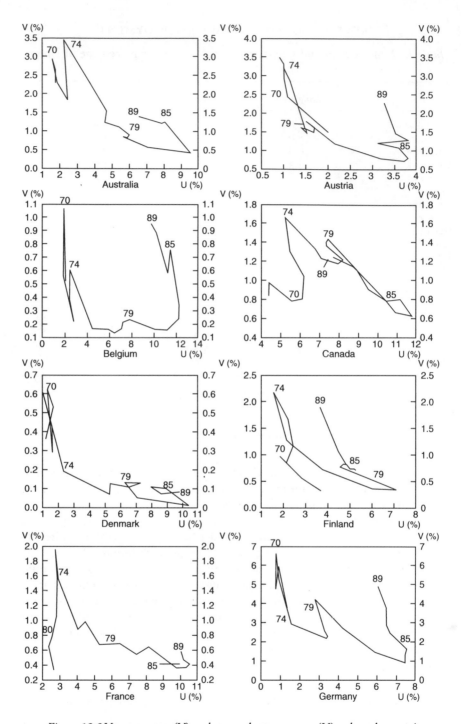

Figure 12.2 Vacancy rates (V) and unemployment rates (U), selected countries

194

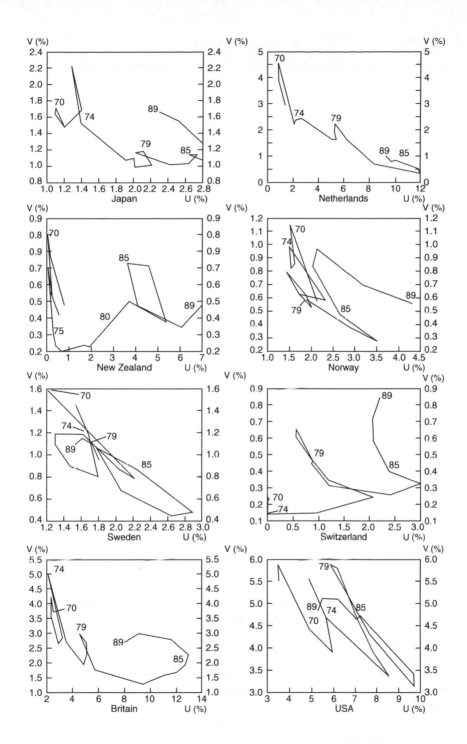

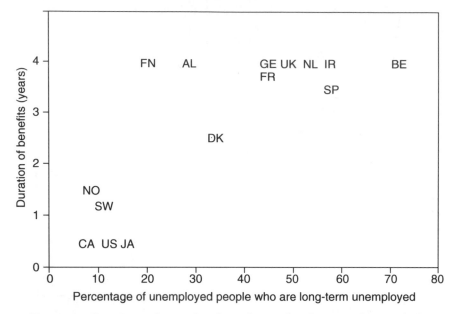

Figure 12.3 Percentage of unemployed people out of work over twelve months by maximum duration of benefits (1984)

individual more employable thereafter. The job subsidy should therefore be available to any employer (private or public). There should also be the least possible restrictions on the kind of work that could be done. Clearly no employer should be allowed to employ subsidized workers if he was at the same time dismissing regular workers. But there should be no condition (as in the UK's former Community Programme and subsequent similar schemes) that the work done should be work that would not otherwise be done for the next two years. Such a requirement is a formula for ineffectiveness. The reason why job creation schemes have so often had these disastrous limiting conditions is the fear of substitution and displacement. This fear is understandable but misplaced.

SUBSTITUTION AND DISPLACEMENT ARE NOT MAJOR PROBLEMS

Most opposition to active labour market measures is based on fears of displacement and substitution. In their extreme form these derive from the 'lump-of-labour fallacy': there is only a certain number of jobs so if we enable X to get one of them, some other person goes without work. It is easy to see how the confusion arises. In the most immediate sense, the proposition is true. If an employer has a vacancy and, due to a job subsidy, X gets it rather than Y, then Y remains temporarily unemployed. But by definition Y is inherently employable. If he does not get this job, he will offer himself for others. Employers will find there are more employable people in the market and that they can more easily fill their vacancies. This increases downward pressure on wage rises, making possible a higher level of employment at the same level of inflationary pressure.[6]

On average over the cycle the level of unemployment is determined by the level needed to hold inflation stable. Active labour market policy increases the number of employable workers and thus reduces the unemployment needed to control inflation. Equally, in the short run a government that has a given inflation target (or exchange rate target) will allow more economic expansion if it finds that inflationary pressures are less than would otherwise be expected. Many people find it difficult to believe that (inflationary pressure being equal) jobs automatically expand in relation to the employable labour force. So it is perhaps worth giving some more general evidence.

MORE EMPLOYABLE WORKERS CAUSE MORE JOBS

People are inclined to suppose that there is some magic in the job-creating powers of the USA and Japan. The truth is that jobs have grown faster there mainly because the numbers available and wanting work have also grown, largely due to births, deaths and migration. In Europe the labour force has grown much more slowly, which is the main reason why employment has grown more slowly.[7] This is illustrated in Figure 12.4. To ram home the point, Figure 12.5 shows that the same applies to 'jobs for men' and 'jobs for women'. They respond with remarkable precision to the ratios of men and women in the labour force. In almost every country the proportion of men aged 16 to 64 wanting to work has fallen and the proportion of women wanting to work has risen. This is the overwhelming source of the change in male/female labour in employment, which has tended to occur within nearly all industries.

However, this evidence clearly relates to the medium run and for some people that is too long to wait. In today's Britain they will not have to wait that long. An increase in the number of employable people shifts the short run trade-off between employment and inflation to the right. More people can be employed at the same level of inflation or, if the same number are employed, inflation will be lower (see Figure 12.6). What will happen depends on monetary policy. If monetary policy is unresponsive, inflation will fall and employment will grow: there will be a 'bit of both'. But if, as in Britain, there is a fixed inflation target, a shift in the trade-off stemming from a rise in the employment rate equilibrium will lead even in the short run to an equal change in employment.

But surely, people will say, it must become more difficult for short-term unemployed to find jobs. The answer is 'not really'. For each month roughly 300,000 people enter and leave unemployment. About 250,000 leave before twelve months are up. So 50,000 flow into long-term unemployment and 50,000 flow out. Under our system no more need flow out. They just flow out faster, so that the stock of long-term unemployed becomes very small.[8]

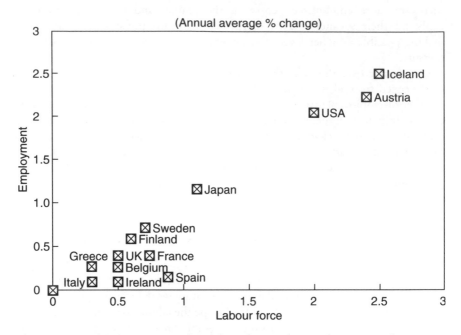

Figure 12.4 Percentage growth in labour force and in employment, 1960–89
Source: OECD

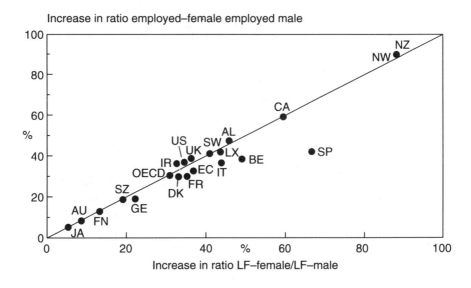

Figure 12.5 Change in relative labour force and change in relative employment: by sex,
1970–90

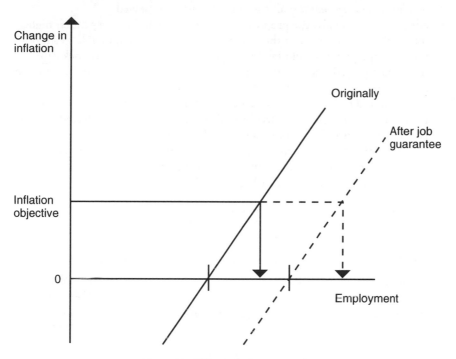

Figure 12.6 The inflation constraint

THE SOCIAL BENEFITS WOULD BE HUGE

We can now proceed to sum up the effects of the scheme and its impact on human welfare. In a formal sense it would abolish long-term unemployment However, this is to overclaim since someone who reverts to unemployment after eighteen months (after a temporary job) is not really short-term unemployed, even though this would be his classification in the statistics. So let us consider the impacts on the flow of a cohort entering unemployment.

- *Up to 12 months*: some people who would not like to accept a programme job may find some other job. Others may delay taking a job because their potential employer has an incentive to wait for the subsidy. It is reasonable to assume these effects cancel out. More important is the hope that a completely new climate would develop in which neither individuals nor the employment service accept the idea that someone should reach the humiliating position of being confronted with temporary work as the only possible source of income. In Sweden in the 1980s typically about 3 per cent of the workforce reached the fourteenth month of unemployment (when benefit ran out). In Britain the figure was about five times larger.

199

- *Twelve to eighteen months*: all the cohort is now employed.
- *After eighteen months*: the proportion employed should be very much higher, due to the employability of those concerned. Thus it is reasonable to suppose that unemployment would fall by roughly the same size as the stock of long-term unemployed, leading to a substantial increase in production. Suppose average unemployment fell to 5 per cent compared with say 9 per cent, output would be at a minimum 2 per cent higher. This is the social gain (not to mention a net gain in psychic well-being among those affected). What is the social cost? Very little. The employment service would need more administrative staff, but this is a tiny cost compared with the gain.[9] The typical EU country spends only 0.1 per cent of GNP on its employment service. All this is illustrated in Figure 12.7.

A Benefits

	Social	Fiscal
Up to 12th month	More job search	Some benefit savings
Months 12–18	Everyone works	Cheaters cost nothing but some deadweight
After 18th month	Higher proportion work	Major savings on benefits + higher taxes

B Costs
Extra administration

Figure 12.7 Benefits and costs of the scheme (to society and to the Exchequer)

THE POLICY WOULD SAVE TAXPAYERS' MONEY

The balance is also acceptable if we focus exclusively on the benefits and costs to the public finances.

- After the twelfth month the taxpayers stop supporting those who are already fraudulently in work or who prefer other jobs to those provided through the subsidy.
- Between the twelfth and eighteenth months, the taxpayers keep paying benefit but now it goes to employers not workers. Any employer who would anyway have hired somebody unemployed between twelve and eighteen months will of course claim the subsidy. So there would on this account be some deadweight (i.e. extra expenditure). However, this deadweight has to be balanced against the fact that some people who would have previously drawn benefit do not now claim subsidized jobs. One should note that the maximum deadweight can be exactly calculated since we know how many of those eligible for subsidized jobs would have found work anyway. (This is never the case for a partial scheme when only some people choose subsidized jobs instead of drawing benefit.)

200

- After the eighteenth month, there will be major savings on benefits and extra taxes received. On any reasonable estimate the total of all these will be a positive saving to the government, and a saving higher than the cost of the employment service. In Annex 2 we give some illustrative calculations which suggest that such a scheme in Britain would save about one quarter of a billion pounds net in a typical year. It would reduce unemployment by around 400,000.

PREVENTION IS BETTER THAN CURE

Why does this analysis seem so much more cost effective than most existing active labour market policy? Because it is much more drastic. Job subsidies without compulsion to accept an offer can easily be ineffective. What is needed is a shift of regime. In passing, note that I have not suggested doing anything extra for the existing long-term unemployed. This is deliberate. Helping people who are already LTU is very difficult and can easily fail. Therefore, prevent long-term unemployment, and let the existing LTU find their own solutions within the existing programmes, as eventually they will.

A PHASED PLAN IS NEEDED

This reform cannot be introduced overnight. The simplest approach would be to phase it by age, starting with those under 25 years of age who reach the twelve-month hurdle. By the end of a parliament it could be extended to people of all age groups reaching the twelve-month hurdle. In Britain and throughout the EU only politicians can decide to abolish the existing system for dealing with unemployed people, which has developed almost by mistake. No one would now design a system like the existing one. But it requires courage and commitment to change it. One thing however is sure. Unless it is changed, we shall in the year 2000 be almost as far from the EU's target for reducing unemployment as we are now.

NOTES

1 I am extremely grateful to Richard Jackman with whom every idea in this paper was developed.
2 A. E. Clark and A. J. Oswald, 'Unhappiness and unemployment', *The Economic Journal*, vol. 104, no. 424, May 1994.
3 Due to the growth of long-term unemployment, total unemployment is now much higher than it used to be at any particular level of vacancies (see Figure 12.2).
4 Layard, Nickell and Jackman (1991) *Unemployment, Macroeconomics Performance and the Labour Market*, Oxford: Oxford University Press, p 55 (see Annex 1). The other variables relate to the replacement ratio, active labour market policy, collective bargaining and the change in inflation.
5 As in Sweden, anyone who failed to find regular work within that period would be entitled to go back onto benefits after six months; but re-entry onto benefits would be conditional on having worked at least fifteen out of the last fifty-two weeks.

6 In Sweden two-thirds of those entitled to temporary jobs because their benefits have come to an end do not exercise their right to subsidized work.
7 To absorb more people requires a downward adjustment of the real wage. But in most countries real wages do not adjust reasonably quickly.
8 The argument is essentially the same even when we allow for the fact that there will be more churning as some of those who get the subsidized jobs will lose them after six months. If this happens they of course need jobs, but at the same time they release existing jobs to be filled by other people. All this is in the steady state. In the transition new jobs get created, which increases the flow of new hirings, as is necessary if the stock of unemployed is to fall.
9 Personally I strongly favour more training, but here I focus on a virtually costless proposal.
10 Layard, P., Nickell, S. and Jackman, R. (1991) *Unemployment, Macroeconomic Performance and the Labour Market*, Oxford: Oxford University Press.

ANNEX 1

Policies whose effects are difficult to forecast

In a book by Layard *et al.* (1991)[10] we show that

1 Social security taxes (or other employment taxes) on employers have an ambiguous effect on average unemployment over the cycle because they are frequently borne by workers – just like income taxes.
2 Job protection rules also have an ambiguous effect, by reducing dismissals as well as reducing hiring.
3 Productivity improvement (based for example on Research and Development) also has an ambiguous effect, since it frequently leads to equal increases in wages.
4 In economies with major union influence, decentralizing wage bargaining may increase rather than reduce wage pressure – and thus increase unemployment.

Our research was based on data up to 1989, but experience since then in Britain and elsewhere provides little reason to change these conclusions about the determinants of average unemployment over the cycle.

ANNEX 2

Effects of the proposals

Here are some approximate calculations on the effects in Britain of the job guarantee as proposed at twelve months. First I give the basic relevant numbers of unemployed (stocks and flows) in the absence of the policy. Then I set out clearly the assumptions about the scheme and its effects, and finally the estimated results.

Table 12.2 Existing unemployment: stocks and flows

	Sept 1990	Sept 1993	Average
Stocks			
At 52–78 weeks	15,709	313,965	214,837
At 78–104 weeks	68,225	211,304	139,764
At 104+ weeks	278,653	499,113	388,883
Flows (quarterly)			
At 52 weeks	88,425	219,972	154,198
At 78 weeks	45,989	131,317	88,650
At 102 weeks	32,206	99,344	65,775

Detailed assumptions about the scheme

The subsidy is offered for six months for all unemployed flowing past fifty-two weeks who accept the job guarantee, which we assume is 80 per cent of those eligible. (This is much higher than in Sweden even in this present recession.) The subsidy equals the benefit, which averages £65 per week (including housing subsidy). The other assumption is that the scheme reduces unemployment beyond seventy-eight weeks by 30 per cent (a rather conservative estimate).

Table 12.3 Results

	At 1990 numbers	At average numbers
Cost to the Exchequer	£	£
Subsidy	480m	830m
Extra administration	120m	220m
Savings on benefit		
at 52–78 weeks	−390m	−720m
at 78+ weeks	−350m	−530m
	−140m	−220m
Fall in unemployment	*People*	*People*
At 52–78 weeks	115k	210k
At 78+ weeks	100k	160k
	215k	370k

13

FULL EMPLOYMENT
The role of the public sector
Chris Trinder[1]

INTRODUCTION

In 1994 the UK government was still by far the largest single employer. Despite a massive privatization programme which dwarfs that of other countries; notwithstanding the reclassification of much of education and training to private sector non-profit-making bodies to deliver; and after allowing for extensive job cuts in core public services such as health and defence, more than five million people at the present time still work in the public sector. This represents one in five of the total workforce in employment in the UK and means that in scale terms alone the public sector's role in helping to achieve and maintain full employment is obviously of critical importance to the success of the overall strategy.

Although it is simple to establish the fact that the role of the public sector in full employment is of considerable significance, explaining the ways that it manifests itself is much more complicated. There are many, multi-faceted and interlocking dimensions. For example, the government has to balance its responsibilities as an employer with those of managing the economy. Although these can complement each other, sometimes there may be trade-offs. Also it is not simply a question of replicating 'good' practice in the private sector. For example, if a firm needs to reduce costs it can cut jobs and lower its payroll, but if the government has to pay the ensuing unemployment benefit of those without work then cutting wage costs only to add to social security payments may make less sense. The complex nature of the public sector's contribution to full employment strategy has in practice in the past often obscured the logic of the argument for it and resulted in it not playing its full role.

In this chapter my aim is to set out clearly the main components of the public sector's role in a full employment strategy, illustrating how they apply, what features of present policies must be preserved, often in the face of threats to change them, what past policies should now be reversed, and some new ideas for the future. The overall message is that while the public sector cannot on its own solve the persistent high levels of unemployment observed in the UK it can, if it so wishes, play a much more major part, directly and indirectly, in the full employment strategy than it has become fashionable to argue.

My approach is as follows: in the first section (pp. 205–12) I show how the public sector can directly influence the level of unemployment prevailing at particular times by the policies it pursues on recruiting and retaining staff. I also expain how, by setting an example to the private sector, it can within limits have an overall influence by its own behaviour greater than the immediate effects of particular actions. In the second section (pp. 212–13) I look at the way in which 'responsible' public sector behaviour on 'pay' has helped to save many jobs that would otherwise have been lost, hence adding to the unemployment problem. This is true of other European countries as well as the UK (OECD1993). In the third section (pp. 213–15) I examine the changing role of special employment measures which were introduced in the 1970s as a response to the rise in youth unemployment, but have been continued to a varying extent ever since. In the fourth section (p. 215) I briefly discuss fiscal policy. Tax, including national insurance policies, can influence the relative cost of labour *vis-à-vis* capital and hence the employment content of any economic growth which may occur in the future. Public expenditure policies on training and unemployment benefits need to be taken into account if all the costs and benefits of alternative strategies for achieving full employment are to be allowed for and the best framework set which creates lasting full employment from a variety of private and public sources over the long term. In the final section (pp. 215–16) I describe the public sector's contribution to structural change in a variety of major European countries and elsewhere. In conclusion I sum up arguments on the role of the public sector for full employment.

PUBLIC SECTOR EMPLOYMENT

In this part of the chapter I look first at the role of the government in its capacity as a direct employer of labour. I start with a description of the latest data available on the current numbers employed and the activities in which they are engaged. I then examine changes over time, distinguishing trends from cycles and explaining the differing roles for the public sector in each case. Second, I examine the extent to which the government, by its example, influences the behaviour of others, or the converse, namely the ways in which the public sector has to respond to forces outside its control. Throughout, the focus is on quantity decisions, the numbers employed; wages are considered in the next section of the chapter.

In mid-1993 public sector employees numbered 5.5 million and made up 20 per cent of the whole economy workforce in employment at that time. The 5.5 million public sector employees consisted of 1.6 million working for central government, 2.7 million employed by local authorities and 1.2 million in public corporations. Figure 13.1 shows the main central government activities, HM Forces, Civil service, Health and 'other' central government and gives the numbers employed on a headcount basis in each case. It also shows the major local government disaggregations, police, education, social services and 'other'

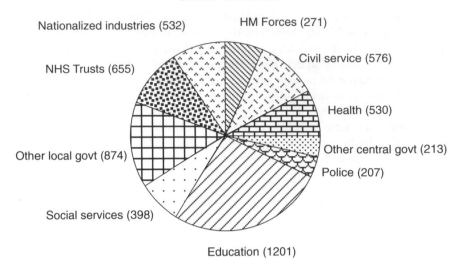

Figure 13.1 Public sector employment, 1993 (mid-year headcount, 000s)
Source: Pearson 1994

local government, which are mainly town hall staff and manual workers, again with the corresponding numbers in thousands in each category shown in brackets. The final part of Figure 13.1 shows public corporations divided into nationalized industries, mainly the Post Office and British Rail, and NHS Trusts which are now the single largest component of this category.

The ten diverse categories of public sector activities shown in Figure 13.1 reflect a similar heterogeneity in the different ways that employment decisions are carried out in the different areas. In the armed forces, for example, there is still considerable centralized control. On the other hand, in the civil service decentralized manpower planning to executive agencies predominates and here, as in the NHS Trusts, there is now considerable scope for local flexibilities in employment policy. Another dimension of variation is between local authorities which are mainly in Labour Party controlled hands and central government and nationalized industries which are primarily steered by Conservative Party philosophy. Of course the elected government still controls a major part of the pursestrings, even in the case of education, police, social services and other local authority activities, but priority on job preservation in this part of the public sector seems to have been higher than in public corporations and central government.

With so many people unemployed and claiming benefit the search is on for innovative policies to provide more opportunities for those in search of work.

There is considerable speculation continuously about new initiatives and no end of suggestions about what they should be. A common factor in many of the proposals is the provision of some additional public sector service jobs for the unemployed so that unused human resources can be put to use, meeting a variety of valuable economic and social needs. This in itself suggests a role for the public sector in job creation as part of a broader strategy to achieve full employment without generating higher inflation. However, the focus on public sector job creation to help prevent long-term unemployment can lead to the neglect of the fact that many jobs are currently being lost from the public sector primarily as a result of the squeeze on budgets. Solutions to unemployment should examine the logic of this job destruction in the public sector as well as schemes for public sector job creation. These issues are discussed in more detail in Trinder (1993).

Of the 5.5 million public sector employees, 3.5 million approximately are women and 2 million are men. Of the females 50 per cent work part-time whereas almost all of the males work full-time. Figure 13.2 shows this disaggregation and the exact number in each category. All the workers are employees as self-employment is as yet rare in the public sector, but there are now some temporary and casual staff and fixed term contracts are being introduced more widely.

Figure 13.3 gives corresponding information on employees in the private sector and shows a slightly higher proportion of full-time and part-time men. In addition to the figures on employees shown in Figure 13.3, there are also three million private sector self-employed.

The present position on employees, with the exception of part-time men, is now fairly similar in the public and private sectors, but this was not always the case. The present similarities mask the fact that the changes over time in the two sectors have been very different. If public sector managers do not give consideration to this they may well find the pattern starts to diverge again sharply, only this time there will be fewer part-time employees in the public sector rather than more as there were in the past. Public sector 'good employment behaviour' should recognize the need for structural change and be innovative in bringing this about via changes in work practices, more use of the self-employed where appropriate and making a place for work sharing.

The present numbers employed in the public sector can be contrasted with the size which prevailed when the Conservative government started its present term of office in 1979. Since 1979 there has been a decline in UK public sector employment of about two million or, in other words, the public sector was about one-third larger in 1979 than it is now. Figure 13.4 shows how these reductions occurred throughout the past fourteen years and that there have been steeper falls at some times rather than others, particularly recently and in 1985, but also that there has been a steady trend reduction throughout this period.

One significant contribution to the reductions in the numbers employed in the public sector since 1979 has been the privatization of many public sector

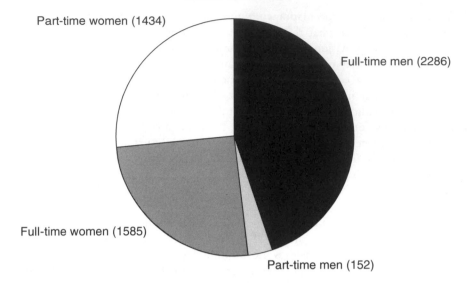

Part-time women (1434)

Full-time men (2286)

Full-time women (1585)

Part-time men (152)

Figure 13.2 Public sector employee types, 1993 (mid-year, 000s)
Source: Pearson 1994

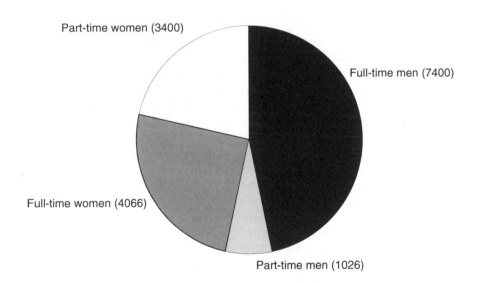

Part-time women (3400)

Full-time men (7400)

Full-time women (4066)

Part-time men (1026)

Figure 13.3 Private sector employee types, 1993 (mid-year, 000s)
Source: Pearson 1994

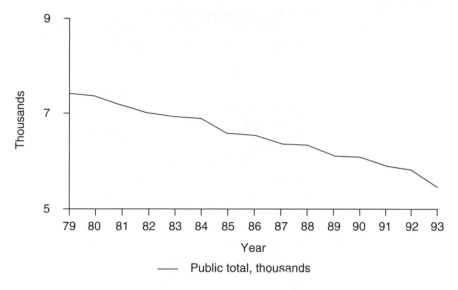

Figure 13.4 Public employment, 1979–93
Source: Pearson 1994

trading activities. Gas, electricity, water and telephones all moved over into the private sector between 1984 and 1990. Table 13.1 shows the major privatizations that have occurred over this period and the number of jobs shifted at the time of privatization from the public to the private sector as a result. If these jobs were merely being reclassified this might not matter, but in fact in the run up to privatization and subsequent to it large numbers of these jobs have disappeared altogether.

A second contribution to the reduction in the size of the non-trading public sector has been the transfer of polytechnics, further education and higher education colleges, which were previously under local government control, out of the public services and into the supposedly non-profit-making private sector. This previously consisted mainly of trade unions, building socities and charities but has now been beefed up considerably by the inclusion of training and enterprise councils and education establishments. These reclassifications are still too recent for the long-term efffects on job numbers to be known, but there must also be a fear here that employment numbers will be reduced, compared to what otherwise would have been the case if they had remained under local authority control. Table 13.2 shows the numbers affected by this process.

A third cause of the reduced size of central governemnt has been the deliberate political decision to reduce the size of the civil service. There were 750,000 civil servants in post when the Conservatives took power, but the number in 1994 was down to below 550,000 and is projected to fall by a further 30,000 by 1996–7. Job reductions in health have been particularly worrying recently. The data for

Table 13.1 Major privatizations

1982	National Freight Company	28,000
	Britoil	14,000
1984	British Telecom	250,000
1986	British Gas	89,000
1987	British Airways	36,000
	Royal Ordnance	17,000
1988	British Steel	53,000
1989	Water	40,000
1990	Electricity	119,000
1991	National Power/Powergen	26,000
	Total	672,000

Source: Pearson 1994

Table 13.2 Reclassifications out of central and local government, 1987–93

1987	Dockyards	16,000
1989	Polytechnics, etc.	60,000
1993	Grant-maintained schools, etc.	23,000
	Further education colleges, etc.	119,000
	Total	218,000

Source: Pearson 1994

the end of 1993 show the numbers employed in health, including NHS Trusts, were down 20,000 on the number employed at the end of 1992. In 1994 local authorities, including schools, reported job losses on an unprecedented scale. Moreover, this can have a built in momentum. The trend to emulate private sector decision-making means that increasingly cash-starved individual management units are making their own policies without regard for the wider implications. An ironic consequence of this is that the resulting job losses are a major factor in driving up public borrowing. This in turn means that the government seeks further to constrain public spending, exacerbating the number of public sector jobs lost next time round and making reductions in public sector employment the single largest influence on the unemployment level.

The policy for the period before 1979 was very different. As can be seen from Figure 13.5, private sector employment fell and rose markedly at different times between 1962 and 1979, but these changes were at least in part compensated for by counter-cyclical changes in the opposite direction in public sector employment. This stabilization policy helped alleviate the worst unemployment effects of recessions and smoothed out the fluctuations that necessarily occur with a country like the UK which is heavily dependent on world trade.

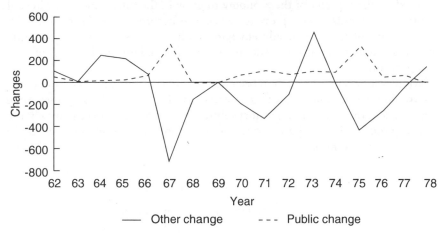

Figure 13.5 Public and other employment, 1962–78 (000s)
Source: Economic trends (annually)

In terms of setting an example to the private sector, the employment policies of the public sector in relation to human resource management have in some areas been encouraging. They have reflected a wider perspective taken by the government on equal opportunities and a determination to utilize suitable people from the whole of society. As an example, the civil service attaches a high priority to promoting opportunities for women, ethnic minorities and people with disabilities. New initiatives have been launched in all these areas. The proportion of ethnic minority employees on 1 April 1993 was 5.2 per cent compared with 4.9 per cent in the whole economy (OPCS 1993). Registered disabled people make up 1.5 per cent which is also slightly above their general representation. The civil service also sets an example to much of private industry in promoting equal opportunities for women to rise to high-ranking jobs. Currently 8.6 per cent of top grades 1 to 3 are women and 8.3 per cent of agency chief executives. In addition, it is more flexible in employing older workers. Upper age limits for candidates have been gradually relaxed and for example for fast stream candidates there is now no upper age limit (House of Commons 1994).

In terms of the timing of its own employment cutbacks, however, the behaviour of the government during the recent recession has been far less appealing. Instead of delaying redundancies until the economic recovery made more likely their redeployment elsewhere, the government pressed on apace with its planned cutbacks giving the okay to private sector employers to behave likewise rather than to try to ride out the storm. Even when the recession turned out to be deeper and longer than foreseen they still persisted with this policy. Moreover, where such behaviour results in older workers prematurely going into early retirement with all the resulting permanent loss of skills and experience, this

211

can reduce the capacity of the economy to grow in the future and result in skill shortages and inflationary pressures when the upturn comes (Trinder 1991). Somes signs of this are already emerging with private sector wages currently increasing at a rate of 4.6 per cent per annum despite headline inflation of only 2.3 per cent.

Moreover, when downsizing becomes the norm this can undermine the motivation and morale of existing workers who feel they are biding their time until their turn for discardment inevitably comes. This can affect adversely the overall productivity of the enterprise and the ability of it successfully to see through its programme.

PUBLIC SECTOR PAY

The relationship between full employment and pay should not be omitted from this chapter, not least because the public sector has in some ways set a good example of preserving jobs in preference to higher pay, particularly on the part of those who are already high earners. Nevertheless, at the outset it should be made clear that the emphasis placed by the government on a simple trade-off between more pay or more jobs within a fixed size paybill is neither helpful to this discussion nor true. Such mechanical basic arithmetic fails to recognize that decisions about cash limits are political and the amount of output that can be financed depends as much on the wider context within which the public sector has to operate and in particular what is happening to private sector pay, as on the behaviour of individual negotiators in the public sector. In Trinder (1994) the relationship between pay, services and jobs in the public sector is explained in considerable detail. Here I want to focus on just one aspect.

In the public sector over the past ten years earnings at all parts of the distribution have increased by roughly the same amount in percentage terms. The highest paid 10 per cent, for example, saw their earnings rise from £249.50 a week in 1984 to £487.40 a week in 1993, a rise of 95 per cent. At the level of the median the corresponding figures were £151.20 a week in 1984 and £292.70 in 1993, a change of 94 per cent over the decade. These public sector figures, which apply to all full-time adult employees, men and women combined, and which have only been produced for the years since 1984, can be contrasted with what happened in the private sector over the same period.

In the private sector while at the level of the median the increase in gross earnings of 94 per cent was the same as in the public sector, when it came to the higher paid their earnings went up much faster, indeed more than 1 per cent per annum faster, and 11 per cent more at the end of the period than at the beginning. The highest paid 10 per cent in the private sector were already paid more than their counterparts in the public sector in 1984 because their earnings were £253.20 a week at that time, but by 1993 they had increased their pay to £522.60 a week, a rise of 106 per cent since 1984 (DOE 1984, 1993).

There is evidence that the large increases in earnings in the private sector at the top have been bought by job reductions elsewhere in the enterprises. In the newly privatized industries, for example, downsizing has been accompanied by significant increases in pay for already relatively high earners. A situation is developing in some instances where half the workforce will lose their jobs over the next few years and those who keep their jobs will see their pay double, the only question being who will be in which half.

By contrast, public sector workers faced first with the 1.5 per cent wage settlement limit in 1993 and a public sector paybill freeze in 1994, with the possibility of continuation until 1997 and even beyond, have, while justifiably complaining about the unfairness and arbitrariness of the policy, nevertheless sought to save jobs rather than strike for higher pay and to share out the inadequate funds in a way that preserved jobs rather than destroyed them.

If the private sector took a leaf out of the public sector's book in this regard then more jobs could have been preserved and unemployment would have been lower. Even if it was simply a matter of timing, the postponement of lay-offs until a firm's downturn was seen to be permanent could be in its own interest due to the expense of recruiting and retraining new employees. But from a wider point of view it offers those displaced a better chance of re-employment elsewhere if the economy is growing and other firms are taking on additional staff.

SPECIAL EMPLOYMENT MEASURES

In the previous two sections of this chapter I have considered what role the government could play as an employer of people at market rates of pay in a co-ordinated attempt to secure full employment. The purpose of this section is to assess what additional contribution, if any, special employment measures can make and how far the public sector, as well as designing them and encouraging their take-up, should also actively participate in directly providing placements in health, education, etc. My conclusion is that while of some value, special employment measures cannot be the main plank of the full employment strategy and in particular that the public sector should not be seen as the employer of last resort making work with low productivity rather than creating and preserving real and good jobs.

The use of special employment measures on social grounds to provide subsidized employment for disadvantaged groups who have exceptional difficulty in finding or holding down a job outside a special scheme is one thing (Jackson and Hanby 1982; Layard and Nickell 1980). However, their use for combatting a general and persistently high level of unemployment is another. Nevertheless there does seem to be widespread cross-party support for special measures of one kind or another.

Special employment measures were introduced in the 1970s as a response to the rise in youth unemployment. As Figure 13.6 shows, youth opportunities made up more than 80 per cent of all starts in 1982–3. In the mid-1980s the total scale of special employment measures was dramatically increased, peaking at just under 1.5 million places in 1987–8. Their scope was also widened with youth training accounting for less than 30 per cent of all placements in that year, with the community programme, aimed primarily at adults, making up 20 per cent. In addition, there were 106,000 self-employed covered by the Business Startup scheme; 124,000 covered by local grants to employers; 108,000 by Training for Enterprise; 148,000 by job training schemes; and a further 106,000 by the Voluntary Projects Programme. Six seperate smaller programmes included National Priority Skills, Open Tech, Industrial Language, Information Technology and Self-standing Work Preparation.

In 1989–90 eleven schemes were discontinued and Employment Training, which had been introduced the previous year, expanded to 50 per cent of the reduced total of 893,000 places. In 1992–3 the total size of SEMs was again at the level of the early 1980s. However, youth training now only accounts for 40 per cent of places and Employment Training has been the largest single programme since 1989–90.

The distinguishing feature of special employment measures is that employment creation is an objective rather than a side effect, that eligibility is restricted to certain categories of worker, that the jobs, training or work experience is temporary and that efforts are made to ensure that other workers are not displaced (OECD 1980; Davies and Metcalf 1985).

The actual content and administration of the schemes has nevertheless come in for some criticism. New schemes have been introduced, only to be replaced after a year or two by further projects with broadly the same objectives. This

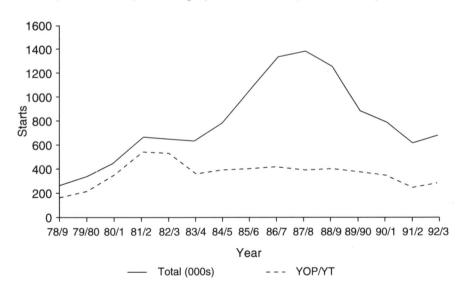

Figure 13.6 Special employment measures, 1978–93 (000s)
Source: Employment Gazette (monthly)

suggests that some schemes have run into administration problems, as one would expect when the objectives for numbers covered, guarantees, etc. were so ambitious. There is a limit therefore to the burden that special employment measures can bear and this applies in the public as well as the private sector (Britton 1986).

FISCAL POLICY

One might expect employment in the public sector to expand as economic growth occurs because public service activities are relatively labour intensive and technical advance in recent years seems to have favoured more capital intensive methods of production in industry and private sector services such as banking and finance (Levitt and Joyce 1988). The main way that dissatisfaction with the level of provision of education and health services can be expressed is political and giving the impression that the costs of provision are lower than in fact is the case only fuels this discontent. It is important therefore that the fundamental reviews of public expenditure currently in progress identify the spending necessary to maintain and improve the quality of public services and that tax and other revenue raising policies are commensurate with this need. In this way public sector employment could be expanded in line with increased output in the economy as a whole.

In addition to getting right the overall fiscal balance, however, there is also the posssibility that micro incentives and levies could alter the balance of advantage between alternative ways of achieving the same objective so as to increase the labour input at the times of high unemployment and favour capital where there are skill shortages. Of course this is not a substitute for reducing supply constraints by adequate training over the medium term, but it recognizes that the economy is often in a state of disequilibrium and that shadow price of labour is a more relevant way of measuring costs for the government than simply taking the prices actually paid. The net cost of employment to the public sector, for example, is less than the gross cost because other social security benefits are reduced and because tax receipts are increased. In practice this 'externality' which affects the position of the public sector as a whole is not evident to the individual decentralized decision-makers in the different parts of central and local government or the nationalized industries or NHS Trusts. The constraints they face and the targets they are set refer to the gross pay bill, total cash spending or the profitability of their enterprise. The decisions they take will not therefore be optimal from the point of view of the public sector as a whole or the representative taxpayer (Britton 1986; Oxley *et al.* 1990).

INTERNATIONAL COMPARISONS

There has been a structural change over the last quarter of a century in the composition of public sector employment in most developed countries. This has involved a rise in the proportion of highly trained employees and a decline in the unskilled and less well qualified categories (ILO 1989). In the drive to full employment the public sector has a responsibility to provide high quality jobs as well as an adequate quantity of them.

Figure 13.7 shows that general government employment in the UK has fallen at a time when in other OECD countries as a whole it has on average remained roughly constant, but in most other major European countries it has been rising. Nevertheless, Figure 13.7 also shows that the UK level is still higher than the OECD average and indeed higher than Germany, Italy and Spain, although it is now below that of France.

The overall comparisons of size mask however the different composition of the public services in the different countries. Defence, for example, accounts for a much higher proportion in the UK than in most other countries except the USA. Figure 13.8 shows this and also that health expenditure is mostly in the private sector in the USA so the overall comparisons need to be supplemented with more detailed analysis.

One area where the UK has clearly pressed on more rapidly than other countries is with its privatization programme for what were previously public corporations. Most other countries are evaluating the UK experience before deciding whether to follow suit. The message from abroad here is to look carefully at the different approaches available and to weigh up the pros and cons of past privatizations before progressing too hurriedly with yet more new ones.

Public service employment also has a long history of providing a stabilizing influence on cyclical fluctuations in private sector employment in most major developed countries (Stevenson 1992). In most of them there is no intention to abandon this in the current deep recession which Europe is experiencing and which has also affected Japan. In the UK, however, this normal safety valve function performed by the public sector has been abandoned.

Similarly on trends in public sector employment the UK is increasingly becoming the odd country out. Government employment has continued to rise in absolute terms, albeit at a slower pace than employment growth in the private sector, in all three of the major European partner countries (i.e. France, Germany and Italy) between 1979 and 1992. Even over the latest two years for which data are available the OECD average shows government employment up 0.9 per cent per annum (1990–92) compared to a reduction of –1.0 per cent per annum in the UK over that same period. Figure 13.9 gives the detailed figures for 1975–9, 1984–9 and 1990–92. Countries following the UK pattern on either cycles or trends can clearly be seen to be the exception rather than the rule.

CONCLUSIONS

Public sector employees now make up about one in five of the working population of 25,000,000. Politics apart, there is no rational objection to increasing this number provided it can be financed; there are areas of the public sector which

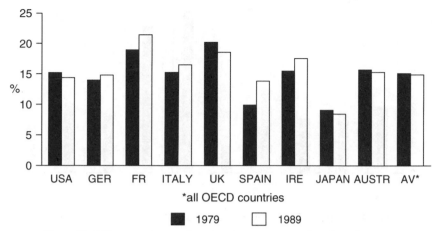

Figure 13.7 Government employment as percentage of total employment
Source: Oxley 1990

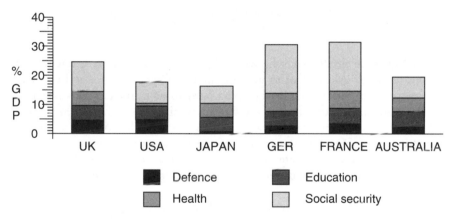

Figure 13.8 Composition of public sector, 1979
Source: Oxley 1990

many feel are under-manned and under-resourced. In addition, it may be necessary to invest in the public sector to facilitate the economic growth that all parties would like to see. Obviously, the public sector should be efficiently managed, so that taxpayers get good value for money and all the population can receive a quality product. Given this situation, the appropriate size of the public sector is determined by considering each individual part of it on its own merits.

At various times in the past, activities have been brought into the public sector in order to allow coherent integrated national strategies to be developed; to increase what was felt to be poor productivity in the private sector; and to

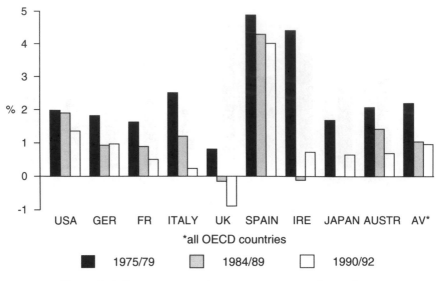

Figure 13.9 Government employment average annual growth rate
Source: OECD 1993

meet legitimate needs that otherwise might not be adequately catered for. It seems to be self-evident that to increase the overall performance and efficiency of any sector in total the removal of extra burdens on it, such as costs associated with competition within that sector, like advertising, would be of benefit. This approach was evident in the case of many local authority services, health and education. However, the fashion of the recent past has been to privatize, contract out and to eliminate public sector activities, but the durability of this approach is not proven and public sector restoration cannot be ruled out over the medium term.

This decrease in the size of the public sector, in politically motivated reductions, takes place in a climate of need and not only fails to stabilize the fluctuations in the economic cycle but also actually accentuates them. In addition, dismantling the public sector removes one of the government's weapons for tackling problematic fluctuations in unemployment; employment in the public sector cannot be a part of any governmental strategy if control of such employment is no longer in its hands. Government is in principle the guardian of the economy and society and should be, and should be seen to be, more mindful of the wider consequences of its actions than a private employer. However, current policy seems to be aimed at creating a disaggregated public service, with each part behaving like a private employer.

The thrust of most currently proposed solutions to unemployment is to encourage a mixture of programmes that either prepare people better to fill new job vacancies when they arise or offer them temporary work placements.

Laudable as such solutions are, and more such programmes are needed, the preservation of existing jobs can achieve both these objectives and in a more direct way. Moreover, the preservation of existing public sector jobs has the added advantage of being less contentious and less prone to economic inefficiency, such as job substitution.

NOTE

1 Paper for TUC/Employment Policy Institute Joint Conference on Tuesday 5 July 1994 to promote the cause of full employment held at Congress House, London, to mark the fiftieth anniversary of the 1944 White Paper on Employment Policy.

REFERENCES

Britton, A. (1986) 'Employment policy in the public sector', in P. Hart (ed.) *Unemployment and Labour Market Policies*, Aldershot: Gower.

Davies, G. and Metcalf, D. (1985) *Generating jobs*, London: Simon and Coates.

Department of Employment (DOE) (1984) *New Earnings Survey, Part A, Streamlined and Summary Analysis*, London: HMSO.

Economic Trends (annually) *Employment in the Public and Private Sectors*, various issues, 1962–78, London: HMSO.

Employment Gazette (monthly) various issues, 1978–94, London: HMSO.

House of Commons (1994) *The Role of the Civil Service: Interim Report*, Paper 390, London: HMSO.

International Labour Organization (ILO) (1989) *Structural Adjustment and Public Service Employment, World Labour Report*, Geneva: ILO.

Jackson, P. and Hanby, V. (1982) *British Work Creation Programmes*, Aldershot: Gower.

Layard, R. and Nickell, S. (1980) 'The case for subsidising extra jobs', *Economic Journal*, March.

Levitt, M. and Joyce, R. (1988) *The Growth and Efficiency of Public Spending*, Cambridge: Cambridge University Press.

OPCS (1993) *Equal Opportunities in the Civil Service for People of Ethnic Minority Origin*, London: HMSO.

Organization for Economic Co-operation and Development (OECD) (1980) *Direct Job Creation in the Public Sector*, Paris: OECD.

—— (1992) *Structural Change and the Public Sector*, Paris: OECD.

—— (1993) *Pay Flexibility in the Public Sector*, Paris: OECD.

Oxley, H. (1990) *The Public Sector: Issues for the 1990s*, Paris: OECD, December.

Pearson, N. (1994) 'Employment in the public and private sectors', *Economic Trends*, CSO, January.

Stevenson, G. (1992) *How Public Sector Pay and Employment Affect Labour Markets*, Washington DC: World Bank, August.

Trinder, C. (1991) 'Older workers and the recession', *Employment Institute Economic Report* 6 (2), May.

—— (1993) 'The public sector and full employment', *Employment Institute Economic Report* 7 (7), March.

—— (1994) *Managing Public Sector Pay: Pay, Services and Jobs*, London: TUC, May.

14

BARGAINING FOR FULL EMPLOYMENT

William Brown

INTRODUCTION

With the economy facing ever more intrusive international competition, Britain's hopes of full employment depend upon maintaining international competitiveness. These hopes are forlorn unless labour costs per unit of output can be kept in line with those of our competitors. It has been conventional to argue that this must imply a national objective of pay restraint. But to give single-minded attention to this objective is ultimately self-defeating. If successful it would lead to a low-wage economy with little incentive for employers to train, less urgency for them to innovate new technologies, and an increasingly degraded workforce.

The central policy challenge is one of sustaining high labour productivity growth, with the restraint of pay within the limits of that growth as a necessary but subordinate objective. It is the argument of this chapter that high productivity growth cannot be achieved by the sort of individualistic pay fixing methods which have received so much official support over the last fifteen years. It is argued that a modern labour market depends unavoidably upon a variety of collective institutions. Central to these in the management of productivity growth and the control of unit costs is the development of responsive collective bargaining.

Collective bargaining has suffered a catastrophic decline in Britain over the past fifteen years. It has also altered substantially in form. If it is to be revived, whether as a grassroots activity or as some sort of nationwide pay co-ordination procedure, the consequences will be very unlike that which we have seen before. In order to suggest why and how such a revival of British collective bargaining might be pursued as part of a full employment policy, it is useful to consider the whys and hows of its recent upheaval.

THE CHANGE IN GOVERNMENT POLICY TOWARDS BARGAINING

Those concerned with future policy should note that recent British governments have pursued a deliberate policy of dismantling collective bargaining. Until the end of the 1970s post-war governments had been largely supportive of it. The efforts of the two ruling political parties to reform what was widely seen to be a defective industrial relations system differed primarily in the emphasis they placed on the role of the law in achieving procedural reform. Governments since 1979 have broken with this tradition. Eight major legislative acts since then have, with growing confidence, undermined the traditional basis of British collective bargaining. They have done this by substantially tightening the procedural requirements for a lawful strike, by altering the legal accountability of union leaderships to their members and by weakening existing arrangements for the recruitment and retention of members. At least as important as this legislation was the active part played by the government in the defeat of trade unions in a series of major strikes in both public and private sectors in the 1980s.

Hostility has deepened towards many other forms of collective institution in the labour market. There has been a general withdrawal of support from tripartite organizations in which unions, employers and the government were involved, notably the Industrial Training Boards, the National Economic Development Council and the wages councils. Official hostility to collectivism has extended to employer organizations. Industry-wide wage agreements arising from voluntary multi-employer bargaining have been sharply criticized by ministers. They have accused them of establishing rigid nationwide wage rates which restrict the downward wage flexibility necessary to promote jobs in those regions of the country with relatively high unemployment.

Employer solidarity, widely seen as a virtue elsewhere in the European Union, has had no place in recent official British philosophy of freer labour markets. In the public sector, as well as having their collective bargaining exposed to sharper product market practices, employers have also come under increasing pressure to dissolve national agreements and to regionalize bargaining structures, thereby reversing a long tradition of centralized public sector pay administration.

THE CONTRACTION AND RESTRUCTURING OF BARGAINING

This abrupt change in official policy has undoubtedly contributed to the contraction of British collective bargaining, although Britain has only been one of the more extreme of many countries experiencing a sharp decline in trade union membership in recent years. Having covered around 45 per cent of the employed workforce from the 1940s until the early 1970s, trade unionism rose to a high point of 55 per cent in 1979, then fell sharply to around 37 per cent at present. Much of this decline has been the result of structural change and, in particular, the decline of traditionally highly organized industries. But recent legislation has made union recruitment and retention substantially more diffficult; unions have not been able to recruit in new industries and firms in the way that they did in the 1970s.

There has been an even greater contraction in the extent of collective

221

bargaining than in the coverage of trade unions. In the private sector, the proportion of the workforce covered by collective agreements has fallen from about three-quarters in the late 1970s to under a half. As well as shrinking in coverage, collective bargaining has also become more fragmented. Two distinct aspects of this are the relative importance of industry-wide bargaining as opposed to enterprise-based bargaining. The second is the level within enterprise-based arrangements at which bargaining occurs. Forty years ago it was possible to describe British collective bargaining almost completely in terms of industry-wide arrangements. The few companies that engaged in formal enterprise bargaining were oddities. But by the time that a Royal Commission considered these things in 1968, this was seen to be changing. Since then there has been a steady spread of enterprise-based bargaining. But since the end of the 1970s, although the proportion of employees in private industry covered by industrial agreements continued to decline, there was not a countervailing increase in those covered by enterprise arrangements. Instead, there has been a sharp rise in the proportion of the workforce not covered by any sort of collective agreement on pay.

The Workplace Industrial Relations Surveys (WIRS) suggest that in 1984, of the six in ten private sector employees covered by pay bargaining arrangements of some sort, four were covered by enterprise and two by industry-wide agreements. By 1990, however, of the barely five in ten employees by then covered by bargaining arrangements, for four they were still enterprise based, but for only one were they industry based. From here on this chapter will draw mainly upon these authoritative WIRS surveys for evidence (Millward *et al.* 1992; Millward 1994).

The second aspect of private sector bargaining levels that has undergone substantial change is within enterprises. The WIRS surveys reveal that, within firms, the fragmentation of bargaining has been diminishing. Multi-establishment firms, especially in service industries, have increasingly been moving to multi-establishment bargaining, rather than single-establishment bargaining. Indeed, by 1990, of all the multi-site firms engaging in bargaining, comprehensive enterprise-wide bargaining accounted for two-thirds of arrangements in manufacturing and over nine-tenths in private services.

This is accompanied by a tightening of corporate control. The decentralization of pay bargaining within an enterprise, whether to divisional or establishment level, increasingly tends to be closely monitored and constrained by higher management at head office. A survey in 1985 reported that in two-thirds of cases where the establishment was ostensibly the most important level of pay bargaining, the local manager was subject to higher level guidelines (Marginson *et al.* 1988). The apparent fragmentation of bargaining structure in the private sector is thus not matched by comparable fragmentation of control over pay. The 1990 WIRS survey confirms that, despite the talk of decentralization of bargaining that has occurred over the 1980s, senior management showed no sign of having relaxed its control.

Effective control over bargained pay in the private sector in Britain may thus, paradoxically, be substantially more concentrated in 1994 through the efforts of independent employers than was the case in, say, 1964, when the bargaining structure relied heavily upon employers' associations struggling to uphold relatively few, but increasingly ineffective, industry-wide agreements. Trade union negotiators in the private sector have increasingly, to use their time-honoured phrase, had to negotiate not with the organ grinder but with his monkey, and the monkey's chain has been getting shorter.

The same cannot be said of the public sector. The civil service has been crumbling into agencies with varied and unclear discretion over pay. Health, education and local government are under similar pressure to devolve pay fixing without any of the central controls in place that self-respecting private sector corporations would consider essential. Added to this has been the proliferation of poorly planned and worse controlled schemes for performance-related pay. A once centralized public sector pay bargaining system is being increasingly broken up without any evidence of the emergence of the necessary substitution of managerial controls.

CHANGE IN THE CHARACTER OF BARGAINING

These changes in the extent and level of bargaining have been accompanied by changes in the underlying character of bargaining. This is true of the public as well as of the private sector. The degree of union security provided by employers is currently changing radically. There has been a substantial decline in the number of workplaces where trade unions are recognized by employers for bargaining. Even in firms where unions are recognized, there has been a decline in the extent of the workforce participation. Specific acts of derecognition in which employers broke existing negotiating arrangements were rare in the early 1980s, but were less rare at the end of the decade and they appear to be becoming common in the 1990s.

The use of closed shops, under which it is accepted that employees have to be union members if they are to keep their jobs, has changed substantially. Although by the 1970s they had come to be treated as managerial devices for procedural discipline rather than as instruments of union power, they declined massively throughout the 1980s, battered by waves of legislative restraint. Between 1980 and 1990 it is estimated that the number of union members in closed shops fell from 3.5 million to 0.5 million. Although this decline is dramatic, it is likely that its implications for trade union organization will be dwarfed by the effects of the 1993 Trade Union Reform and Employment Rights Act in spoiling 'check-off' arrangements whereby members can have their union dues collected by employers.

Both surveys and detailed case studies suggest that there has been a decline in the depth of union involvement in the administration of bargaining. Union organization has been eroding severely where it was weakly based. The 1990

223

WIRS survey does suggest, however, that in the diminishing number of places where collective bargaining is still strong, the formal involvement of unions has been maintained, at least in terms of such things as the presence of consultative committees, office facilities and the collection of union subscriptions by employers. But this is misleading. Better formal institutions and better facilities do not necessarily imply greater depth of union involvement even where unions continue to have a strong presence. On the contrary, it probably indicates that the workplace union organization has become less effective by becoming more dependent upon management for legitimacy and other resources.

Another crucial aspect is the scope of bargaining, that is the range of issues upon which effective bargaining takes place. For manual workers in manufacturing, for whom workplace bargaining has traditionally tended to offer an especially wide range of issues, there was a substantially smaller proportion of managers reporting negotiations on the issues they were asked about at the establishment level in 1990 than in 1984. The scope of bargaining appears to have declined across the whole unionized sector.

A final aspect of the changed character of collective bargaining is that agreements tend to be more precisely implemented and controlled. Traditionally, British industrial agreements offered neither obligatory standards nor effective machinery to see that the standards were observed. On the other hand the *de facto* system of workplace regulation was fragmented, informal, had inadequate disputes procedures, and many issues were left to custom and practice. There is no doubt that the shift to enterprise bargaining has greatly increased the degree of control of agreements on both pay and non-pay issues. Companies have generally tightened their machinery of monitoring and this has been reflected in the fact that formal procedures for discipline, dismissal, grievance and pay had become almost universal in unionized workplaces by 1990.

UNDERLYING CAUSES

These aspects of the change in collective bargaining over the past decade or so are well documented. But it would be a mistake to attribute the driving force behind them to government policy. Government policy has certainly weakened trade unions. They have become far more cautious and have faced greater difficulties in recruiting and in gaining recognition. But what has driven the change in employer policy predates the legislative changes. It has seen the rise of enterprise bargaining, a phenomenon which has recently been apparent to some degree in most industrialized market economies.

Lying behind the move to enterprise bargaining has been the desire of individual employers, under the increasing competitive pressures of an ever more internationalized world economy, to gain more control over unit wage costs. The once powerful advantages of industry-wide employer solidarity at the national level have been eroded. This has been especially true in countries such as Britain where industry-wide training arrangements have been largely abandoned.

Furthermore, employers have found that enterprise bargaining can permit more precise and flexible management of labour in pursuit of tighter control of wages and labour productivity. There has been increasing reliance upon in-house training and on a variety of other techniques which increase the insulation of internal labour markets and wage structures from the labour market outside. They include a move to more fluid job descriptions, particular to the firm; a shift from payment according to task to payment by salary structures related to career trajectories; and widespread experimentation with varied forms of performance-related pay, not linked to physical output but to other indicators of individual performance and to company profitability.

These accompaniments of enterprise bargaining tend to weaken both the potential grip of collective agreements and also the ability of unions to mobilize the collective sentiments and power of their members. Domestic union organizations thus become distanced from the wider union movement. Enterprise bargaining does this independently of governmental action. Where governmental opposition to collective bargaining becomes important is in making it harder for trade unions to deal with these more difficult circumstances and harder for them to gain and retain essential employer recognition in a climate of official disapproval.

CONSEQUENCES OF THE UPHEAVAL IN BARGAINING

What consequences can we attribute so far to these massive recent alterations in collective bargaining? The most obvious change for most British people has been the substantial decline in strike activity. Working days lost per thousand workers, which had averaged 570 per year in the 1970s and 330 per year in the 1980s, have tumbled to around 50 per year so far in the 1990s. Legislation and other government action is likely to have contributed substantially to this fall; certainly strike ballots appear to have gone some way to displacing strike action as both a sanction and safety valve. The economic consequences of strike action and strike avoidance are, however, notoriously complex, and it would be rash to attempt a judgement on the economic consequences of a decline in strike levels.

An apparently more tractable question which econometricians have addressed is how far, in the few years since their implementation, these radical changes in labour market policy have improved competitiveness. From a mass of fairly inconclusive studies it is, however, hard to point to any clear findings. There is consistent evidence that during the 1980s the average level of pay rises was higher in non-unionized than in unionized firms. The greater decentralization of pay controls in non-unionized than in unionized firms appears to have contributed to this. There is also evidence that during the 1980s firms with decentralized bargaining were more willing to link pay settlements to changes in working arrangements. It would, however, be a mistake to assume that produc-tivity related pay deals necessarily promote sustained productivity growth. In some bargains, the brittle intensification of labour effort may have discouraged investment in technological innovation and improved labour skills.

There had been speculation in the 1980s that there might be a new style of collective bargaining, characterized by some combination of single union deals, single-status employment conditions, flexibility agreements, consultative committees and pendulum arbitration. The WIRS surveys suggest this to have been illusory; their number was almost insignificant.

CONSEQUENCES OF NON-UNIONISM

Even if one could identify immediate consequences of a policy concerned with dismantling collective bargaining, it might be foolish to expect any. The reform of such deep-rooted institutions of labour management would be slow to effect and slow to have effect. Instead we turn to consider the rapidly growing sector of the economy where collective bargaining has died or has never developed. On this, the three WIRS surveys provide rich and authoritative data.

Was there a blossoming of human resource management (HRM) techniques in non-unionized firms in the 1980s? These techniques, with their emphasis on individualistic treatment of employees and the pre-empting of collective grievances, would be characterized by sophisticated methods of direct communication with employees, by harmonization of employment conditions and by 'high trust' time-keeping procedures. The WIRS surveys suggest that, although 'top-down' briefing had increased, consultative committees had declined over the 1980s. There was little concerted move towards harmonization and high trust time-keeping practices had become less popular.

There was no evidence that the very substantial growth in non-unionism in the 1980s was accompanied by a growth in HRM or more progressive management practices. Indeed, arrangements at workplace level to consult, communicate with and inform employees, including briefing groups and employee surveys, were more, not less, widespread and more highly developed in unionized workplaces than in the non-union sector. On a wide range of matters that could be expected to be of interest to employees, the WIRS survey analysis concludes,

> Our results showed that managers in the non-union sector were much less likely to disseminate that information to employees than was the case in the unionised sector. Furthermore, we could find no evidence that there was any growth in the amount of information disseminated in the non union sector. . . . Britain is approaching the position where few employees have any mechanism through which they can contribute to the operation of their workplace in a broader context than that of their own job. There is no sign that the shrinkage in the extent of trade union representation is being offset by a growth in other methods of representing non managerial employees' interests and views.

(Millward 1994: 97)

This confirms the view that without the stimulus of a trade union presence the great bulk of employers tend to manage labour poorly. It echoes what has been found by researchers on health and safety, training, unfair dismissal and on consultation, not just in Britain but in other countries. Without a trade union to assert employee rights and to press for best practice, personnel management standards tend to slide. Enlightened employers of non-union labour do exist and exemplary cases can be cited among firms both large and small. What the surveys show is that they appear to be the exception and not the norm.

Nor are the issues the immediate ones of employee welfare; there are dynamic factors underlying productivity growth at stake. A union presence, contrary to common prejudice, appears to be seen by employers to be conducive to technical innovation. An analysis of the 1984 WIRS by Daniel (1987), for example, which explored attitudes to technical innovation, concluded not only that trade unions were not perceived by employers as being obstacles to change, but also that both shop stewards and full-time officers tended to be more strongly in favour than ordinary workers of technical changes in the office and on the shop floor. A structure of employee representation appears to facilitate the painful process of helping a skilled workforce to adjust its skills.

There is also the more familiar issue of the role of employee collectivities in encouraging skill acquisition. For centuries, guilds, trade unions and professional associations have existed to protect the jobs and earnings of those who have acquired slowly learned skills. By offering at least a partial guarantee of occupational and income security for the skilled, they have strengthened the incentive to invest time and money in training for the potential trainee. By offering such protection across whole labour markets, they have reduced the scope for free-riding employers to poach skilled labour, and thus weaken the incentive to train held among their more far-sighted competitors.

There can be no doubt that legislative change has weakened trade unions. A succession of government sponsored defeats has probably weakened them more. In some of the public sector industries such as printing and television, this weakening has probably been important in enabling employers to introduce change faster than they might otherwise have done. But it has not been replaced by a substantially new and coherent system of managing labour. We are not witnessing the emergence of a brave new world of non-union HRM but a tired old world of unrepresented labour. Many employers will find their union-free systems of employee relations to be inarticulately aggressive in an economic upturn.

THE SCOPE FOR SOCIAL PARTNERSHIP

How can an employment promoting economic policy be built on this changed bargaining landscape? Policy-makers face a scene that has been transformed since the 1970s. Collective bargaining has contracted dramatically and its decline continues. In the private sector it survives largely in the form of enterprise bargaining in which individual employers deal with largely isolated union organizations through tight agreements on limited issues. The broadening areas of non-unionism appear to be characterized by backward employment practices and heavy reliance upon performance-related pay. In the public sector, a once relatively controlled bargaining system is being dismantled and once fairly stable pay relativities are being scrambled. It would be hard to design a pay-fixing scene more prone to uncontrolled inflation in an economic upturn.

It would be attractive to argue for the promotion of the sort of national co-ordination of bargaining so strongly advo cated by Layard (1990) and others. But we have to face the fact that the task of co-ordination is harder than ever before. Wage bargainers are now a minority and their ranks are in disarray. It is true that in those parts of the private sector where enterprise bargaining continues, it is more tightly under management control than in the past. But the same certainly cannot be said of the public sector, nor of the widening areas of employment where no bargaining takes place. What guidelines might assist in the rebuilding of labour market institutions in such a way that the prime aim of productivity enhancement might be combined with the controlled growth of pay? One key component suggested, in the light of international experience, by Soskice (1990) among others, lies in the fostering of a degree of national employer solidarity in the pay fixing process. Such a task is likely to be assisted by the acceptance of the spurned Social Chapter of the Maastricht Agreement and also by involving major employers in stronger national training initiatives.

Another key component would be a co-ordinated public sector pay fixing procedure, the main elements of which had been emerging from the actions of successive governments (not least Mrs Thatcher's) until the obsession with frag-menting public service power became dominant. Such a procedure would extend and link the work of the present pay review bodies. It would enhance public service productivity by the cultivation of professional commitment rather than by tinkering with largely inappropriate performance-related cash rewards.

A third key component would address the pay and productivity relationship at the workplace level by encouraging, rather than harassing, collective bargaining. A clear shift in government attitude, accompanied by relatively minor legislative changes, could do much to reverse the ebbing support of employers and poten-tial members from trade unions. The objective, for which enterprise-based bargaining is particularly well-suited, would be the recreation of an articulate workforce, able to respond intelligently to the strains of innovation and to put pressure on employers to manage labour efficiently. If the experience of the past decade or so has anything to show, it is that the denying of a collective voice to a workforce tends also to deny it effective labour management.

This chapter has not attempted to sketch anything like a fully fledged full employment policy. On the contrary, it has tried to demonstrate that building such a policy from the wreckage of old institutions will be more difficult than is generally imagined. Instead, it has picked over that wreckage to argue that an essential feature of such a policy in Britain will have to be a renaissance of collective institutions – for employers, for employees, and for collective bargaining between them.

In asking our workforce to accept change in their employment circumstances at an internationally dictated pace and price we are making a massive political demand. Progress towards it will come neither from untrammelled individualism nor from brute imposition. The social partnership that will be necessary will have to acknowledge the essentially political nature of this demand and the consequent need for representative discussion and negotiation at workplace, enterprise, and national levels.

REFERENCES

Daniel, W. W. (1987) *Workplace Industrial Relations and Technical Change*, London: Frances Pinter.

Layard, R. (1990) *Wage Bargaining and Incomes Policy*, Discussion Paper 2, Centre for Economic Performance, London: London School of Economics.

Marginson, P., Edwards, P. K., Martin, R., Purcell, J. and Sisson, K. (1988) *Beyond the Workplace*, Oxford: Blackwell.

Millward, N. (1994) *The New Industrial Relations?*, London: Policy Studies Institute.

Millward, W. W., Stevens, M., Smart, D. and Hawes, W. R. (1992) *Workplace Industrial Relations in Transition*, Aldershot: Dartmouth (WIRS3).

Soskice, D. (1990) 'Wage determination: the changing role of institutions in advanced industrialised countries', *Oxford Review of Economic Policy* 6 (4).

INDEX

230

to, 214; and the long-term
unemployed, 190; National Insurance
contributions (NICs), 16, 17; subsidies
to, 192–6, 199–200; and unit wage
costs, 224
employment conditions, 171
Employment in Europe 1993 (EC), 85–6
employment growth (1961–94), 10
Employment and Growth (Australian
  White Paper) xvii
employment policy, xv, 121–7, 167–8
Employment Policy (1944 White Paper)
  xvii–xviii, 2, 25, 30, 32, 33, 40, 41,
  46, 70
Employment Policy Institute (EPI) xiii,
  xvii
employment protection, xiii, 12, 13, 168,
  171, 202; qualifying period for, 89
employment rights, 90
employment services, 20
employment subsidies, 42, 44, 45,
  192–3, 199–200; for recruiting new
  workers, 89
employment taxes, and benefits reform,
  16–20, 202
Employment Training, 214
enterprise bargaining, 184, 185, 224–5,
  227–8
environmental issues, 129, 171
equal opportunities, 77, 78, 94, 211
Equal Opportunities Commission, Hours
  of Work Survey 82 Fig. 5.1, 83
Etzioni, A., 119
Euro-monetarism, 24–5
Europe, 36, 127–8, 146, 216; Eastern,
  118, 174; and flexibility, 163–5;
  long-term unemployment, 191–2;
  regulation vs. deregulation, 177–89
  Western, 113; globalization and
  low-skilled workers, 132–50
European Union (EU), xiii, 12, 14, 24,
  138, 169; female labour market
  participation, 65–8; hours of work,
  (1991), 76; model of regulation and
  welfare, 9, 167, 168–9; poverty
  definition, 50; unemployment 5 per
  cent target, 190; unemployment in
  the, 5, 154–9, 163
Exchange Rate Mechanism (ERM), 40,
  100, 153
exchange rates, 105, 106
Exchequer costs of unemployment,
  59–60 Table 3.3

factor price equalization, 139–41, 144,
  147
fair employment, 167, 168–9; and
  economic success, 170–2
family: 'job rich' and 'job poor', 18–19
  men and, 83–4, 90, 94 and
  unemployment, 53–4
Family Credit, 18, 19, 44–5, 69–70, 74,
  82, 91, 92–3
family wage, assumptions about, 91–2
Farrington, D.P., 54
female labour market participation;
  European Union 65–8, 116;
  generational analysis, 68
female unemployment, 55
Field, F., 56
financial markets, 24, 41
Finland, 160
fiscal policy, UK, 32, 205, 215
flexibility, 81, 83–4, 171, 178;
  agreements, 226; Europe and USA,
  163–5; 'fair', 88, 90; various forms of,
  115–20
flexibilization, and gender, 71–2
flexible working, 14, 181–2, 187
flexitime, 119
Ford, Henry, 172
Fordism, 112, 118, 119
forecasting, 152–4
Fox, J.A., 54
France, 84, 85, 97, 106, 107, 132,
  161–2, 169, 170, 180, 184, 216;
  unemployment (1960–93) 159 Fig.
  9.4
free market xiii, 47, 151, 164
free trade, 127, 133
Freeman, Christopher, 7, 14, 109–31
Freeman, Richard B., 7–8, 9, 132–50
full employment, 1–29; bargaining for,
  220–9; definitions of, 65, 121; in a
  market economy, 30–48; and mass
  unemployment, 2–3; for men and
  women, 81–95; role of the public
  sector in, 204–19; significance of
  37–9; UK (1945–60), 33–4; without
  low pay, 167–76; and women, 63–80
further education, 15

Gallie, D., 58
game theory, 183
'gender blindness', 4, 63–80
General Agreement on Tariffs and Trade
  (GATT), 8, 133

94; flexible, 76, 112, 119; preferences, 84; UK, 168, 169
working lifetime, changes in the, 90–1
Working Nation: Policies and Programmes (Australian government) xvii, 12
'working poor', 179
working time: contracts, 82–3; 'fair' flexibility in, 14; women and, 68–70
Working Time Directive (EC), 87–92
Workplace Industrial Relations Survey (WIRS), 222–4, 226, 227

works councils, 183, 184, 185–6
'Workstart' programme, 21
World Bank, 138
world economy, 127–8
World Employment Report (1995) (ILO) xvii, 24

youth unemployment, 205, 213–14, 213–15

zero hours contracts, 82, 119